A
Twenty-Something's
Guide
to
Spirituality

A Twenty-Something's Guide to Spirituality

Questions You Hesitate to Ask, Answers You Rarely Hear

Edited by Jacob Werrett & David Read

DESERET
BOOK

SALT LAKE CITY, UTAH

Library of Congress Cataloging-in-Publication Data

A twenty-something's guide to spirituality / compiled by Jacob Werrett and David Read.
    p. cm.
  Includes bibliographical references and index.
  ISBN-13: 978-1-59038-794-8 (pbk.)
  1. College students—Religious life. 2. Spirituality—Church of Jesus Christ of Latter-day Saints. 3. Spirituality—Mormon Church. I. Werrett, Jacob. II. Read, David Haxton Carswell.
  BX8656.T88 2007
  248.8'34—dc22   2007019217

Printed in the United States of America
Publishers Printing, Salt Lake City, UT

10 9 8 7 6 5 4 3 2 1

Contents

Preface

College life is not for the faint of heart. It has long been known by college students that among the toughest tests are those without multiple choices—with answers that are not clearly defined, which cannot be simply stated or easily recognized, and where there may be many shades of alternative answers. When Latter-day Saint college students register for life, they find that the tests come without ample study time, test preview, or even a syllabus. College life presents taxing examinations containing questions such as—

How can I become scholarly while remaining meek and teachable?

As a female, to what extent should I pursue an education?

What is the relationship between truth, knowledge, and faith?

Are some aspects of science, ancient history, and philosophy a threat to the premises of Latter-day Saint philosophy?

Is it possible to pursue tough scholarly questions without disrespecting priesthood authority?

How can I balance spirituality with the demands of college life?

The college experience represents perhaps the most crucial time of life for the student to receive doctrinal direction and academic answers. As eager students, we enter the lecture hall with the hope of learning and increasing in knowledge. In turn, the teachings sounding from behind the lectern may well bring a host of questions, rather than firm, fixed answers, and the student's subsequent exploration may lead to areas of thought that could have disastrous consequences. As Aristotle taught in his *Ethics*, this could "make a vast difference, or rather all the difference in the world."[1]

Determined to unearth universal answers to these individual questions, we turned to respected LDS authors and scholars found in both academia and the Christian community. We spent two years requesting and gathering essays from professionals in varying fields. Everyone we approached held an advanced degree; additionally, all of them were experienced, devoted, and determined disciples of Jesus Christ. We also gathered inquisitive articles from students to take the spiritual temperature of college campuses nationwide. Their essays help crystallize the common questions and concerns found among Latter-day Saint college students. In this compilation we have combined thoughtful questions from students with answers from those who know.

The edict "Thou shalt love the Lord thy God with all thy *heart*, and with all thy *soul* and with all thy *mind*" (Mark 12:30; emphasis added) requires the student to develop reason and knowledge to defend and deepen his faith in Christ. Additionally, Peter counseled us to "add to your faith virtue; and to virtue knowledge" (2 Peter 1:5). Hence, we must not separate our faith and the acquisition of earthly knowledge, for one necessarily builds upon the other. Evidence is at the core of our knowledge and grows into the foundation of our faith. So having refused to separate the spiritual and the temporal, the college student must make tough decisions about the correlation, collaboration, and association of truths in order to construct a healthy relationship between faith and reason.

This compilation represents our desire to reconcile education with faith in the Lord Jesus Christ and ultimately sustain President Gordon B. Hinckley's challenge to "rise up and discipline [ourselves] to take advantage of educational opportunities."[2] As a result, we hope this collection of essays will address some of the many queries found in the latter-day classroom and encourage a lifestyle and promote principles that can be universally utilized to direct the individual Christian college student.

—Jacob Werrett and David Read

Notes

1. Aristotle, *Nichomachean Ethics* (New York: Penguin, 2004), 32.

2. Gordon B. Hinckley, "Rise Up, O Men of God," *Ensign,* November 2006, 61.

The Meek Disciple-Scholar

Ryan Thompson

Resident Physician, Massachusetts General Hospital,
Harvard Medical School

Question:

I remember feeling a profound sense of gratitude the evening I found out about a significant academic achievement during medical school. That same night, however, I recall making some judgmental and cynical comments about a neighbor. I thought these comments were innocent enough—I was simply stating my observations about a particular situation. How wrong I was. It did not take long for the gratitude and satisfaction I felt to give way to feelings of pride and negativity.

My reflection on this brief but poignant experience led me to two scriptures. The first was a teaching of the Savior to His disciples: "For what is a man profited, if he shall gain the whole world, and lose his own soul?" (Matthew 16:26). The second was a somewhat chilling phrase recorded by the prophet Mormon: "For none is acceptable before God, save the meek and lowly in heart" (Moroni 7:44). Such statements are quite indicting of one who is prideful, arrogant, or self-serving. As I reflected on my life, I was struck at how my pride had placed me at serious risk to "lose [my] own soul" and to be found "unacceptable unto God."

I have found meekness to be a rare and unpopular virtue in today's academic world. It may be easy to cultivate meekness when engaged in scripture study or Church service. Yet when I pass through a stressful week, when the burdens of school or work are bearing down, Satan always seems to appear with his subtle yet effective tactics: the urge to criticize, the desire to self-promote or to gain recognition, the need to outdo or outperform someone, the tendency to take shortcuts or cut corners. When I cave in to such temptations, it is usually because my focus has shifted onto myself rather than the Lord and his work. My cultivation of meekness and other gospel virtues gets tossed to the wayside in favor of my "vain ambition" (D&C 121:37). In short, my pride too often renders me "unacceptable unto God" and at risk of losing my "own soul."

This spiritual tug-of-war between pride and meekness seems to rage on day after day as I strive to be both a successful scholar and meek disciple. How is it, then, that I can develop this Christlike quality of meekness and at the same time maintain the academic rigor and competitive advantage necessary to achieve academic and professional success? How can I be meek when it's a stressful Thursday afternoon, when I'm overwhelmed that two tests are quickly approaching and an important project is shortly due? What about when I get passed over for an "A" grade or for a scholarship or for some academic recognition I believe I deserved? Conversely, how do I maintain a spirit of meekness when academic success, awards, or adulation come my way? To whom can I look for a modern-day example of meek, Christlike living in today's academic world?

I am young in my career, and I believe it is important to achieve success in my field. But "what is a man profited" (Matthew 16:26) if success comes at the expense of meekness? Thus the most fundamental question for me regarding the pursuit of an education is this: How can I be a successful scholar and professional and yet remain "meek and lowly in heart" and acceptable unto God?

* * *

Elder Neal A. Maxwell

Late Member of the Quorum of the Twelve Apostles,
The Church of Jesus Christ of Latter-day Saints

Answer:[1]

I call your attention to the scripture which describes the terrestrial kingdom as including the honorable individuals of the earth. What so many honorable individuals do is certainly useful and even commendable. But their focus is not on the celestial, and hence they may be "taken in" by the world and are not "valiant in the testimony of Jesus" (D&C 76:75, 79).

Given all of your talents and opportunities, I hope you will not settle for being among the "honorable" men and women of the earth. Furthermore, along with your many gifts and talents, you have been given much; hence much is "required" (D&C 82:3). The word is *required*, not the words "hoped for," "expected," or the phrase "it would be nice if. . . ."

My regard is for what you now are, but also for what you have the power to become. This causes me to speak to you of overarching and undergirding things. For instance, the distinguishing and facilitating quality of meekness will be noted more than once in these remarks. How you treat those *around* you, *below* you, and *behind* you in life will matter greatly in your lives.

No Conflict between Faith and Learning

The Lord sees no conflict between faith and learning in a broad curriculum:

... that you may be instructed more perfectly in theory, in principle, in doctrine, in the law of the gospel, in all things that pertain unto the kingdom of God, that are expedient for you to understand;

Of things both in heaven and in the earth, and under the earth; things which have been, things which are, things which must shortly come to pass; things which are at home, things which are abroad; the wars and the perplexities of the nations, and the judgments which are on the land; and a knowledge also of countries and of kingdoms. . . .

And as all have not faith, seek ye diligently and teach one another words of wisdom; yea, seek ye out of the best books words of wisdom; seek learning, even by study and also by faith (D&C 88:78–79, 118).

The scriptures see faith and learning as mutually facilitating, not separate processes. Robert Frost's line "Something there is that doesn't love a wall" is applicable regarding a wall between mind and spirit.

Are All Truths of Equal Importance?

Since truth is highly and rightly valued in the learning process, please allow me to present a few graphic illustrations about the gradations of truth. These points may seem obvious, but it is so easy to look "beyond the mark" (Jacob 4:14).

The restored gospel of Jesus Christ gives us a different view of truth. To begin with, there is no democracy among truths. They are not of equal significance. These gradations might be represented geometrically by a wide circle (see figure 1).

The outer edges of the circle would include truths which are accurate descriptions of reality. These facts, such as airline schedules and exchange rates, have only a momentary utility and relevancy, a short shelf life. They are useful, and they cannot be ignored, but they are simply not on the same footing as other kinds of truth. You could supply your own and better illustrations.

FIGURE 1: GRADATIONS OF TRUTH—There is no democracy among truths

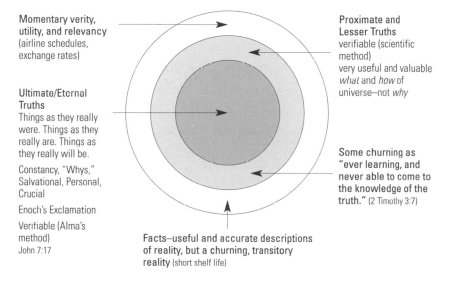

Momentary verity, utility, and relevancy (airline schedules, exchange rates)

Ultimate/Eternal Truths
Things as they really were. Things as they really are. Things as they really will be.
Constancy, "Whys," Salvational, Personal, Crucial
Enoch's Exclamation
Verifiable (Alma's method)
John 7:17

Proximate and Lesser Truths verifiable (scientific method) very useful and valuable *what* and *how* of universe—not *why*

Some churning as "ever learning, and never able to come to the knowledge of the truth." (2 Timothy 3:7)

Facts—useful and accurate descriptions of reality, but a churning, transitory reality (short shelf life)

The next concentric circle inward would include more important truths. These are proximate and important truths, however, not ultimate truths. Some of these, for instance, are verifiable by the very serviceable scientific method. These truths can be very useful and valuable. For instance, in the realm of astrophysics they tell us much about the *what* and *how* of the universe, but they cannot (and do not even presume to) tell us *why* it exists.

In this same middle circle—the suburbs, so to speak—there is a churning and revising among some of these truths. Life in the suburbs may mean one can be "ever learning" but still "never able to come to the knowledge of *the* truth" (2 Timothy 3:7; emphasis added). Even so, these truths are important and valued.

In the very center of the circle of truth lie the "deep things of

God" (1 Corinthians 2:10, 14). These come to us only by revelation from God, and they clearly have a greater significance than other truths and fleeting facts.

These truths concern things as they really were, really are, and really will be (D&C 93:24). There is constancy, not churning, among these strategic truths. These truths, for instance, are revealed from God and tell us *why* the universe exists. They are also very personal and crucial, such as is contained in Enoch's exclamation (Moses 7:30). They represent the highest order of truth.

These truths are likewise verifiable. Jesus describes how: "If any man will do his will, he shall know of the doctrine, whether it be of God, or whether I speak of myself" (John 7:17; see also Alma 32:26–43).

Prioritizing Truths

Thus we constantly need to distinguish between the truths which are useful and those which are crucial, and between truths which are important and those which are eternal. The restored gospel gives us this special sense of proportion.

Stephen Hawking, displaying that meekness which is found in great scientists, wrote: "Although science may solve the problem of how the universe began, it cannot answer the question: Why does the universe bother to exist? I don't know the answer to that."[2]

Hawking also raised some ultimate questions pertaining to the innermost zone of figure 1. He wrote:

What is the nature of the universe? What is our place in it, and where did it and we come from? Why is it the way it is? . . .

. . . If we do discover a complete theory, . . . then we shall all . . . be able to take part in the discussion of the question of why it is that we and the universe exist. If we find the answer to that, it would be the ultimate triumph of human reason—for then we would know the mind of God.[3]

Such questions are answered only by revelation, not solely by reason. Certain high-grade knowledge, as Paul taught, is "spiritually discerned" (1 Corinthians 2:14). Only when mind and spirit combine can we penetrate the inner realm.

Nephi lamented over those who "will not search knowledge, nor understand great knowledge" (2 Nephi 32:7). Clearly he was referring to a particular gradation of knowledge. Jesus lamented that some had lost the "key of knowledge." Joseph Smith translated the word *key* as "the fulness of the scriptures" (JST Luke 11:53; see also D&C 84:19–20).

Yes, we are nourished in many helpful ways by certain facts and feelings, but as Jacques Maritain observed: "Poetry (like metaphysics) is spiritual nourishment; but of a savor which has been created and which is insufficient. There is but one eternal nourishment. Unhappy are you who think yourselves ambitious, and who whet your appetites for anything less than the [divinity] of Christ. It is a mortal error to expect from poetry the super-substantial nourishment of man."[4]

Scholarship As a Form of Worship

For a disciple of Jesus Christ, academic scholarship is a form of worship. It is actually another dimension of consecration. Hence one who seeks to be a disciple-scholar will take both scholarship and discipleship seriously—and, likewise, gospel covenants. For the disciple-scholar, the first and second great commandments frame and prioritize life. How else could one worship God with all of one's heart, might, *mind,* and strength? (Luke 10:27). Adoration of God leads to emulation of Him and Jesus: "Therefore, what manner of men ought ye to be? Verily I say unto you, even as I am" (3 Nephi 27:27; see also 2 Peter 3:11).

So much tutoring is required, however, in order for the disciple to become "as a child, submissive, meek, humble, patient, full of love, willing to submit to all things which the Lord seeth fit to inflict upon him, even as a child doth submit to his father" (Mosiah 3:19).

The disciple-scholar also understands what kind of community he or she should help to build. Its citizens openly and genuinely desire to be called God's people. They are not secret disciples, but bear one another's burdens, mourn with those that mourn, comfort those in need of comfort, and witness for God at all times, and in all places, and in all things (Mosiah 18:8–9). Hubris, including intellectual pride, reflects the ways of hell, not of heaven! No wonder a true community of scholars would qualify to be part of a larger community of Saints.

The disciple-scholar also understands Jesus' style of leadership, which includes persuasion, long-suffering, gentleness, meekness, love unfeigned, kindness, pure knowledge—all being achieved without hypocrisy and guile (D&C 121:41–42; Mosiah 3:19). There again, wholeness and meekness are emphasized.

Consecrated Scholarship

The attribute of *knowledge* reflects more than the accumulation of assorted, uneven facts. It is "pure," and it is also not something apart; rather, it is closely associated with all other redeeming virtues (D&C 4:6; 107:30; 121:41; 2 Peter 1:5–9).

Jesus is "the way, the truth, and the life" (John 14:6). Since He has received a fulness of truth, we rightly seek to have "the mind of Christ" (D&C 93:26; 1 Corinthians 2:16). If we keep His commandments, the promise is that we will receive "truth and light" until we are "glorified in truth and [know] all things" (D&C 93:28). Would either a true scholar or disciple settle for less?

In writing of C. S. Lewis, Paul L. Holmer wrote, "We can also say that in living right, we will also think right."[5]

Consecrated scholarship thus converges the life both of the mind and of the spirit!

Christ and the Creation

Restoration theology is expansive, not constraining. We do not face the problems Copernicus faced, when many mistakenly believed that the earth was the center of the universe.

For instance, through revelations we learn that Jesus played a remarkable role even premortally. Yet, given His stunning past, He was so meek! Under the direction of the Father, before His birth at Bethlehem, Jesus was actually the creating Lord of the universe. Clearly, God the Father is not the God of merely one planet!

Putting our planet in perspective, Stephen W. Hawking wrote: "The earth is a medium-sized planet orbiting around an average star in the outer suburbs of an ordinary spiral galaxy, which is itself only one of about a million million galaxies in the observable universe."[6]

Figure 2 shows the placement of our comparatively tiny solar system in the suburbs of the Milky Way galaxy. The visuals relate to the hymn we sing, "If You Could Hie to Kolob."

Figure 3 is the brightest portion of our "ordinary" Milky Way galaxy. This breathtaking view brings to mind the Lord's words about His having created "worlds without number" (Moses 1:33).

Figure 4 is a spiral galaxy—much like our galaxy, with millions of stars. This recalls the divine words that "there is no end to my works" (Moses 1:38).

Figure 5 is the Doradus Nebula. If it were as close to us as is very distant Orion, it would cover one-fourth of the night sky. Think of the words about how God's creations "cannot be numbered unto man; but they are numbered unto [Him]" (Moses 1:37).

Figure 6 is called Baade's Window. These myriad stars in just one region of the Milky Way galaxy recall the words "and the stars . . . give their light, as they roll upon their wings . . . , and any man who hath seen any or the least of these hath seen God moving in his majesty and power" (D&C 88:45, 47).

When we contemplate the stunning vastness, it is wise to remember, "Behold . . . all things are created and made to bear record of me" (Moses 6:63). Alma similarly declared, "All things denote there is a God . . . all the planets which move in their regular form do witness that there is a Supreme Creator" (Alma 30:44). It is a witnessing and overwhelming universe!

At the other end of the spectrum of size we also see divine design in the tiny but significant DNA molecule. This molecule (figure 7), which performs so many large chores, is formed by a double, intertwined helix.

It is instructive that the Lord told Moses, "But only an account of this earth, and the inhabitants thereof, give I unto you" (Moses 1:35). Even so, the Lord has told us some soaring, salvational things: "That by [Christ], . . . the worlds are and were created, and the inhabitants thereof are begotten sons and daughters unto God" (D&C 76:24).

Truly, "The heavens declare the glory of God; and the firmament sheweth his handywork" (Psalm 19:1), including the announcing star of Bethlehem.

Amid such cosmic *vastness* overseen by God and Jesus, however, we can also have faith in their loving *personal-ness*.

FIGURE 2

FIGURE 3

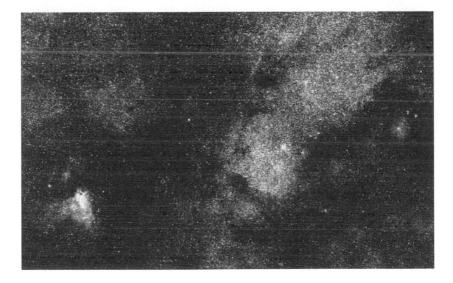

FIGURE 4

FIGURE 5

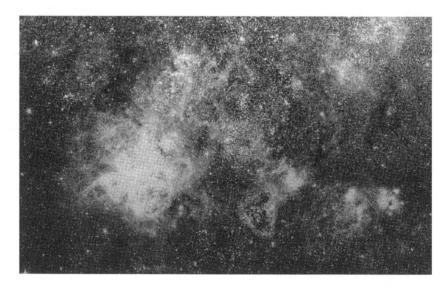

FIGURE 6

FIGURE 7

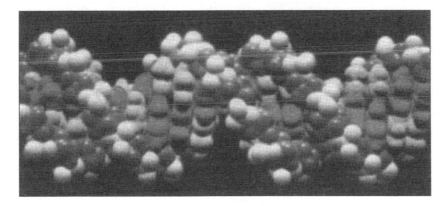

Does the Creator of the Universe
Care about Us Individually?

We want to be assured that God is there, but also to know what He is like. We yearn to know what His and life's purposes are. Does He really know us and really care about us individually? The reassuring reality was confirmed in Enoch's exclamation: "And were it possible that man could number the particles of the earth, yea, millions of earths like this, it would not be a beginning to the number of thy creations; and thy curtains are stretched out still; and yet thou art there, and thy bosom is there; and also thou art just; thou art merciful and kind forever" (Moses 7:30).

The most important thing for meek Enoch to know was not how many worlds there were, but that God was really *there!* Moreover, Enoch also learned that God is *just, true,* and *merciful* (Moses 6:31; 7:30, 33, 37). We have an exemplifying Lord. Will we, however, follow His example?

When meek Enoch was first called by the Lord of the universe, he was unsure of himself: "And when Enoch had heard these words, he bowed himself to the earth, before the Lord, and spake before the Lord, saying: Why is it that I have found favor in thy sight, and am but a lad, and all the people hate me; for I am slow of speech; wherefore am I thy servant?" (Moses 6:31). Yet much later meek Enoch had so deepened his discipleship that he actually came to know "that he pleased God" (Hebrews 11:5). Imagine the satisfaction of that knowledge!

Jesus gives such striking attention to individuals. To a woman from Samaria: "The woman saith unto him, I know that Messias cometh, which is called Christ: when he is come, he will tell us all things. Jesus saith unto her, I that speak unto thee am he" (John 4:25–26). Jesus disclosed His true identity to an audience of one.

After His resurrection, Jesus, the Lord of the universe, visited

Paul in a castle jail: "And the night following the Lord stood by him, and said, Be of good cheer, Paul; for as thou hast testified of me in Jerusalem, so must thou bear witness also at Rome" (Acts 23:11). Another audience of one!

It shouldn't surprise us that God gives so much individual attention to humans or to the divine design in the tiny DNA molecule. God "is in the details"—of the galaxies, of the DNA molecule, but, even more important, He "is in the details" of our lives.

Primary Attribute of the Disciple-Scholar: Meekness

There is as much vastness in the theology of the Restoration as in the stretching universe. "There is space there" for the full intellectual stretching of any serious disciple. There is room "enough and to spare" for all the behavioral development one is willing to undertake. No wonder, therefore, personal wholeness is required in discipleship. Genius without meekness is not enough to qualify for discipleship.

The portions of the key attributes lacking in each of us vary from person to person. It is meekness which facilitates working on what is lacking. For instance, the rich, righteous young man, otherwise clearly a high achiever, who came to Jesus asking what he might do to have eternal life, was told, "One thing thou lackest" (Mark 10:21; see also Luke 18:22). His lack was not of marketplace acumen or of honesty in business affairs; instead, he lacked meekness. This, alas, kept him from doing that customized thing which Jesus asked him to do—sell all that he had, give to the poor, and come follow Him. The young man lacked consecration.

Oliver Cowdery, who devotedly helped the Restoration in so many other ways, couldn't translate as he had hoped. He apparently lacked intellectual diligence, thinking all he had to do was ask. Also he "did not continue as [he] commenced"; he also feared, and "the time is past" said the Lord (D&C 9:5, 11). How many times in life do opportunities pass us by for want of meekness, never to return?

Moses was meek enough but needed to make a major change in his leadership style—for both his and the people's sake. He was advised by Jethro to delegate—not only in order to be a more effective leader but also so he could better serve others by focusing on the things that mattered most in his ministry. "And thou shalt teach them ordinances and laws, and shalt shew them the way wherein they must walk, and the work that they must do" (Exodus 18:20; see also 18:17–22).

Moses changed. No wonder he was referred to in the scriptures as "very meek, above all the men which were upon the face of the earth" (Numbers 12:3).

Peter was courageous and, understandably, thought he would never desert Jesus. Later, in an excruciating exchange, lack of full faith was underscored. This brought back Jesus' invitation to a humbled Peter—that when Peter was fully converted, he was to strengthen his brethren (Luke 22:32; see also John 21:15–17). So often the invitation to greater consecration comes by means of painful, personal experiences.

As Michael Polyani noted, "To learn by example is to submit to authority."[7]

Ponder what Brigham Young said of his tutorial relationship with Joseph Smith: "An angel never watched [Joseph] closer than I did, and that is what has given me the knowledge I have today. I treasure it up, and ask the Father, in the name of Jesus, to help my memory when information is wanted."[8]

May I shift for a few minutes to the secular scene. In the opinion of Clement Attlee, Winston Churchill was England's greatest wartime leader ever. Nevertheless, Churchill often neglected and was insensitive to his wartime coalition cabinet colleagues, including Attlee. At times Churchill put on a "one-man show." In frustration, Attlee, Deputy Prime Minister, once wrote a sharp letter to Churchill. " . . . I should have thought that you would have reposed some confidence in your Cabinet colleagues, but on the contrary you exhibit a very scanty respect for their views."[9] Attlee then spelled out an irrefutable bill of particulars. Churchill was "thunderstruck" and indignantly checked the feedback with his wife, Lord Beaverbrook, and another friend—all of whom quickly and candidly confirmed its accuracy.

Winston Churchill was wise in many respects, however. He presciently chose as the motto for his last volume of World War II history these words: "How the Great Democracies Triumphed, and so Were Able to Resume the Follies Which Had so Nearly Cost Them Their Life."[10]

One great individual who had considerable meekness was George Washington. Of him, his biographer wrote: "In all history few men who possessed unassailable power have used that power so gently and self-effacingly for what their best instincts told them was the welfare of their neighbors and all mankind."[11]

Washington's was "the charisma of competence," wrote Richard Norton Smith. Unlike Churchill, Washington was not an orator, and he knew it, saying: "With me it has always been a maxim rather to let my designs appear from my works than by my expressions."[12]

We are in a period in which so many are fascinated by charisma or seek for empowerment. Power to do what, however? This is the relevant question. Clever and evil, Hitler and Stalin (along with their combined henchmen) certainly had vast power. They helped to account for the premature losses of life in Greater Europe between 1930 and 1953 of an estimated 40–50 million people—as a result of wars and famine, massacres, purges, and exterminations. This man-made destructiveness is without precedent in human history![13]

What Fyodor Dostoevsky wrote about power in "Notes from the House of the Dead" surely applies, and not alone to Hitler and Stalin:

> Whoever has experienced the power, the complete ability to humiliate another human being . . . with the most extreme humiliation, willy-nilly loses power over his own sensations. Tyranny is a habit, it has a capacity for development, it develops finally into a disease. . . . Blood and power are intoxicating. . . . The human being and the citizen die within the tyrant forever; return to humanity, to repentance, to regeneration, becomes almost impossible.[14]

Hitler had a certain charisma, all right, which Washington did not. But what about consequences?

Lincoln wrote of the incessant strivings for glory, especially among the talented:

> It is to deny, what the history of the world tells us is true, to suppose that men of ambition and talents will not continue to spring up amongst us. . . . Towering genius disdains a beaten path. It seeks regions hitherto unexplored. It sees no distinction in adding story to story, upon the monuments of fame, erected to the memory of others. It denies that it is glory enough to serve under any chief. It scorns to tread in the footsteps of any predecessor, however illustrious. It thirsts and burns for distinction; and, if possible, it will have it, whether at the expense of emancipating slaves, or enslaving freemen.[15]

Power is safest, therefore, with those most Christlike, and heaven's power is accessible only to such individuals. No wonder the Lord warns us that power and authority, as used by the natural man, are abused by "almost all"! (D&C 121:34–46).

Thomas Merton noted Gandhi's searching question: "How can he who thinks he possesses absolute truth be fraternal?"[16] Obviously, the answer is for truth to company with love and meekness—as exemplified for us in the character of Jesus.

Do we have adequate faith in Jesus' character and in His atonement to strive genuinely to become more like Him, including in meekness?

The Great and Spacious Building

Do you remember the great and spacious building in the Book of Mormon? The trendy, self-congratulating multitudes were "politically correct" as they unmeekly mocked and pointed at those who clung to the gospel's iron rod. A few whose hands had once grasped the iron rod ended up in the great and spacious building pointing fingers of scorn at former friends. Strange as it seems, the scriptures do not indicate that these individuals let go of the iron rod for any objective reasons, or because they were in truth intellectually persuaded by the views of those in the great and spacious building. They were simply ashamed and embarrassed to be separated from the worldly multitudes, whose contempt they would not endure. "And after they had partaken of the fruit of the tree they did cast their eyes about as if they were ashamed" (1 Nephi 8:25).

No wonder Jesus, who "endured the cross, despising the shame" (Hebrews 12:2), asks us to do likewise (D&C 56:2). Jesus "gave no heed" to temptations either (D&C 20:22).

There is a certain security which comes of spiritual wholeness. Thomas More's words to his mortal judges reflected both his integrity and his generosity. Having been sentenced to die, he said to his judges: "Like the Blessed Apostle St. Paul, as we read in the

Acts of the Apostles, was present, and consented to the death of St. Stephen, and kept their clothes that stoned him to death, and yet be they now both twain Holy Saints in heaven, and shall continue there friends forever, so I verily trust and shall therefore right heartily pray, that though your lordships have now here in earth been judges to my condemnation, we may yet hereafter in heaven merrily all meet together, to our everlasting salvation."[17]

More gave no heed to the contempt in which he was held by his accusers, but was not contemptuous of them.

The Path to Discipleship

The sooner we are on the way to serious discipleship, therefore, the sooner the needed spiritual and personal reinforcements and intellectual reassurances will come to us personally. If one chooses to live out his life without God, however, it will be as if he had been sentenced to remain a permanent resident in an airport transit lounge—consigned there, briefly and expectantly, to mingle with the ever-changing, lonely crowds. Somehow, in that forlorn situation, even being granted a cot and a hot plate in the corner of the transit lounge would not ease either the sense of anomie or futility.

Someday, in the search for wholeness in thought and behavior, we shall see much more clearly how orthodoxy "is our reward, not solely our goad."[18]

Genius is safest when it is accompanied by meekness. Competency is most useful when accompanied by humility. The qualities of love, mercy, patience, meekness, and spiritual submissiveness are portable. These—to the degree developed—will go with us through the veil of death; they will also rise with us in the resurrection.

No matter how many talents or gifts we now have, God will still seek to remodel us, if we will let Him. Borrowing a parable from George MacDonald, C. S. Lewis wrote of such painful remodeling:

> Imagine yourself as a living house. God comes in to rebuild that house. At first, perhaps, you can understand what He is doing. He is getting the drains right and stopping the leaks in the roof and so on: you knew that those jobs needed doing and so you are not surprised. But presently he starts knocking the house about in a way that hurts abominably and does not seem to make sense. What on earth is He up to? The explanation is that He is building quite a different house from the one you thought of—throwing out a new wing here, putting on an extra floor there, running up towers, making courtyards. You thought you were going to be made into a decent little cottage: but He is building a palace.[19]

Long before being a General Authority, I remarked on how in the world some academic men and women are blind in one eye. These are quick to see dangers coming from the one direction, but not from other directions. Only the eyes of faith permit us to see "things as they really are, and . . . things as they really will be" (Jacob 4:13). The disciple-scholar is concerned with knowing and responding to such reality. He also values history. But history, by itself, has its limitations, as Churchill observed:

> History with its flickering lamps stumbles along the trail of the past, trying to reconstruct its scenes, to revive its echoes, and kindle with pale gleams the passion of former days. . . . The only guide to a man is his conscience; the only shield to his memory is the rectitude and sincerity of his actions. It is very imprudent to walk through life without this shield, because we are so often mocked by the failure of

our hopes and the upsetting of our calculations; but with this shield, however the fates may play, we march always in the ranks of honor.[20]

The Holy Ghost, which gift the disciple has, provides precious proportion. Otherwise, as Owen Barfield wrote, there occurs a "whisper" which "Memory will warehouse as a shout."[21]

To be a disciple-scholar in our time is a call to high adventure! Just as one's quest for knowledge should be unending, so too should the quest for greater love, meekness, and patience.

Consecration and the Disciple-Scholar

In considering consecration, it is well to remember that under this principle nothing is held back—whether turf, attitude, or hobbies. One's will is to be swallowed up in the will of God—just as occurred with Jesus (Mosiah 15:7).

Though I have spoken of the disciple-scholar, in the end all the hyphenated words come off. We are finally disciples—men and women of Christ (3 Nephi 27:27).

But is consecration asking too much? It is certainly asking more than but a few finally achieve. It certainly involves a submission to authority, but what an Authority!

When we consecrate, individuality is actually enhanced, not lost. Our quirks and impurities go, but who would want to come into the Inner Court trailing such obsolete trinkets anyway? Besides, it is easier to be a character than to have character!

Why is it all so slow? Because God will not impose upon us.

In opting for discipleship, we have nothing to fear but the disapproval of the natural man and his like-minded, preoccupied friends—with their pointing fingers.

Most forms of holding back are rooted in pride or are prompted by the mistaken notion that somehow we are diminished by sub-mission to God. Actually, the greater the submission, the greater the expansion!

Where will the journey take us? "Unto a perfect man, unto the measure of the stature of the fulness of Christ" (Ephesians 4:13). One who "continueth in God, receiveth more light; and that light groweth brighter and brighter until the perfect day" (D&C 50:24). There isn't any shortcut. The straight and narrow is the quickest and most direct way. It is also the only way!

Will there be perplexities? Yes, indeed. "I know that [God] loveth his children; nevertheless, I do not know the meaning of all things" (1 Nephi 11:17). Indeed, we too will not always know the "meaning" of things happening to us and around us. Therefore, whatever knowledge we may have, we still need to have faith to see us through those puzzling moments. Because of past verifying experiences, we can know that we have proven God "in days that are past,"[22] thus giving us faith for the challenges of the present.

God bless you who are in the vanguard of special spirits in these the last days.

Notes

1. This essay was originally given as part of the Discipline and Discipleship Lecture Series presented to participants in the Brigham Young University Honors Program in 1994–95; published in Henry B. Eyring, ed., *On Becoming a Disciple-Scholar* (Salt Lake City: Bookcraft, 1995), 1–22.

2. Stephen W. Hawking, *Black Holes and Baby Universes* (New York: Bantam Books, 1993), 99.

3. Stephen W. Hawking, *A Brief History of Time* (New York: Bantam Books, 1988), 171, 175.

4. Jacques Maritain, *Frontiers of Poetry* (New York: Charles Scribner's Sons, 1962), 132.

5. Paul L. Holmer, *C. S. Lewis, The Shape of His Faith and Thought* (New York: Harper and Row, 1976), 115.

6. Hawking, *A Brief History of Time*, 126.

7. Michael Polyani, *Personal Knowledge: Towards a Post-Critical Philosophy* (Chicago: The University of Chicago Press, 1958), 53.

8. Brigham Young Papers, 8 October 1866 sermon.

9. Kenneth Harris, *Attlee* (London: Weidenfeld and Nicolson, 1982), 242.

10. Winston S. Churchill, *The Second World War, vol. 6: Triumph and Tragedy* (Boston: Houghton Mifflin Company, 1953), ix.

11. James Thomas Flexner, *Washington, the Indispensable Man* (New York: Plume, 1984), xvi.

12. Richard Norton Smith, *Patriarch: George Washington and the New American Nation* (Boston: Houghton Mifflin Company, 1993), 8, 12.

13. See Alan Bullock, *Hitler and Stalin* (New York: Vintage Books, 1993), 969.

14. In Bullock, *Hitler and Stalin*, 971–72.

15. Don E. Fehrenbacher, ed., *Abraham Lincoln: A Documentary Portrait through His Speeches and Writings* (New York: The New American Library, 1964), 41.

16. In Neal A. Maxwell, *A More Excellent Way* (Salt Lake City: Deseret Book, 1967), 31.

17. Anthony Kenny, *Thomas More* (New York: Oxford University Press, 1983), 88.

18. Holmer, *C. S. Lewis, The Shape of His Faith and Thought*, 115.

19. C. S. Lewis, *Mere Christianity* (New York: Macmillan, 1952), 174.

20. In Robert Rhodes James, ed., *Churchill Speaks* (New York: Chelsea House, 1980), 734.

21. Wayne Martindale and Jerry Root, eds., *The Quotable C. S. Lewis* (Wheaton, Ill.: Tyndale House Publishers, 1989), 424.

22. From William Fowler, "We Thank Thee, O God, for a Prophet," in *Hymns of The Church of Jesus Christ of Latter-day Saints* (Salt Lake City: The Church of Jesus Christ of Latter-day Saints), no. 19.

How We Know:
The Delicate Relationship
between Evidence and Faith

Aaron Titus

Juris Doctor, George Washington University Law School

Question:

My physics professor started the semester by asking our large class, "What is truth?"

Several students raised their hands. The first said, "Truth is universal."

"Wrong!" the professor retorted. "In physics, truth is specialized."

Stunned, another student answered, "Truth is something you know but can't prove."

"Wrong!" he shot back. "Nothing is true without proof."

The next student ventured, "Truth never changes."

Clearly in a rhythm the professor bellowed, "Wrong! Truth constantly changes as we learn new things."

A half-dozen students offered answers to the professor's question before I could muster the courage to raise my hand. I decided to try Jacob's answer in the Book of Mormon. "Truth is the way things really are," I said.

The professor's rhythm broke, and he gave no rebuttal.

My university education stretched my mind in ways I never could have imagined. College is a time of intellectual experimentation, and while most minds expand, a few narrow. Some spiritually suffocate in an intellectual atmosphere where "miraculous" is always considered "mythical." For some reason, academic discussion tends to selectively reject spiritual vocabularies. I have met many who believed that strength comes from cynicism and skepticism. How do I share spiritual truths using a vocabulary of numbers, calculations, formulas, and observations? How can I defend my faith when I can't talk about the "still, small voice," faith, or the fruits of the Spirit?

I recently became friends with an older man of great intellectual capacity and international repute. Decades of his work have culminated in a complex taxonomic database of design concepts. As an abstract sculptor, his ponderous, figure-like stone pieces exhibit a surprising counterpoint to his analytic talents.

During dinner, our discussion turned toward finding and knowing truth. He asked, "What is truth?" His resigned tone intimated a lifelong and vain pursuit of the question. He continued detachedly, "I don't know that truth exists." His question was not disingenuous or born of intellectual haughtiness, but the product of a seasoned and fatigued mind, weary of asking questions with no apparent answers. It seemed he had long since turned his mind inward in a futile search for truths that cannot exist in solitude.

Humbly and frankly I replied, "Well, that's easy." Then relying again on Jacob and Joseph Smith, I said, "Truth is the way things really are, the way things really were, and the way things really will be. That is truth" (Jacob 4:13; D&C 93:24).

He thought for a moment and said, "Yes, I can accept that definition. But what is the 'way things really are,' and how can I know it?" Then he asked intensely, "How do you know your mind does not distort the truth?"

His words reminded me of Korihor's doctrine that spiritual truths are nothing more than the effect of a "derangement of your minds" (Alma 30:16). He told me how unsatisfied and empty he felt, wanting to know truth but unable to bring himself to trust his own mind.

I bore testimony of the Book of Mormon and its miraculous origins. He listened thoughtfully and respectfully—as one does when someone relates a religious myth. Then, just as respectfully, he said, "That is very interesting, but did it really happen?"

I said, "Well, yes. I can show you the book; it is really here."

For the remainder of our conversation, we talked about ways to discover the "way things really are": By gathering empirical, logical, or spiritual evidence. I believe that though we are unable to know everything, we are capable of understanding at least some things. I told him that I know God lives and that He loves me. Unexpectedly, I saw a glimmer of admiration in his eyes. For a flash, I could see he believed that I knew what I said; but just as quickly his eyes again became detached and resigned. By the end of our conversation I was poignantly grateful for the things I know.

Expressing spiritual knowledge is always a challenge, especially in an intellectual setting, where spiritual vocabularies are taboo. When I'm at church, it's okay to use spiritual words to explain spiritual things, but in college I occasionally find it hard to breathe spiritually in the academic atmosphere. How do I share the things I know with someone who does not speak a spiritual language?

* * *

Robert L. Millet

Professor of Ancient Scripture at Brigham Young University

Answer:

Some time back I sat in my home ward and listened with much interest as four children moved to the front of the chapel and in turn bore their testimonies. The first one could not have been more than seven years old, and yet she spoke with a confidence that one might expect from a seasoned adult member of the Church. She said, essentially, "I want to bear my testimony that I know that the Church is true, that Joseph Smith was a prophet of God, and that President Gordon B. Hinckley is our living prophet today." She then shared some personal feelings and sat down. I pondered on her words, on the depth of sincerity evident in her voice, and I wondered: Does she know? Does she *really* know? How much could she know? Later during the day I reflected on the experience again and again and had affirmed to my mind and heart that little children can come to know the things of God, by the power of the Spirit of God (1 Corinthians 2:11–14), and can speak words of truth and wisdom just as their adult counterparts can (Alma 32:23). A testimony is not something you either have or don't have, but rather an impression of the Spirit as to the truthfulness of eternal things, an inner awareness that ranges along a spiritual continuum from a simple, peaceful feeling to a perfect knowledge.

It has wisely been observed that the strength of this Church lies not alone in the powerful witnesses of the fifteen men we sustain as prophets, seers, and revelators, but also in the deep reassurance and resolve that rest in the souls of individual Saints of the Most High from Alabama to Zanzibar. A testimony may begin through trusting in and relying upon the witness of another, of one who knows for sure—to believe on the faith of another is indeed a spiritual gift, a gift that can lead to eternal life (D&C 46:13–14). And yet surely each one of us desires to possess our own witness, an independent knowledge of the reality of God our Father, the redemptive mission of Jesus the Christ, and the divine call of Joseph Smith and the work of the Restoration. It was President Heber C. Kimball who warned us of a test to come, a test that would separate out those who professed membership in the Church but did not possess a personal testimony sufficient to see them through hard times. "The time will come when no man or woman will be able to endure on borrowed light," he said. "Each will have to be guided by the light within himself. If you do not have it, how can you stand?"[1]

Faith and Evidence

My memories of the first class I took in religion at an eastern university are still very much intact. It was a course entitled "Seminar in Biblical Studies" and dealt with such issues as scripture, canon, interpretation, authorship, eschatology, prophecy, and like subjects. We were but weeks into the seminar when the professor was confronted by a question from an Evangelical Protestant student on the reality of miracles among ancient Israel. The response was polite but brief: "I'm not going to state my own position on the matter in this class. Let me just say that I feel it doesn't really matter whether the Israelites actually crossed the Red Sea on dry ground as a result of some miracle performed by Moses. What matters is that the Israelites then and thereafter *saw* it as an act of divine intervention, and the event became a foundation for a people's faith for centuries."

About a year later I found myself in a similar setting, this time in a seminar entitled "Critical Studies of the New Testament," the first half of a two-semester encounter with a literary-historical study of the New Testament. The composition of the students in the seminar made for fascinating conversation: a Reformed Jew, two Methodists, two Southern Baptists, a Roman Catholic, a Nazarene, and a Latter-day Saint. The professor was a secular Jew. By the time we had begun studying the passion narratives in the Gospels, the question of "historical events" versus "faith events" had been raised. The professor stressed the importance of "myth" and emphasized that miraculous events in the New Testament— because in them the narrative detaches itself from the ordinary limitations of time and space such that the supernatural "irrupts" into human history—should be relegated to the category of faith events or sacred story. And then came the punchline, a phrase that had a haunting familiarity: "Now, for example: Whether or not Jesus of Nazareth came back to life—literally rose from the dead— does not matter. What matters is that the Christians thought he did. And the whole Christian movement is founded on this faith event."

What we are dealing with is historicity—in simple terms, whether something significant truly took place, whether it was an actual event in actual history. Few normal people doubt, for example, that Jesus lived. His appearance on the stage of history is too well attested to doubt. But what is so often doubted is His divinity—His divine Sonship, His miracles, His ability to forgive sins and heal and regenerate human souls, His power over life and death.

In 1966 Elder Gordon B. Hinckley said: "*Modern theologians strip [Jesus] of his divinity and then wonder why men do not worship him.* These clever scholars have taken from Jesus the mantle of godhood and have left only a man. *They have tried to accommodate him to their own narrow thinking. They have robbed him of his divine sonship and taken from the world its rightful King.*"[2] Some five years later, President Harold B. Lee explained to a group of students at Utah State University: "Fifty years ago or more," he said, "when I was a missionary, our greatest responsibility was to defend the great truth that the Prophet Joseph Smith was divinely called and inspired and that the Book of Mormon was indeed the word of God. But even at that time there were the unmistakable evidences that *there was coming into the religious world actually a question about the Bible and about the divine calling of the Master himself.* Now, fifty years later, our greatest responsibility and anxiety is to defend the divine mission of our Lord and Master, Jesus Christ, for all about us, even among those who claim to be professors of the Christian faith, are those not willing to stand squarely in defense of the great truth that our Lord and Master, Jesus Christ, was indeed the Son of God."[3]

Who was Jesus of Nazareth? To what degree can we trust the canonical Gospels in regard to what Jesus said and did? Has the Christian Church transformed a lowly Nazarene into a God? Is it possible to tear away the faithful film of believing tradition and get back to the way things really were? Indeed, the question of the ages is, "What think ye of Christ?" (Matthew 22:42). I add my voice to the growing throng of tens of thousands of irritated Christians and to an increasing number of religious leaders and serious scholars who certify

• that Jesus was and is who He and the Gospel writers say He was—the literal Son of God, the Only Begotten Son in the flesh of the Eternal Father;

• that we have every reason to believe that the four Gospels are true and accurate and that the essential message of historical Christianity—that Christ lived, taught, lifted, strengthened, renewed, healed, prophesied, communed with Deity, suffered, died, rose from the dead, appeared thereafter to hundreds, and will come again in glory—is to be taken seriously;

• that efforts to demythologize or debunk Jesus will in time be shown to be what they in actuality are—shams and charades on the part of people who dare not believe and who work endlessly to proselyte others to share their doubts. Too often the undergirding assumption of those who cast doubt on the historical Jesus as set forth in scripture, in whole or in part, is a denial of the supernatural and a refusal to admit of prophecy, revelation, and divine intervention.

C. S. Lewis, in speaking of biblical critics, observed: "These men ask me to believe they can read between the lines of the old texts; the evidence is their obvious inability to read (in any sense worth discussing) the lines themselves. They claim to see fernseed and can't see an elephant ten yards away in broad daylight." Lewis also noted that the typical biblical scholar does not have immediate access to the truth any more than the average man on the street. "Scholars as scholars," he added, "speak on it with no more authority than anyone else. The canon 'If miraculous, unhistorical' is one they bring to their study of the texts, not one they have learned from it. *If one is speaking of authority, the united authority of all the Biblical critics in the world counts here for nothing. On this they speak simply as men;* men obviously influenced by, and perhaps insufficiently critical of, the spirit of the age they grew up in."[4]

Indeed, why should modern biblical scholars scoff at the findings of the Jesus Seminar? Is not this the logical extension of what began as the quest for the historical Jesus? Have we not now come face to face with where the naturalistic presuppositions eventually bring us?

How is my belief in present-day healing, for example, affected by what did or did not take place in the first century? Can I believe that the power to heal is real in our own day if in fact such powers were not operative in the first century or in the days of Joseph Smith's Nauvoo, if the stories of the healing of the blind, the halt, the maim, and even the dead being raised are prevarications? Faith is based on evidence, and the stronger the evidence the stronger the faith. To what extent can I trust in a power of redemption if in fact

Jesus was not the Savior of humankind? How should I view death if in fact Jesus did not rise from the tomb three days after his crucifixion? To what degree do my religious beliefs need to be both true and reasonable?

Can Jesus be a Galilean guru and not the Son of God? Can He play the role of Samaritan Socrates and not be divine? In short, what of the idea so prevalent among the humanists that Jesus was a great moral teacher, a mere man, albeit a brilliant and inspired man, but not the promised Messiah? In short, is there a difference between the "historical Jesus" and the "Christ of faith"? Do the extant sources allow such a distinction? Did Jesus?

There's a simple syllogism that applies to some of the current claims about Jesus. It goes something like this: He was a great moral teacher. He claimed to be the Son of God. He was not the Son of God. Therefore, He could not be a great moral teacher. Robert Stein has written: "On the lips of anyone else the claims of Jesus would appear to be evidence of gross egomania, for Jesus clearly implies that the entire world revolves around himself and that the fate of all men is dependent on their acceptance or rejection of him. . . . There seem to be only two possible ways of interpreting the totalitarian nature of the claims of Jesus. Either we must assume that Jesus was deluded and unstable with unusual delusions of grandeur, or we are faced with the realization that Jesus is truly One who speaks with divine authority, who actually divided all of history into B.C.-A.D., and whose rejection or acceptance determines the fate of men."[5]

One of the most famous statements on this matter, one that forces the issue and exposes the shallowness of many a person's thinking, was made by C. S. Lewis. "I am trying here," he explained, "to prevent anyone saying the really foolish thing that people often say about Him: 'I'm ready to accept Jesus as a great moral teacher, but I don't accept His claim to be God.' That is the one thing we must not say. A man who was merely a man and said the sort of things Jesus said would not be a great moral teacher. He would either be a lunatic—on a level with the man who says he is a poached egg—or else he would be the Devil of Hell. You must make your choice. Either this man was, and is, the Son of God: or else a madman or something worse. You can shut Him up for a fool, you can spit at Him and kill Him as a demon; or you can fall at His feet and call Him Lord and God. But let us not come with any patronizing nonsense about His being a great human teacher. He has not left that open to us. He did not intend to."[6]

Stripped of His divinity, His teachings concerning His own Godhood, forgiveness of sins, resurrection, and Second Coming, why would Jesus of Nazareth be so controversial? Why would people dislike such a man? Why on earth would He be crucified? I have wondered over the years how so many who read the same New Testament I do could conjure up a Jesus who is basically a simple, nondirective counselor, a sensitive ecologist who came to earth to model quiet pacifism. Given, Jesus of Nazareth was indeed the caring, compassionate, forgiving, serving man described by Matthew, Mark, Luke, and John. He was also, however, God Incarnate, the discerning, fearless, assertive, confrontive, excoriating, and at times sarcastic Being who had little patience with hypocrisy and self-righteousness. John Meir observed: "While I do not agree with those who turn Jesus into a violent revolutionary or political agitator, scholars who favor a revolutionary Jesus do have a point. A tweedy poetaster who spent his time spinning out parables and Japanese koans, a literary asthete who toyed with first-century deconstructionism, or a bland Jesus who simply told people to look at the lilies of the field—such a Jesus would threaten no one, just as the university professors who create him threaten no one. The historical Jesus did threaten, disturb, and infuriate people—from interpreters of the Law through the Jerusalem priestly aristocracy to the

Roman prefect who finally tried and crucified him. . . . A Jesus whose words and deeds would not alienate people, especially powerful people, is not the historical Jesus."[7] In addition, as Scot McKnight pointed out, "A social revolutionary would have been crucified (and this partly explains Jesus' death, in my view), but it is doubtful that such a revolutionary would have given birth to a church that was hardly a movement of social revolution."[8]

President Howard W. Hunter noted that "there are those who declare it is old-fashioned to believe in the Bible. Is it old-fashioned to believe in Jesus Christ, the Son of the Living God? Is it old-fashioned to believe in his atoning sacrifice and the resurrection? If it is, I declare myself to be old-fashioned and the Church to be old-fashioned. . . .

"In this world of confusion and rushing, temporal progress, we need to return to the simplicity of Christ. We need to love, honor, and worship him. To acquire spirituality and have its influence in our lives, we cannot become confused and misdirected by the twisted teachings of the modernist. We need to study the simple fundamentals of the truths taught by the Master and eliminate the controversial. Our faith in God needs to be real and not speculative. The restored gospel of Jesus Christ can be a dynamic, moving influence, and true acceptance gives us a meaningful, religious experience. . . . We can be modern without giving way to the influence of the modernist. If it is old-fashioned to believe in the Bible, we should thank God for the privilege of being old-fashioned."[9]

Faith in the Unseen

Let's come at this from a different angle. A few years ago a Baptist minister friend and I were driving through Boston in an effort to get to the LDS Institute of Religion at Cambridge. As has been my custom nearly every time I have been there, I was absolutely lost and had no idea where we were. We stopped several times for directions, and each helpful person would point to us the way and say with much assurance, "You can't miss it." After having heard that phrase five or six times, I asked our seventh helper for directions and began my question with "Please don't say 'You can't miss it,' because I assure you we can, for we have done it again and again."

During our scavenger hunt of sorts, we chatted. My colleague commented on a matter we had discussed several times, namely the idea that Latter-day Saints are more prone to rely upon feelings than tangible evidence for truth of religious claims. Being just a bit frustrated, I asked, "Do you believe in the literal bodily resurrection of Jesus Christ?"

The look he gave me was similar to that which a sixteen-year-old would give to someone who had asked what the teenager felt to be an inane question. "Of course I believe in the resurrection, Bob. I'm an ordained minister."

I followed up: "Why do you believe in the resurrection? How do you know it really happened?"

He answered, "Because the New Testament teaches of the resurrection of Jesus."

I shot right back, "But how do you know that the New Testament accounts can be trusted? How do you know the Bible can be trusted? Maybe someone just made all of this up. Maybe the Bible is a giant hoax."

"No," he said, "there is strong evidence to support the truthfulness of the Bible."

"Like what?" I asked.

"Well, there are archaeological, historical, and cultural evidences that what is being described actually happened."

I then queried. "And so that's how you know the resurrection is real?"

"Yeah, I suppose so," he said.

At this point my mind began to race. And I found myself saying something I hadn't planned to say. "You know, I feel a great sense of sadness right now."

My Evangelical friend was surprised and asked, "Sadness? Why are you sad?"

"I was just thinking of a good friend of mine, an older woman in Montgomery, Alabama."

My companion asked, "What about her?"

I then said, "Well, I was thinking of how sad it is that this wonderful and devoted Christian, a person who has given her life to Jesus and studied and memorized her Bible like few people I know, a woman whose life manifests her complete commitment to the Savior, is not really entitled to have a witness of the truthfulness of the Bible."

"Why is that?" he followed up.

"Well, she knows precious little about archaeology or languages or culture or history or manuscripts, and so I suppose she can't really know within her heart that the Bible really is the word of God."

"Of course she can," he said. "She can have her faith, her personal witness that the Bible is true."

I pulled off to the side of the road and stopped the car. I turned to him, smiled, and stated, "Do you mean that she can have the power of the Holy Spirit testify to her soul that her Bible is completely trustworthy and can be relied upon as God's word?"

"Yes, that's what I mean."

My smile broadened as I added, "Then we've come full circle."

"What do you mean by that?" he asked.

I said, "You're telling me that this good woman, one who has none of the supposed requisite background or knowledge of external evidence, can have a witness of the Spirit, including deep personal feelings about the Bible, and that those feelings are genuine and heaven-sent."

At that point my friend looked into my eyes and he smiled. "I see where you're going with this."

We then engaged in one of the most productive conversations of our time together as friends. We agreed between us that it is too easy to yield to the temptation to categorize and pigeonhole and stereotype and even demonize persons whose faith is different from your own. It is too easy to overstate, to misrepresent, to create "straw men" in an effort to establish your own point.

We agreed that Evangelical Christians and Latter-day Saint Christians both base their faith on evidence—both seen and unseen. While, as we observed earlier, saving faith is always built upon that which is true, upon an actual historical moment in time, upon something that really existed in the past, true believers will never allow their faith to be held hostage by what science has or has not found at a given time. I know, for example, that Jesus fed the five thousand, healed the sick, raised the dead, calmed the storm, and rose from the dead—not just because I have physical evidence for each of those miraculous events (because I do not), nor even because I can read of these things in the New Testament, which I accept with all my heart. But I know these things actually happened because the Spirit of the Living God bears witness to my spirit that the Lord of Life did all that the scriptures say He did, and more.

Many years ago on a Sunday morning I opened the door and reached down to pick up the morning newspaper when I saw beside the paper a plastic bag containing a paperback book. I carried both inside and laid the newspaper aside as I browsed through the paperback. The cover was a lovely picture of a mountain stream, but the title of the book revealed to me what in fact the book was all about—it was an anti-Mormon treatise. Many of the arguments in the book against The Church of Jesus Christ of Latter-day Saints were old and worn-out ones, dead horses that have been beaten since the days of E. D. Howe. Latter-day Saints had responded to the issues posed scores of times, but they continued to crop up.

One section of the book, however, did prove to be of some interest to me. Let me paraphrase what was essentially said about 130 pages into the text. The author pointed out that eventually two Mormon missionaries would come to the reader's door. If they do come, he pleaded, don't let them in. If, however, you do let them in, then don't listen to them. If they are allowed to tell you about their message, about Joseph Smith and angels and golden plates, they will ask you to kneel and pray about the truthfulness of these things. Whatever you do, don't pray! The writer then made this unusual observation: In ascertaining the truthfulness of a religious claim, there are three things a person can never trust: (1) your thoughts; (2) your feelings; (3) your prayers.

I was all ears at this point, wondering how we could ever know anything. I didn't have to wait long, for the writer then noted that the only thing that could be trusted was the Holy Bible itself. I shook my head and felt a deep sense of sadness for the author, for I wondered how indeed a person could even know of the truthfulness of the Bible if he or she could not think, feel, or pray. I had a collage of feelings at that moment. As indicated, I felt sad for the writer, for it was obvious that he could not see the blatant inconsistency and irrationality of his own words. I tried to put myself into the place of a reader who was not a Latter-day Saint and wondered how I might feel upon reading such things. To be honest, I would feel insulted, knowing that I could not be trusted enough in my pursuit of truth to rely upon my mind, my heart, or even the most tried and true method of obtaining divine direction—prayer itself.

True believers will always be challenged by those who refuse to see. In a very real sense, believing is seeing. No member of the Church need feel embarrassed when he or she cannot produce the golden plates or the complete Egyptian papyrus. No member of this Church should ever feel hesitant to bear testimony of those verities that remain in the realm of faith, that are seen only with the eyes of faith. Elder Neal A. Maxwell wrote: "It is the author's opinion that all the scriptures, including the Book of Mormon, will remain in the realm of faith. Science will not be able to prove or disprove holy writ. However, enough plausible evidence will come forth to prevent scoffers from having a field day, but not enough to remove the requirement of faith. Believers must be patient during such unfolding."[10]

Similarly, President Ezra Taft Benson pointed out: "We do not have to prove the Book of Mormon is true. The book is its own proof. All we need to do is read it and declare it. The Book of Mormon is not on trial—the people of the world, including the members of the Church, are on trial as to what they will do with this second witness for Christ."[11]

"We are not required to prove that the Book of Mormon is true or is an authentic record through external evidences—though there are many. It never has been the case, nor is it so now, that the studies of the learned will prove the Book or Mormon true or false. The origin, preparation, translation, and verification of the truth of the Book of Mormon have all been retained in the hands of the Lord, and the Lord makes no mistakes. You can be assured of that."[12]

President Gordon B. Hinckley put things in proper perspective when he taught: "I can hold [the Book of Mormon] in my hand. It is real. It has weight and substance that can be physically measured. I can open its pages and read, and it has language both beautiful and uplifting. The ancient record from which it was translated came out of the earth as a voice speaking from the dust. . . .

"The evidence for its truth, for its validity in a world that is prone to demand evidence, lies not in archaeology or anthropology, though these may be helpful to some. It lies not in word research or historical analysis, though these may be confirmatory. The evidence for its truth and validity lies within the covers of the book itself. The test of its truth lies in reading it. It is a book of God. Reasonable individuals may sincerely question its origin, but those who read it prayerfully may come to know by a power beyond their natural senses that it is true, that it contains the word of God, that it outlines saving truths of the everlasting gospel, that it came forth by the gift and power of God."[13]

While we seek to make friends and build bridges of understanding where possible, we do not court favor, nor do we compromise one whit on what we believe. Some doctrines, like the doctrine of "the only true and living church" (D&C 1:30), by their very nature arouse antagonism from those of other faiths. Would it not be wise to avoid or at least downplay such divisive points? Perhaps, some say, we should consider focusing on matters we have in common and put aside, for the time being, the distinctive teachings of the Restoration. Elder Boyd K. Packer declared: "If we thought only in terms of diplomacy or popularity, surely we should change our course. But we must hold tightly to it even though some turn away. . . .

"It is not an easy thing for us to defend the position that bothers so many others. Brethren and sisters, never be ashamed of the gospel of Jesus Christ. Never apologize for the sacred doctrines of the gospel. Never feel inadequate and unsettled because you cannot explain them to the satisfaction of all who might inquire of you. Do not be ill at ease or uncomfortable because you can give little more than your conviction. . . .

"If we can stand without shame, without hesitancy, without embarrassment, without reservation to bear witness that the gospel has been restored, that there are prophets and Apostles upon the earth, that the truth is available for all mankind, the Lord's Spirit will be with us. And that assurance can be affirmed to others."[14]

Conclusion

In the end, the only way that the things of God can and should be known is by the power of the Holy Ghost. These things are what the scriptures call the "mysteries of God." Another way of stating this is to suggest that the only way that spiritual truths may be known is by the quiet whisperings of the Holy Ghost. How did Alma the younger know? Was it because he was struck to the ground by an angel? Was it because he lay immobile and speechless for three days while he underwent a confrontation with himself and his sinful and rebellious past? No, Alma knew as we know: he may have undergone a serious turnaround in his life through the intervention of a heavenly messenger, but the witness that drove and directed this magnificent convert was the witness of the Spirit. In his own words: "Behold, I testify unto you that I do know that these things whereof I have spoken are true. And how do ye suppose that I know of their surety? Behold, I say unto you *they are made known unto me by the Holy Spirit of God.* Behold, I have fasted and prayed many days that I might know these things of myself. And now I do know of myself that they are true; for the Lord God hath made them manifest unto me by his Holy Spirit; and this is the spirit of revelation which is in me" (Alma 5:45–46; emphasis added).

On the other hand, we can come to sense the *significance* of a spiritual reality by the loud janglings of opposition it engenders. For example, what do the following locations have in common: Portland, Dallas, Atlanta, White Plains, Nashville, Denver, Stockholm, and Ghana? Clearly, in each of these places the announcement that a Latter-day Saint temple was to be built there brought opponents and even crazed zealots out of the woodwork.

Brigham Young is reported to have said once that "every time we announce the erection of a temple, all the bells of hell begin to ring." President Young then added the following (and it must have been with a smile): "And oh how I love to hear those bells."[15] If I did not already know by the quiet whisperings of the Spirit within me that what goes on within temples is true and is of eternal import, I just might sense the significance of the temple by the kind of opposition that seems to flow almost naturally from those who refuse to see.

Consider another illustration. Why is it that so many people throughout the world write scathing books, deliver biting addresses, and prepare vicious videos denouncing the Book of Mormon? What is it about black words on a white page, all of which are uplifting and edifying, that invite men and women to come unto Christ and be perfected in Him, that would arouse such bitter antagonism? Once again, if I did not already know, by the quiet whisperings of the Spirit, that the Book of Mormon truly is heaven-sent and indeed Another Testament of Jesus Christ, I would recognize its significance—its power to settle doctrinal disputes, touch hearts, and transform men and women's lives—by the loud and hostile reactions people tend to have toward it.

Hugh Nibley, one of the great defenders of the faith, stated: "The words of the prophets cannot be held to the tentative and defective tests that men have devised for them. Science, philosophy, and common sense all have a right to their day in court. But the last word does not lie with them. Every time men in their wisdom have come forth with the last word, other words have promptly followed. The last word is a testimony of the gospel that comes only by direct revelation. Our Father in heaven speaks it, and if it were in perfect agreement with the science of today, it would surely be out of line with the science of tomorrow. Let us not, therefore, seek to hold

God to the learned opinions of the moment when he speaks the language of eternity."[16]

I have learned a few things as I have learned a few things over the years. I thank God for the formal education I have received, for the privilege it is (and I count it such) to have received university training and to have earned bachelors, masters, and doctoral degrees. Education has expanded my mind and opened conversations and doors for me. It has taught me what books to read, how to research a topic, and how to make my case or present my point of view more effectively. But the more I learn, the more I value the truths of salvation, those simple but profound verities that soothe and settle and sanctify human hearts.

I appreciate knowing that the order of the cosmos points toward a Providential Hand; I am deeply grateful to know, by the power of the Holy Ghost, that there is a God and that He is our Father in Heaven.

I appreciate knowing something about the social, political, and religious world into which Jesus of Nazareth was born; I am deeply grateful for the witness of the Spirit that He is indeed God's Almighty Son.

I appreciate knowing something about the social and intellectual climate of nineteenth-century America; I am grateful to have, burning within my soul, a testimony that the Father and the Son appeared to Joseph Smith in the spring of 1820 and that The Church of Jesus Christ of Latter-day Saints is truly the kingdom of God on earth.

In short, the more I encounter men's approximations to what is, the more I treasure those absolute truths that make known "things as they really are, and . . . things as they really will be" (Jacob 4:13; compare D&C 93:24). In fact, the more we learn, the more we begin to realize what we do not know, the more we feel the need to consider ourselves "fools before God" (2 Nephi 9:42).

Those who choose to follow the Brethren, believe in and teach the scriptures, and be loyal to the Church—no matter the extent of their academic training or intellectual capacity—open themselves to ridicule from the cynic and the critic. Ultimately, doctrinal truth comes not through the explorations of scholars, but through the revelations of God to apostles and prophets. And if such a position be labeled as narrow, parochial, or anti-intellectual, then so be it. I cast my lot with the prophets.

I am one who sincerely believes that education need not be antithetical to conversion and commitment; it all depends on where one places his or her trust. "True religion," Elder Bruce R. McConkie testified, "deals with spiritual things. We do not come to a knowledge of God and his laws through intellectuality, or by research, or by reason. . . . In their sphere, education and intellectuality are devoutly to be desired. But when contrasted with spiritual endowments, they are of but slight and passing worth. From an eternal perspective what each of us needs is a Ph.D. in faith and righteousness. The things that will profit us everlastingly are not the power to reason, but the ability to receive revelation; not the truths learned by study, but the knowledge gained by faith; not what we know about the things of the world, but our knowledge of God and his laws."[17]

Notes

1. Orson F. Whitney, *Life of Heber C. Kimball,* 4th ed. (Salt Lake City: Bookcraft, 1973), 446, 449–50.

2. Gordon B. Hinckley, in Conference Report, April 1966, 85; emphasis added.

3. Harold B. Lee, LDS Student Association Fireside, Utah State University, 10 October 1971.

4. C. S. Lewis, *Christian Reflections* (San Francisco: Harper Collins, 1967), 197, 198; emphasis added.

5. Robert Stein, *The Method and Message of Jesus' Teachings* (Philadelphia: Westminster, 1978), 118–19.

6. C. S. Lewis, *Mere Christianity* (New York: Macmillan, 1952), 55–56; emphasis added.

7. John Meir, *A Marginal Jew: Rethinking the Historical Jesus*, 3 vols. (New York: Doubleday, 1991), 1:177.

8. Scot McKnight, "Who Is Jesus? An Introduction to Jesus Studies," in *Jesus Under Fire: Modern Scholarship Reinvents the Historical Jesus*, Michael J. Wilkins and J. P. Moreland, eds. (Grand Rapids: Zondervan, 1995), 61–62.

9. Howard W. Hunter, *That We Might Have Joy* (Salt Lake City: Deseret Book, 1994), 23, 25–26.

10. Neal A. Maxwell, *Plain and Precious Things* (Salt Lake City: Deseret Book, 1983), 4.

11. Ezra Taft Benson, *A Witness and a Warning* (Salt Lake City: Deseret Book, 1988), 13.

12. Benson, *A Witness and a Warning*, 31.

13. Gordon B. Hinckley, *Faith: The Essence of True Religion* (Salt Lake City: Deseret Book, 1989), 10–11.

14. Boyd K. Packer, in Conference Report, October 1985, 104, 107.

15. A paraphrase of Brigham Young, *Journal of Discourses*, 26 vols. (Liverpool: F. D. Richards & Sons, 1851–86), 8:355–56.

16. Hugh Nibley, *The World and the Prophets* (Salt Lake City: Deseret Book and FARMS, 1987), 134.

17. Bruce R. McConkie, in Conference Report, April 1971, 99.

LDS Women and Education

Emily Mabey Swensen

Master of Writing and Publishing, Emerson College (Boston)

Question:

My dad has had more formal education than my mom, but I learned more about *continuing* education from her. She was always reading a book, even while she ate her morning bowl of cereal. She has always belonged to book groups, study groups, quilting groups, and even an investment group, and has kept her nursing license current. She reads the newspaper, news magazines, and Church magazines. Like her mother before her, she is a student of life and always ready for a heated discussion. I admired my dad's study of the law, but it was my mom's constant *informal* education that drove me on to extensive formal education.

Though my parents had four daughters and no sons, I don't think it occurred to them to limit our aspirations to domestic pursuits. We talked around the dinner table about serving missions, going to graduate school, and dreaming big dreams as much as any family of boys might have. We also talked about getting married, having kids, and being home with them. In our house and in our minds, these goals were not mutually exclusive. I wasn't sure how

I'd manage the details, but I was sure I could be a Supreme Court Justice, Relief Society President, and Terrific Mom all in time, if not all at once. I always understood Latter-day Saint doctrine to back up what I was learning at home. After all, I knew Brigham Young had said that, forced to choose, he would educate his daughters rather than his sons.[1]

Continuing my education through college and beyond was about the pure love of learning, more than career goals. I remember thinking when I finished my bachelor's degree at BYU, "Am I done already?" I didn't feel all that smart, and I still felt that unquenchable desire to keep learning. I decided to pursue a master's degree in writing because at the time it scared me more than anything else. I thought I had a wee knack for writing, but I was terrified to test it, and I knew only formal education could force me to do so. Graduate school did challenge me, emotionally, spiritually, and creatively. Obviously, to be a married Mormon girl at a very liberal graduate school in Boston made me stand out. (I was even present in a class once when a fellow student used Mormonism as an example of a peculiar modern philosophy.) But it was worth every odd look. I learned to think and read more critically and to understand my beliefs and my own experiences well enough to present them to others in a way they could relate to and understand. Now, five years later, I find myself wanting to continue my education and to expand my mind again.

At thirty, I have been Relief Society president of a struggling ward, and am working at the Mom part. After a few years home with my children, I find that the Supreme-Court-Justice desire still lives within me. And now I stand at a crossroads. As I consider law school, I am torn between the desire to follow that dream and the needs to support my husband in these important years of his career and to spend my hours with my small children.

I realize what a great gig it is to be the full-time parent, and I'm not willing to give it up. I guess I'm still hoping to have it all. But can I?

An LDS woman once referred derisively to my oldest sister, who has a Master's of Fine Arts in acting, as an "expensive waitress," alluding to the cost of her graduate school versus her ability to earn money at the time. We as LDS women often judge rather than support each other in this subtle balance between aspiration and family. So, from time to time my confidence is shaken and I find myself wondering: Should I continue my educational pursuits, even if I can't be sure how I'll use them throughout my life?

* * *

Camille Fronk Olson

Associate Professor of Ancient Scripture at Brigham Young University

Answer:

Several years ago, I visited high school business classes as a representative for LDS Business College. My presentation focused on the importance of education, independent of one's life path. At one school with a high concentration of Latter-day Saint students, I asked an accounting class whether they deemed post–high school education as important for women as men. I have not forgotten the spontaneous response by one young man, "Are you kidding? How much education do you need to run a washing machine?" From the erupting laughter and high-fives that followed, I sensed that he was not alone in his opinion.

Education has always been encouraged and valued in the LDS faith both for the here and now and for eternity. The Lord instructed Joseph Smith that "if a person gains more knowledge and intelligence in this life through his diligence and obedience than another, he will have so much the advantage in the world to come" (D&C 130:19). Similarly, B. H. Roberts wrote, "The Mormon point of view in education . . . has regard not only to the preparation of man for the duties and responsibilities of the moment of time he lives in this world, but aims to prepare him for eternal life in the mansions and companionship of the Gods."[2]

Do these statements apply to women as well as men? Does God desire His daughters to be educated, or do scriptures and counsel from latter-day prophets discourage education for women? Furthermore, are certain disciplines more or less appropriate for women according to Latter-day Saint directives?

With a university faculty position in a predominantly male department, my bias on this subject is hard to disguise. But my life's experiences have also exposed me to reactions that create mixed messages about the value of education for women. Observations from those opposed to women earning advanced degrees and working in disciplines traditionally pursued by men are particularly curious in light of Latter-day Saint teachings. A sample of such comments illustrates types of disparaging messages young women may receive pertaining to education and career and the potential confusion that these opinions create.

• From an institute teacher when I was twenty-three years old and considering a master's degree: "You already have two strikes against you (completion of a bachelor's degree and a full-time mission). If you complete a graduate degree, no LDS man will want to marry you."

• From a fellow seminary teacher when I was a new Church Educational System hiree and the only full-time female seminary teacher in the state: "I've been trying to figure out why you were hired to teach seminary. The only reason I can think of is to protect the Church from discrimination lawsuits."

• From a student: "I'm struggling to know whether I should take a class from you. You obviously chose education and a career rather than marriage and family as prophets have admonished women."

• From a student at the end of a semester: "You're not married? And you have a Ph.D.? But you're happy—how can that be? I understood that women can be happy only when they marry."

Because such assumptions have questioned the direction and confirming witness I received at the time from the Spirit, I have sought answers and explanations from authoritative sources. The findings are most encouraging. Affirming statements are plentiful and deepen one's appreciation for the reasons why education in general is valuable and, for women, particularly beneficial.

Scriptural Evidence of Educated Women

During His mortal ministry, the Savior actually sought out individual women to whom He could teach His gospel. His approach indicates that He knew these women could understand truths that went beyond their cultural religious teachings. For example, when He met a Samaritan woman at a well, Christ taught her spiritual truths of deep import, by which she recognized Him as the Messiah. She became the first person in recorded scripture to hear the Savior verbally identify Himself as the Redeemer. Armed with this intelligence, she returned to her village and taught her neighbors of Christ. The Savior did not command the Samaritan woman to "tell no man," but confirmed her witness when the villagers subsequently sought Him to hear Him themselves (John 4).

Likewise, Christ taught two sisters from Bethany named Mary and Martha. While Martha was involved in a stereotypical activity for women (preparing a meal), she complained to Jesus that her sister should be helping her rather than sitting, pondering, and learning at Jesus' feet. Without denigrating Martha's service, Jesus assigned virtue to Mary's choice to quietly listen to learn during dinner preparations, an activity typically ridiculed in women. Jesus complimented a woman's choice to study and learn when He taught, "Mary hath chosen that good part, which shall not be taken away from her" (Luke 10:42).

Missionary efforts in the early Christian Church support the existence of educated women among the first believers. Paul the Apostle found rare success among the intellectuals of Athens, but a woman, Damaris, was among those converted (Acts 17:34). Similarly, Paul found appreciative minds in Thessalonica among the "chief women" (17:4), the "honourable women" of Berea (17:12), and a seller of expensive purple dye—a businesswoman named Lydia—who was his first convert in Philippi (16:14–15).

From the beginning, God's sons and daughters have reflected educational influence, as recorded in scripture. Our first parents taught literacy to their children. "Adam and Eve . . . called upon the name of the Lord, and they heard the voice of the Lord. . . . And he gave unto them commandments. . . . And Adam and Eve . . . made all things known unto their sons and their daughters" (Moses 5:4–5, 12). As ones who "called upon God," Adam and Eve were "given . . . to write by the spirit of inspiration; and by them their children were taught to read and write" (6:5–6). And Huldah, a "prophetess" during the reign of Judah's King Josiah, read a newly uncovered manuscript and declared it to be the word of God (2 Chronicles 34:21–28).

Rationale for Women's Continued Education

Exploring reasons why education benefits women provides motivation and conviction to women of all ages to pursue meaningful learning. I will discuss four of many reasons why education blesses a woman and her family and community.

1. To Fulfill Our Foredesignated Assignments

President Brigham Young pursued a view not popular in his day when he encouraged women to extend their efforts outside the daily maintenance of the home to vocational and academic pursuits. He recognized that such efforts prepared women for God's greater purpose for them.

> We believe that women are useful, not only to sweep houses, wash dishes, make beds, and raise babies, but that they should stand behind the counter, study law or physics, or become good bookkeepers and be able to do the business in any counting house, and all this to enlarge their sphere of usefulness for the benefit of society at large. In following these things they but answer the design of their creation.[3]

Each individual, man or woman, has a different mission to fulfill. Education will substantially help individuals to prepare for their unique situations in life.

The Lord instructed us to allow for Christ's enabling power in learning the gospel and all other disciplines: "Teach ye diligently and my grace shall attend you, that you may be instructed more perfectly in theory, in principle, in doctrine, . . ." The study list continues with a multitude of subjects in the sciences, history, law, and current world affairs; then the Lord gives this explanation for our study: "That ye may be prepared in all things when I shall send you again to magnify the calling whereunto I have called you, and the mission with which I have commissioned you" (D&C 88:78–80).

President Spencer W. Kimball reminded men and women of

these premortally assigned responsibilities that require mortal preparation:

> Remember, in the world before we came here, faithful women were given certain assignments while faithful men were foreordained to certain priesthood tasks. While we do not now remember the particulars, this does not alter the glorious reality of what we once agreed to. You are accountable for those things which long ago were expected of you just as are those we sustain as prophets and apostles!
>
> . . . This leaves much to be done by way of parallel personal development—for both men and women.[4]

Without knowing the specifics of our unique, foredesignated missions, education is a fundamental part of our preparation. When we possess the appropriate tools and hold fast to our faith in Christ, God can direct His sons and His daughters where He wishes. That is why in the end we will discover that our education is not for our own merits and pursuits but for the Lord's purposes.

2. To Enhance Financial Security

A practical rationale for a woman to receive education is the most commonly expressed, but considered alone, it is not particularly convincing. Learning skills to prepare for a salaried occupation is a side benefit of education, not the core purpose.

Elder James E. Faust addressed Brigham Young University students with a message he prepared for his granddaughters to "help bring [them] identity, a sense of value, and happiness as a person." He spoke about the unique endowments given to women so that "becoming like men is not the answer; being who you are and living up to your potential and commitment is." Continual education helps us learn who we really are. With education and faith in Christ, we are more confident in becoming our true selves rather than compensating for fears by attempting to acquire masculine characteristics. Elder Faust encouraged his granddaughters to go to college, but to use that time wisely by learning a marketable skill:

> Your grandmother and I urged your mothers to get an education, not only to help them in their homemaking but also to prepare them to earn a living outside the home if that became necessary. Going to college is a wonderful experience, but the dollars, the effort, and the time are much better used if the education also prepares the student with a marketable skill.[5]

As BYU president, Dallin H. Oaks spoke to students and to faculty after "conversations with . . . women students and with faculty, administrative, and staff women" led him to detect "some uneasiness and confusion about where we stand on education for women, especially vocationally oriented education." Without marginalizing the blessings of motherhood, which he called women's "highest calling and opportunity for service," President Oaks described the reality of our world:

> Many of our young women will need to earn a living for themselves because they do not marry, because they do not marry until after some years of employment, or because they have been widowed or through other circumstances have been compelled to assume responsibilities of the family breadwinner. A mother who must earn a living for the family in addition to performing the duties of motherhood probably has as great a need for education as any person in the world.[6]

No one can predict when and how a woman will need skills

and degrees. A woman who values marriage and family must exercise faith to pursue advanced schooling when marriage or motherhood could take precedence at any time. Assigned research, homework, writing deadlines, and examinations are not often as "fun" as the alternatives nonstudent friends receive. At least for a moment many young women are tempted to avoid the challenges, discipline, and often criticism that accompany the pursuit of more schooling in the hopes that a strict focus on home décor and preparing for a family will bring the marriage proposal sooner and negate her need to prepare for a career. President Oaks recognized the frustrations that young women face in planning their educational future when the future holds so many unknowns. He requested improved educational advisement for women students as a result.

> It is clear that we need better educational counseling for our young women than for our young men, because a young woman has a much wider range of contingencies than a young man who is obligated to take the initiative to marry and support a family. Despite the preferred alternative of marriage and children, a young woman never knows whether she will remain single, or be married and childless, or widowed—or what special educational needs she may have in the years after her family is raised.[7]

From President Gordon B. Hinckley's recent address to young women, these frustrations and questions still exist. With the expanding vocational opportunities available to women and with successful women role models in nearly every field, a young woman finds increased options to balance her hope to become a mother one day. President Hinckley admonished:

> Find purpose in your life. Choose the things you would like to do, and educate yourselves to be effective in their

pursuit. For most it is very difficult to settle on a vocation. You are hopeful that you will marry and that all will be taken care of. In this day and time, a girl needs an education. She needs the means and skills by which to earn a living should she find herself in a situation where it becomes necessary to do so.

Study your options. Pray to the Lord earnestly for direction. Then pursue your course with resolution.

The whole gamut of human endeavor is now open to women. There is not anything that you cannot do if you will set your mind to it. You can include in the dream of the woman you would like to be a picture of one qualified to serve society and make a significant contribution to the world of which she will be a part.[8]

Earning credentials and developing skills to secure a salaried job, if needed, will reduce stress in times of uncertainty and increase confidence to face unforeseen challenges.

3. To Encourage Active Participation in the Church

An added benefit of education for Latter-day Saint women is the motivation toward deeper involvement in their faith.

In response to secularization theory, which claims that people become less religious as society becomes more modern and industrialized, researchers Stan L. Albrecht and Tim B. Heaton conducted a study in the early 1980s on education level and religiosity for Latter-day Saints in the United States in contrast to Christians in general.[9] Their study focused on one key aspect of the theory, which links a decline in religion with the rise in science, empirical testing, and rational thought. A review of similar studies conducted among other U.S. Christian communities led them to summarize that "the most prevalent view [among Christians in general] . . . seems to be

Table 1: Relationship between Education and Religiosity Indicator[10]

	Weekly Attendance (%)		Full Tithing (%)		Daily Prayer (%)		Gospel Study (%)		Beliefs Important (%)		Number	
	M	F	M	F	M	F	M	F	M	F	M	F
Grade School	34	48	40	50	52	72	3	56	71	95	94	102
Some High School	48	52	51	48	44	61	37	45	75	82	181	265
High School Graduate	43	54	42	49	44	58	37	44	70	85	620	919
Some College	65	71	57	59	54	63	46	53	81	88	620	795
College Graduate	71	82	68	73	60	75	48	52	81	93	241	205
Graduate School	80	76	71	73	68	62	61	48	87	83	377	131
Correlation	.24*	.20*	.22*	.14*	.15*	.02	.17*	.04	.12*	.02		

*P<.05

that educational achievement impacts negatively on religious commitment and that increased levels of education often lead to apostasy as individuals encounter views that deemphasize spiritual growth and elevate scientific and intellectual achievement."[11]

In contrast to Christians in general, who show a decrease in religious devotion with increased education, Albrecht and Heaton found a positive relationship between level of education and various indicators of religiosity among Latter-day Saints. Overall, Latter-day Saints (especially those with a college degree) had the highest church attendance of any other denomination considered. The correlation between higher religiosity and increased education continued to hold independent of whether or not the respondents attended a Church university or resided in Utah or another part of the country.

The Church's lay clergy and the expectation that every adult member would serve in a Church calling proved to be a "key link" between education and Church attendance among Latter-day Saints in this study. Certainly the volume of literature Latter-day Saints are encouraged to study would arguably be less intimidating for the more educated than those who have little exposure to foreign languages, literature from earlier eras, or research requirements. Literacy is highly valued among Latter-day Saints because members are expected to regularly "study" all four standard works of scripture. The objective for such study is not merely to report that you have read them all, but to discover gospel insights and connections to personal life that bring relevance to God's word in our modern world.

One anomaly emerged in the Albrecht-Heaton study. When comparing Latter-day Saint men and women in various education levels, religiosity measures were always higher for women than for men—with one exception: postgraduate women. In other words, when Latter-day Saints achieve a high school diploma, some college, or even a bachelor's degree, the attendance level, payment of a full tithing, degree of gospel study, frequency of daily prayer, and stated importance of their religious beliefs all increase as the amount of education increases—and these things are also all higher for women than for men. Only when LDS women pursue post-graduate education do they collectively manifest a reversal in the trend toward greater religiosity. By contrast, LDS men with graduate-school education manifest the highest evidence of religiosity in comparison to any lower level of educational attainment.

No hypothesis was given or test reported in the Albrecht-Heaton study to explain why LDS women with advanced college degrees show a slight decline in religiosity. I offer a few suggestions for contemplation. Perhaps LDS men in Church callings sense greater encouragement from fellow members to draw on their educational training than LDS women do in their auxiliary callings. Perhaps women who complete graduate degrees are more likely to be single or marry later, finding themselves in yet another way to be different from the traditionally described LDS woman. Highly educated women may be judged as choosing school over family when Church leaders often identify family as a woman's greatest responsibility and opportunity.

A scholar who studies communication patterns that differ between men and women has described women as seeking for common ground to establish comfortable societies, while men identify a linear hierarchy among them. She described a woman's typical connection with the world to more likely be "where individuals negotiate complex networks of friendship, minimize differences, try to reach consensus, and avoid the appearance of superiority, which would highlight differences."[12] If specifically Latter-day Saint women reflect this tendency to identify commonalities among themselves, perhaps they are less likely to feel sisterhood with women who place such a high priority on formal education.

Perhaps women with graduate school experience tend to ask more questions dealing with women and religion where answers are not accessible or addressed, which in turn gives them a sense of unimportance. Then again, perhaps LDS women with advanced degrees are more likely to marry out of the Church as the probability of meeting a compatible, single LDS man dwindles.

Whatever the reason, the prophetic encouragement for Latter-day Saint men and women to study and comprehend their Church doctrine remains, as this 1903 admonition by President Joseph F. Smith reflects: "The word and the law of God are as important for women who would reach wise conclusions as they are for men; and women should study and consider the problems of this great latter-day work from the standpoint of God's revelations, and as they may be actuated by his Spirit, which it is their right to receive through the medium of sincere and heartfelt prayer."[13]

The tie between college education and Church participation was further stressed by then BYU President Dallin H. Oaks:

> One of the most important purposes of a university education is to prepare men and women to be responsible and intelligent leaders and participants in the life of their families, their Church, and their communities. That kind of education is needed by young men and young women alike. In short, we make no distinction between young men and young women in our conviction about the importance of an education and in our commitment to providing that education.[14]

4. To Cultivate the Mind for a Lifetime of Learning

Arguments for education that see beyond the vocational and financial benefits are most compelling to me. Certainly the highest salaries earned are neither a reflection of the highest level of education attained nor the greatest intellect developed. What happens to a society when skills are learned merely for the economic return associated with that skill? Credentials to earn money are not the only benefits gained through a good education. Discipline to sit still and read thoughtfully, ability to do critical thinking, exposure to different perspectives and viewpoints, and capacity to broaden and deepen our understanding of the world are among the greatest strengths of a sound education. These are also skills associated with recognizing personal revelation from the Spirit.

"Will education feed and clothe you, keep you warm on a cold day, or enable you to build a house?" President Brigham Young inquired. "Not at all. Should we cry down education on this account? No. What is it for? The improvement of the mind; to instruct us in all arts and sciences, in the history of the world, in the laws of nations; to enable us to understand the laws and principles of life, and how to be useful while we live."[15]

As mindless activities become increasingly available, the attraction to "veg out" in front of the TV, surf the Internet, or endlessly telephone (or Internet) chat for no particular reason can be intoxicating. Thinking and visualizing from words and abstract ideas is hard when one is accustomed to finding life's answers through fashion trends, pop culture, and neighborhood gossip. Likewise, it is easier to attend a fireside or class where emotional stimulation is the draw than one where the audience is invited to consider a different perspective and explore what they really understand and believe. For example, educational maturity is evident in the ability to become completely engaged in a lecture where the presenter has a completely opposite viewpoint from mine. Yet I can come away fed and enlightened because the presenter's cogent thinking helped me to better crystallize my own beliefs by contrast and to articulate them more clearly.

Cultivating the mind is much more than memorizing facts to

pass an exam. It is beyond fulfilling the requirements for a degree. Developing reading, thinking, and researching skills are priceless, because the greatest learning takes place independent of a formal educational setting. Formal schooling's greatest contribution may therefore be teaching the skills and developing discipline to find answers to questions we will encounter long after the final school bell sounds, when no one is around to assign a deadline and a grade. Learning to recognize the beauty and power in the abstract, the uncommon in the natural world around us, and the magic and clarity in the world of words are gifts from learning to study and think.

Additionally, failure to value education for the joy of learning creates unnecessary roadblocks in our life's progression and potential. What a tragedy to hear a bright young college student agonize over choosing a major because she can't find a discipline that can be mastered now and remain unchanged twenty years later when her family is reared and she finally wants to apply her knowledge in a career. Does she think insight will not be gleaned and heightened in every discipline every year? Does she think that her mind will go into cold storage and the world won't change while she is at home with her family? Does she think that school is the only place one can learn?

By contrast, one of the brightest and most capable women I know has not received any formal college education, yet she has learned how to learn. She is disciplined, quick to observe, and confident that answers are found when you ask and seek. She always has a book or two that she is reading—on health, nutrition, nature, Church doctrine, history, relationships, psychology, human development, and more. Her children know that she is fascinated in what they are learning, and she encourages them to share their new insights with her. She is a frequent patron of the local library and quickly finds ways to apply her new knowledge into her personal or family life. Most of all, she generously shares what she learns with a humble confidence that draws many people to seek her sage advice. True education isn't teaching a specific vocation; it is teaching someone how to learn independently, how to find answers to life's unique challenges that are never discussed in any textbook.

BYU President Oaks stressed reasons to become educated for more than merely financial motives, such as my friend reflects. "Education is more than vocational," he taught. "Education should improve our minds, strengthen our bodies, heighten our cultural awareness, and increase our spirituality. It should prepare us for greater service to the human family. Such an education will improve a woman's ability to function as an informed and effective teacher of her sons and daughters, and as a worthy and wise counselor and companion to her husband."[16]

President Gordon B. Hinckley has long encouraged young women to develop lifelong learning skills. "Educate your hands and your minds," he advised. "To you young women may I suggest that you get all the education you can. Train yourselves to make a contribution to the society in which you will live. There is an essence of the divine in the improvement of the mind. . . .

"In the process of educating your minds, stir within yourselves a greater sensitivity to the beautiful, the artistic, and the cultivation of the talent you possess, be it large or small."[17]

Influences That Encourage Education in Women

Much can be done to reinforce the value that Latter-day Saint tenets place on education for women. Knowing and citing prophetic and other authoritative teachings on the subject is an important start, but reflecting those teachings in our daily attitudes and behavior will go far to influence future generations.

In the mid-1990s, a BYU study was conducted to test various family and religious influences on current and expected post–high school academic achievement in Latter-day Saint teenagers.[18] No attempt was made to design a model considering every possible reason for a youth's academic success or failure, but the researchers, Brent L. Top and Bruce A. Chadwick, noted that "peer and family influences" are key indicators of success in school.[19] More specifically, they considered the father's educational level; public and private religious practice and attitudes; peer influence; parental regulation; parents' use of psychologically controlling behaviors; family connection; whether or not the mother was employed outside the home; and family structure (reside in a two-parent, stepparent, or single-parent home).

Of all the influences tested, private and public religiosity proved to be the strongest predictor of academic performance in Latter-day Saint teenagers. The more active teenagers were in their religion, the higher their actual and expected academic achievement. Peer influence was significant only if the teen's friends were low academic achievers. "None of the family factors were directly related to school performance for young men, and only family connection and granting of psychological autonomy were significant for young women."[20] The researchers were surprised that the father's education proved insignificant in the equation, since it has been particularly important in research with national samples of American teens.

The study provokes suggestions beyond those tested in their model for influencing academic success among Latter-day Saint youth. For example, I am curious about the influence of a mother's education. More important, what about a mother's attitudes about education and current educational practices? How often does she read for her own satisfaction? What does she read? How varied are her interests? How confident is she in her ability to find answers? How often does she read to her children? How motivated and disciplined is she to learn?

Whether a mother found biology or math her favorite subject in school or whether it was child development and home economics is insignificant. If she develops a passion for learning, she will undoubtedly influence her children to enjoy the process. Whether or not she uses her degree in a salaried career, she will bring unparalleled relevancy to any subject that her children learn in school when they come home and see her still enthusiastic to learn.

Conclusion

In summary, education for women is clearly supported in authorized Latter-day Saint teachings. Consequently, rank and file members can significantly help by refraining from disguising or misrepresenting that message. As a young woman seeks direction for her education through personal revelation from God, she will build confidence and faith that will lead her through the even more important decisions that will surely come her way.

Attention to several actions and attitudes can make this message easily accessible to Latter-day Saint young women. First, we can help both young men and young women see that marriage and motherhood are not the end of education for a woman but in many ways the beginning of her need to apply educational skills to finally study in the most meaningful ways. Second, we can communicate that education is as valuable for women as for men, whether a woman marries early in life, later, or not at all. Encouraging the importance of cultivating the mind and finding purpose in education far beyond the financial value will promote greater joy in learning.

Third, we can teach and model sincere religious devotion and activity. Regular and meaningful scripture study that spills into exploring teachings of modern prophets, establishing a historical context, and learning definitions of words will instill a contagious joy into gospel study. Furthermore, as we establish a personal testimony of Christ in our youth, the gospel becomes an integral part of learning every other subject or discipline.

Finally, let us communicate that every family benefits from two parents who have developed the skills and motivation to continue their education when no homework is assigned and no public recognition is promised. In so doing, we will be prepared to answer in the affirmative whenever and in whatever capacity God calls us to serve, knowing He will continue to teach us along the way.

Notes

1. Gordon B. Hinckley, "Our Responsibility to Our Young Women," *Ensign,* September 1988, 10.

2. B. H. Roberts, "The Mormon Point of View in Education," *Improvement Era,* December 1898, 126.

3. Brigham Young, *Discourses of Brigham Young,* edited by John A. Widtsoe (Salt Lake City: Deseret Book, 1973), 217.

4. Spencer W. Kimball, "The Role of Righteous Women," *Ensign,* November 1979, 102.

5. James E. Faust, "A Message to My Granddaughters: Becoming 'Great Women,'" *Ensign,* September 1986, 19.

6. Dallin H. Oaks, BYU Devotional, February 12, 1974; "Statement on the Education of Women at BYU," BYU President's Assembly, September 9, 1975.

7. Oaks, "Statement on the Education of Women at BYU," September 9, 1975.

8. Gordon B. Hinckley, "How Can I Become the Woman of Whom I Dream?" *Ensign,* May 2001, 95.

9. Stan L. Albrecht and Tim B. Heaton, "Secularization, Higher Education, and Religiosity," in *Latter-day Saint Social Life: Social Research on the LDS Church and Its Members,* edited by James T. Duke (Provo, Utah: BYU Religious Studies Center, 1998), 293–314.

10. Ibid., 305; used by permission.

11. Ibid., 298.

12. Deborah Tannen, *You Just Don't Understand: Women and Men in Conversation* (New York: Ballantine Books, 1990), 26.

13. Joseph F. Smith, *Gospel Doctrine* (Salt Lake City: Deseret Book, 1977), 290.

14. Oaks, BYU Devotional, February 12, 1974; "Statement on the Education of Women at BYU," September 9, 1975.

15. Brigham Young, in *Journal of Discourses,* 26 vols. (London: Latter-day Saints' Book Depot, 1854–86), 14:83.

16. Oaks, BYU Devotional, February 12, 1974.

17. Gordon B. Hinckley, "Rise to the Stature of the Divine within You," *Ensign,* November 1989, 96.

18. Brent L. Top and Bruce A. Chadwick, "Seek Learning, Even by Study and Also by Faith: The Relationship between Personal Religiosity and Academic Achievement among Latter-day Saint High School Students," *The Religious Educator,* vol. 2, no. 2, 2001, 121–37.

19. Ibid., 125.

20. Ibid., 130.

The Lord's Plan for Learning

John LeBaron

Master of Social Work, Columbia University (New York)

Question:

I have never been a fan of teachers who propose subjective questions to a class, while inwardly relying on an arbitrary set of objective answers to make their point. In preparing to teach my Old Testament Gospel Doctrine class on birthright blessings, I wondered if the "golden nugget" I planned on conveying would inadvertently set up the kind of "I'm asking questions that only *I* know the answers to" scenario that predictably rubs me the wrong way as a student.

Then it happened. My class was gathered in the basement of the chapel in a poor Brooklyn neighborhood. I had just set up the million-dollar question: "Why was Abraham so insistent that Isaac marry a woman from his kindred rather than from the Canaanites, in whose land Abraham and Isaac lived?" A brother at the back of the class raised his hand and delivered the golden nugget more beautifully than I could have imagined. He articulately explained how Noah had cursed his grandson Canaan, the son of Ham, and thus, by mixing his seed with the Canaanites, Isaac (a descendant of

69

Noah's second son, Shem) would be unable to perpetuate the Abrahamic covenant. Indeed, the descendants of Japheth (Noah's eldest son) were not able to receive that covenant until the meridian of time (Acts 11:7–18), and Ham's descendants had to wait until this dispensation (D&C Official Declaration 2).

The brother who answered the question was a descendant of Ham. He and I did not share the same native tongue. He was born into the poorest country in the Western Hemisphere; I was born into the richest. I was certain that we did not share the same educational or economic upbringing. I now faced my own million-dollar question: Why was I so surprised that he, despite our apparent differences, knew the answer?

More, what did my surprise really say about me? Was my higher education truly making me a "more educated" person? Or was it slowly but convincingly blinding my eyes and heart to the source of all true education and light—the Spirit?

Up to that point, I had focused primarily on the tangibles of my education. Painfully aware of my small mortgage of mounting tuition, I had often grappled with questions like, "As a future family provider, how do I reconcile pursuing a vocation that might fail to provide?" Or, "Is it reckless to get an education that you might not ever use?" Or, "How do I justify this kind of debt for a *second* college degree?"

That Sunday in Gospel Doctrine, I was reminded to look beyond the peripherals of my education and focus on the process. This intense self-reflection led to questions such as, "How do I avoid thinking that I am better or smarter than someone else?" "As a future provider, how will my educational experiences help me provide for my family's temporal *and* spiritual welfare?" "Is it reckless to get caught up in popular opinions of self-determination and social justice when the Lord has made it clear that they are against His plan?" "How do I justify the kind of spiritual debt I might incur if I allow my education to instill pride in my heart instead of charity?" (2 Nephi 9:42–43). And ultimately, "When I am inclined to believe that there is an arbitrary set of objective answers to my subjective educational dilemmas, in whose plan am I really trusting?"

* * *

Kim B. Clark

President, BYU–Idaho

Answer:

Latter-day Saints are committed to learning and education. For us, it is a commandment to seek knowledge, to enlarge our understanding, to learn throughout our lives. This certainly includes learning about the scriptures and the gospel, but the reach of this responsibility includes knowledge of all kinds. Coupled with the scriptural mandate to develop and strengthen our faith, this means that the Lord's word to the Latter-day Saints is clear: be educated and be faithful.

This is a challenging mandate. To be educated means more than attending school or acquiring credentials. By "educated" I have in mind something Henry Rosovsky, former dean of the faculty of Arts and Sciences at Harvard, wrote several years ago:

> An educated person must . . . be able to communicate with precision, cogency and force; should . . . be trained to think critically . . . have a critical appreciation of the ways we gain knowledge . . . an informed acquaintance with the . . . methods of the . . . sciences; the historical and

quantitative techniques needed for investigating . . . modern society; with some of the important scholarly, literary and artistic achievement of the past; and with the major religious and philosophic conceptions of mankind; . . . cannot be provincial in the sense of being ignorant of other cultures and other times; . . . have some understanding of . . . moral and ethical problems; . . . should have achieved some depth in some field of knowledge.[1]

To be educated in this sense is much more than knowing facts or having skills. It is also about habits of mind, approaches to problems, and perspective on our lives and the world around us. Likewise, to be faithful is more than attending church and participating in religious worship. For Latter-day Saints it also means being obedient to the commandments, following the counsel of a living prophet, seeking and listening to the Spirit of the Lord in making decisions, devoting priority time and energy to family, being honest, serving others, paying tithing, living the Word of Wisdom, and in general living the gospel in practice. It, too, is about habits of mind, but faithfulness is also about heart, about approaches to problems, and about our perspective on our lives and the world around us.

Neither being educated nor faithful is easy to achieve in its own right. Doing them both is yet more difficult. As I have reflected on that challenge over the years, I have seen in my own life and in the lives of my Latter-day Saint colleagues a pattern of behavior, a set of practices, that if followed raise substantially the likelihood that challenge will be met. This essay is about that challenge and those patterns. My hope is to shed some light on what it means for Latter-day Saints to be "educated and faithful."

Education in LDS History and Doctrine

The emphasis on education among the Latter-day Saints has roots both in the doctrines of the Church and in its history. From the founding of the School of the Prophets by Joseph Smith in 1833, to the creation of the Church Educational System for high school and college students, to the ongoing support of the three campuses of Brigham Young University, the leaders of the Church have created an institutional history of commitment to learning and education.[2] Moreover, the prophets and Apostles have created in their personal lives a living witness of the importance of learning, knowledge, and education. We have, of course, the example of Joseph Smith and Brigham Young, both of whom were largely self-taught and invested in learning throughout their lives. Among the current First Presidency and Quorum of the Twelve Apostles, a college education is common, and many of these leaders have advanced degrees in medicine, engineering, law, education, business, political science, and the humanities. Gordon B. Hinckley, President of the Church, framed his personal commitment this way:

> I love to learn. I relish any opportunity to acquire knowledge. Indeed, I believe in and have vigorously supported, throughout my life, the pursuit of education, for myself and for others. I was able to obtain a University education during the Great Depression and from that time forward I have never been satiated with the pursuit of knowledge. From my point of view, learning is both a practical matter and a spiritual one.[3]

A commitment to learning and education plays an important role in the daily lives of members of the Church. In fact, Latter-day Saints spend a lot of time in classes. I know this from personal experience. Consider what a bird's–eye view of a fairly typical

Mormon household (ours) reveals about this commitment to education: As the sun creeps over the horizon twenty LDS teenagers (sixteen to eighteen years old) show up at the house; it is 6:15 A.M. They are there for early morning seminary, a fifty-minute class on the scriptures (this year it is the New Testament) that meets every school day. Later that day the family gathers for family home evening where the lesson is on the plan of salvation. As the week progresses, we see the mother preparing her lesson and activity for her nursery class on Sunday; the teenage daughters heading off to a Tuesday night class on service in the community; and the father preparing for a talk he has to give on Sunday evening at the LDS institute of religion, which serves multiple college campuses in the area. For the children in the family, this participation in Church classes and lessons comes in the midst of hours spent in college and high school, completing research projects and working on homework (for parents too!). If we extend the view a bit we can see a beautiful new Latter-day Saint temple close to the family's home, where the adults in the extended family gather early on Saturday morning to complete an endowment session in the temple. Here, in what for them is the most sacred place on earth, the central activity is learning: about the purpose of life, God's plan for our eternal progression, and the eternal nature of the family.

Indeed, it is precisely in these principles of eternal progression that we find the doctrinal roots for the Church's commitment to education. We are commanded to learn and to gain knowledge because that is an important part of our purpose here on earth and in the eternities. In a revelation given to Joseph Smith in 1843, the Lord connects knowledge and our eternal progression:

> Whatever principle of intelligence we attain unto in this life, it will rise with us in the resurrection. And if a person gains more knowledge and intelligence in this life through

his diligence and obedience than another, he will have so much the advantage in the world to come (D&C 130:18–19).

In addition to their impact on our personal progression, knowledge and learning allow us to more effectively serve God and His children, including our families. Brigham Young taught the Latter-day Saints that education was important in building the kingdom of God and had the power to improve the lives of people in the world. It should be sought for those purposes. Quoting Brigham Young, Hugh Nibley made clear this connection between education and strengthening God's kingdom (the words in quotation marks come from Brigham Young):

> "The business of the Elders of this Church (Jesus, their elder brother, being at their head), is to gather up all the truths in the world pertaining to life and salvation, to the Gospel we preach, to mechanisms of every kind, to the sciences, and to philosophy, wherever they may be found in every nation, kindred, tongue and people, and bring it to Zion." The "Gathering" was to be not only a bringing together of people, but of all the treasures surviving in the earth from every age and culture; "Every accomplishment, every polished grace, every useful attainment in mathematics, music, in all science and art belong to the Saints, and they rapidly collect the intelligence that is bestowed upon the nations, for all this intelligence belongs to Zion. All the knowledge, wisdom, power, and glory that have been bestowed upon the nations of the earth, from the days of Adam till now, must be gathered home to Zion." "What is this work? The improvement of the condition of the human family."[4]

The Lord's Plan for Learning: "Even by Study, and Also by Faith"

A commitment to education is in our history and in our beliefs. But in the passage of scripture noted above, the Lord also makes clear that in His calculus education and faith are connected: one gains knowledge and intelligence through diligence: digging, seeking, studying; and through obedience: exercising faith by keeping the commandments of the Lord. Indeed, whenever the Lord talks to us about education He always connects study and faith. Consider, for example, these words from a revelation given to Joseph Smith in 1835, in which the Lord lays out instructions for those who would embark in His service:

> Call a solemn assembly, even of those who are the first laborers in this last kingdom. . . . And I give unto you, who are the first laborers in this last kingdom, a commandment that you assemble yourselves together, and organize yourselves, and prepare yourselves, and sanctify yourselves. . . . And I give unto you a commandment that you shall teach one another the doctrine of the kingdom. Teach ye diligently and my grace shall attend you, that you may be instructed more perfectly in theory, in principle, in doctrine, in the law of the gospel, in all things that pertain unto the kingdom of God, that are expedient for you to understand; of things both in heaven and in the earth, and under the earth; things which have been, things which are, things which must shortly come to pass; things which are at home, things which are abroad; the wars and the perplexities of the nations, and the judgments which are on the land; and a knowledge also of countries and of kingdoms—that ye may be prepared in all things when I shall send you again to magnify the calling whereunto I have called you, and the

mission with which I have commissioned you. . . . And as all have not faith, seek ye diligently and teach one another words of wisdom; yea, seek ye out of the best books words of wisdom; seek learning, even by study and also by faith (D&C 88:70, 74, 77–80, 118).

Preparation for the work involves the mind and the spirit. It is about building a life of faith and obedience, and a life of learning. Gaining knowledge of all kinds is important (notice the connections between Doctrine and Covenants 88 and Rosovsky's description of an educated person above), and that knowledge is to be had through reason (study) and revelation (faith).

Why does the Lord connect study and faith in this way? Why this linking of reason and revelation, of the intellect and the spirit? It might have been different. He could have said: "Study is study and that you do in school; faith is faith and that you do in church." But he didn't. He connected them. Why? Part of the answer is that inspiration from God is a powerful way to gain the kinds of knowledge and intelligence essential to our education here on earth. Latter-day Saints believe in personal revelation, that God can speak to us in many ways to help us in our lives. We believe in the power of prayer and that these times of personal meditation and reflection can yield new understanding and insight. A life of faith can, therefore, create habits of prayerful contemplation and quiet reflection that open our minds and our hearts to revelation and inspiration.

Many times I have sat in Church and listened to faithful Latter-day Saints talk about walking out after an exam, or solving a particularly knotty research problem, or finding a way to write something quite difficult, and feeling they had been blessed with insight and understanding beyond their capacity. I have had these experiences myself, and I am confident they would not have happened without a lot of studying and work (this is what I emphasize to my children). But I also believe that faith plays an important role in what are very important learning moments.

So, part of the purpose for connecting faith to study is the Lord's desire to help us learn through inspiration. But it is also true that using our minds to actively seek knowledge in the way that the Lord outlines helps prepare our minds to receive that inspiration. This principle is at the heart of the reprimand received by Oliver Cowdery, who served as scribe to Joseph Smith during the translation of the Book of Mormon. Oliver had sought permission to try to translate and had not had success. The Lord said:

> Behold, you have not understood; you have supposed that I would give it unto you, when you took no thought save it was to ask me. But, behold, I say unto you, that you must study it out in your mind; then you must ask me if it be right, and if it is right I will cause that your bosom shall burn within you; therefore, you shall feel that it is right (D&C 9:7–8).

The Lord promises confirmation, but only after hard thought and study. Joseph Smith taught the same principle and emphasized the connection between the intellect and the spirit:

> We consider that God has created man with a mind capable of instruction, and a faculty which may be enlarged in proportion to the heed and diligence given to the light communicated from heaven to the intellect.[5]

And again:

> The things of God are of deep import; and time, and experience, and careful and ponderous and solemn thought can only find them out. Thy mind, O man! If thou wilt lead

a soul unto salvation, must stretch as high as the utmost heavens.[6]

The Prophet thus taught that our intellect receives "light from heaven"; that we can expand our capacity to learn from that light if we are diligent; and that our minds are essential to finding out the things of God, as we ponder and learn from our experience; but they must be connected to heaven if we are to achieve all that God has in store for us. There is no distinction here between secular and religious knowledge or between the spirit and the intellect.[7] We may have separated the spirit and the intellect into different compartments of our lives, but according to the Prophet, that is not our true nature. In that sense, connecting study and faith is the Lord's plan for learning because it is precisely the best way to learn. The process He gives us for gaining knowledge–study, seek, ponder, pray, keep the commandments—is thus intended to help us integrate the intellect and the spirit.

Dangers in the Search for Knowledge

The Lord's plan does more than give us a powerful way to learn. It also serves as a protection against the dangers that lie in the path of our search for knowledge. And there are dangers. Jacob, an ancient prophet on the American continent, had this to say about knowledge and learning:

> O that cunning plan of the evil one! O the vainness, and the frailties, and the foolishness of men! When they are learned they think they are wise, and they hearken not unto the counsel of God, for they set it aside, supposing they know of themselves, wherefore, their wisdom is foolishness and it profiteth them not. And they shall perish. But to be

learned is good if they hearken unto the counsels of God
(2 Nephi 9:28–29).

To be learned, to search for and attain knowledge is good, but
things can go terribly wrong if one is not careful. Some of the dangers one faces are matters of the mind and some affect our hearts. I
will discuss four here: shallow thinking, cynicism, pride, and greed.
Each poses a serious challenge to being educated and faithful.

Danger: Shallow Thinking

Acquiring education, really searching for knowledge the way
the Lord has commanded us, can be hard and difficult work. It
takes time and energy and focus. One of the great dangers we face
in this journey is never to start. Or if we start, to be content with a
surface understanding of things, or worse, with an imitation of the
real thing.

Part of the difficulty here lies in the fact that some ideas we
might encounter on our journey are uncomfortable. Sometimes
those who write and teach about "the wars and the perplexities of
the nations, and the judgments which are on the land" or things "in
the earth, and under the earth" may proclaim ideas that contradict
(or appear to contradict) things we learned (or thought we learned)
in Sunday School or in the scriptures or in the teachings of the
prophets. And some that proclaim such ideas may actively seek to
undermine religious faith.

The learned, particularly those who uncover new ideas and
create new knowledge, "think they are wise" for a reason: the ideas
they create do have power to explain and illuminate. From the earliest days of the Church the prophets have taught that the gospel
encompasses all truth, whether religious or secular, and that we
should seek after it. In this sense reason and revelation are two
paths to the same end. In the end, there will be no conflict between

revealed truth and truth established through reason. But in the meantime, some ideas created through reason create real dissonance, as well as, sometimes, doubt and discomfort.

For those who would be educated and faithful, there really are two dangers here. One is to avoid discomfort by not searching at all, never embarking on the journey, or if embarking, never getting beyond the surface of things. One may be comfortable on the surface, but shallow thinking does not fulfill the Lord's mandate. The other danger is to give so much allegiance to new, uncomfortable ideas (they are, after all, powerful) that one abandons one's religious faith. But in our day when new ideas supplant old ones at a significant rate, basing one's behavior, let alone one's life, on such ideas amounts to putting one's faith in the "wisdom of men" (1 Corinthians 2:5).

Neither staying on the surface of ideas nor abandoning religious faith is attractive. If Latter-day Saints follow the Lord's plan they do neither one. Rather, the solution is to forge ahead. Jeffrey R. Holland, writing at a time when he served as president of BYU (he is now a member of the Quorum of the Twelve) captures the essence of this forging in mind and spirit:

> If we knew all that God knew and we had all the light and all the truth, I am confident it would be both perfectly rational and perfectly revelatory. The rub is we do not have all the truth and the light. It is in that ignorance, in that falling short, that we have challenges. We grope and we grasp. . . . We ought to feel free to use any tool we can to pursue any avenue we find, to employ any process that is legitimate in order to stretch, to grow, and move ahead. . . . We want to have faith and . . . rigorous scholarship. We hope to have wide-open inquiry and strong religious faith.[8]

Danger: Cynicism

As we forge ahead on the path of knowledge and learning, there are other dangers lurking on the journey, perhaps more subtle and potentially more difficult to see and overcome. The very process of education is one of them. Sometimes people learn in very passive ways. They read or listen to someone else or watch a teacher solve a worked-out problem. But active modes of learning—writing papers, formulating hypotheses, running experiments, developing evidence and argument, presenting ideas and discussing them, opening up oneself and one's ideas to critique—are far more effective and thus are widely used. This is especially true where teachers seek to impart a deeper understanding of fundamental principles and to develop critical habits of mind, rather than simply to transmit certain facts. In that context, prevalent in colleges and universities, students and teachers treat each other's ideas with a practiced skepticism.

I have lived and taught and learned in such an environment for over thirty years. All of my experience has taught me the importance of carefully scrutinizing ideas, of attention to methodology, of asking hard questions about evidence and logic. Putting students through such educational experiences helps them become what William James called "tough minded."[9] But early in my years as a student I saw the dark side of this process, a side that can have serious consequences for one's spiritual welfare. I once participated in a seminar in which a doctoral student presented the results of his research to other students and to faculty. It did not take long to realize that the students in the seminar were primed to find the flaws in the work (and, as is often the case, there were flaws to be found). But the comments from some were sharp and biting. They attacked the methods, as they should, but their sarcasm, even when tinged with humor, cut the person as well. I left that seminar with an uneasy feeling, because I realized how easy it would be for me to fall into that pattern of behavior.

As the years passed, I became a teacher and witnessed (and lived) the tension between the value of a rigorous examination of ideas and the development of a climate of respect for each other in the learning process. Without strong attention to the latter, a misguided emphasis on the former can turn healthy skepticism into cynicism and a mean-spiritedness that can, if not recognized and addressed, become a canker on the spirit, affecting not only one's behavior in the world of the classroom, but in everything one does.

Such cynicism and meanness is not productive of real learning, and it surely is not what Latter-day Saints are required to develop if they are to serve God. The Lord said it clearly in these words:

> Wherefore, be not weary in well-doing, for ye are laying the foundation of a great work. And out of small things proceedeth that which is great. Behold, the Lord requireth the heart and a willing mind; and the willing and obedient shall eat the good of the land of Zion in these last days (D&C 64:33–34).

The challenge for Latter-day Saints (and anyone else for that matter) who would be educated and faithful, then, is to be tough-minded, but not hard-hearted. I shall return to that challenge below.

Danger: Pride

We have talked about the dangers in the search for knowledge; we now must look more closely at the possession of knowledge itself. Here, Jacob was most emphatic: a little learning goes a long way to make one proud and arrogant. If such were the case several hundred years before Christ's birth in the society depicted in the

Book of Mormon, it is certainly true in the world of the early twenty-first century.

Knowledge is wonderful. When my son hurts his shoulder (as he did) and needs a difficult operation (also true), I want the very best surgeon with the most advanced knowledge to perform the operation. The difference between the best and the average is enormous, all the more so when the problem is challenging and difficult. For those individuals who have such knowledge, it is natural to feel an intrinsic sense of accomplishment: one has to work hard to acquire it, having it expands one's perspective and sense of purpose, and knowledge allows one to deliver real solutions.

But this sense of accomplishment may be a slippery slope; one also must deal with what the scriptures call "the honors of men" (D&C 121:35). Learning brings recognition from society and from the communities of practice (engineers, lawyers, doctors, leaders, scientists, artists, officials, teachers, and so forth) one may aspire to join, or to which one already belongs. Moreover, within such communities there is often a hierarchy of status and influence based on knowledge and expertise.

Communities of practice with knowledge-based influence and status can have a very positive impact on society. Those with significant knowledge and learning can offer to society service of great value and can help to establish high standards of practice that, when transferred to others, can lift up the quality of work everywhere. But such a position in a community and in society can breed in those who possess such knowledge a self-importance and conceit that may degenerate into willful pride and arrogance. The scriptures describe such people as "stiffnecked" (Jacob 2:13). In effect, those who receive great honor from their colleagues, who receive accolades from society, begin to believe their own press releases. And "the honors of men" may, in particular, lead them to place their own wisdom or understanding ahead of the words of the prophets and the counsels of God.

The challenge is to have high standards without being stiff-necked.

Danger: Greed

Society confers status and honor on those who are knowledgeable. It has ever been thus. But in our day, society goes even further. We live in an economy that places increasing economic value on knowledge, at least on the kinds of knowledge that are critical to the creation of new technologies, new forms of entertainment, and new products and services. And with a modern capital market that translates future value into current wealth, some in our modern society have accumulated wealth on a truly remarkable scale. And they have in turn become the models for many, many others. When one lives in a knowledge economy, Jacob's warning becomes even more salient. Because now, in addition to "the honors of men," learning and education could—and likely will—bring wealth as well.

This is dangerous ground. Here again Jacob cuts to the heart of the problem:

> But wo unto the rich, who are rich as to the things of the world. For because they are rich they despise the poor and they persecute the meek, and their hearts are upon their treasures; wherefore, their treasure is their god. And behold, their treasure shall perish with them also (2 Nephi 9:30).

> And the hand of providence hath smiled upon you most pleasingly, that you have obtained many riches; . . . ye are lifted up in the pride of your hearts, and wear stiff necks

and high heads because of the costliness of your apparel, and persecute your brethren because ye suppose that ye are better than they.

. . . Before ye seek for riches, seek ye for the kingdom of God.

And after ye have obtained a hope in Christ ye shall obtain riches, if ye seek them; and ye will seek them for the intent to do good—to clothe the naked, and to feed the hungry, and to liberate the captive, and administer relief to the sick and the afflicted (Jacob 2:13, 18–19).

If education becomes the brass ring, if it becomes a ticket to wealth and nothing more, then it becomes a way, albeit a socially acceptable way, to give expression to greed. If, however, one's search for knowledge and learning has a higher purpose—to serve others and God—then one may use the wealth that comes along for good purposes. But the danger is clear. The challenge, then, is always to do good, whether one does well or not.

Following the Lord's Plan for Learning

These are the dangers on our journey to acquire learning and knowledge. We may encounter uncomfortable ideas and stop searching altogether, or we may fail to dig deep. We may lose our way, paradoxically placing too much faith in the wisdom of men. Moreover, the process of education and the possession of knowledge may breed within those who learn a cynicism, a pride and arrogance, a greed that can be destructive of the spirit and of faith. If your own voice, or the voice of your colleagues in your circle of practice, or the many voices of the world, are so loud that you cannot hear the Lord, you will fail to learn all you can and will fall prey to the "cunning plan of the evil one" as Jacob warned long ago.

The Lord's plan for the Latter-day Saints to "seek learning, even by study and also by faith" is designed to help us avoid the dangers and overcome the challenges, so that we can be both educated and faithful. So, how does this work in practice? Over the years I have observed a set of practices and a pattern of behavior in the lives of many of my Latter-day Saint friends and colleagues that help to make the Lord's plan a reality. This is an ideal type based on a personal assessment, of course, but I believe a close look at Latter-day Saints who are educated and faithful would highlight the kinds of practices I lay out here. And for Latter-day Saints still on the journey, they are simply good advice.

Humility

I begin with a short but important story. Early in my college years my uncle told me a story and taught me what I will call "the sacrament meeting test." It was designed to help one, especially one seeking learning, to maintain perspective and avoid both cynicism and pride. First the story: Many years ago my uncle (who at the time was a professor at a prominent university) was sitting in sacrament meeting listening to a talk given by a member of his congregation. As the man talked, my uncle noticed several errors of grammar and very poor sentence structure. The man's delivery was awkward, and the logic of his talk was at best incomplete. These problems attracted my uncle's attention. By the time the man finished his talk, my uncle had developed a devastating critique of the logical structure of the argument and the methods of presentation.

As he walked from the meeting, however, my uncle's conscience kicked into gear and he heard that "still, small voice" telling him that something was wrong. On reflection, he realized that he had brought the tools and methods of his classroom into sacrament meeting and had failed to hear the man's message. Then he remembered that his father had taught him that the really important questions are always these: What is the message of this talk? What is the speaker trying to teach me? What would the Lord have me learn? This is a far more productive approach to sacrament meeting in general. But it also helps to avoid cynicism and intellectual arrogance. For my uncle this was a defining moment. The lesson stayed with him. For me, sacrament meeting has become a litmus test: Whenever I find myself analyzing sacrament meeting talks rather than listening for the message in them, I know I am on dangerous ground and need to focus on what the Lord wants me to learn.

My uncle's story motivates the first element in the pattern I want to describe. Those Latter-day Saints who succeed in combining study and faith seek to develop humility. No matter what the circumstance, they ask: What can I learn from this experience? What is the Lord trying to teach me? What does He want me to learn? They accept and embrace opportunities to serve others (especially as home teachers) because they know that in doing so they serve God. And they attend the temple, not only because it is the Lord's house and a house of learning, but because they leave behind the distinctions of the world and stand equal before God with all their brothers and sisters. An attitude of humility is important in helping us maintain high standards while avoiding a stiff neck.

Focused Prayer

Being teachable, serving others, making the temple a central part of one's life—these are the activities that foster an attitude of humility. And humility helps us to not take ourselves too seriously and ignore the counsels of God. The second element in the pattern—prayer—also protects against intellectual arrogance and cynicism.

Prayer is an essential part of a life of faith. But I have in mind here a particular kind of prayer, a prayer that brings to God the specific, practical, mundane issues and problems of one's study. In this pattern, one lays before God the specific issues with which one is wrestling and seeks His guidance. The wrestling and the seeking are important. One goes before God without all the answers and acknowledges that God has them, all of them. It does not matter what the subject is or how big the issues are, the prophets tell us to take them to the Lord in prayer.

A specific prayer to God for help acknowledges our need for Him. But it is incomplete. It is also very important to thank Him for His mercy and blessings. Such specific, focused prayers of thanksgiving evoke in us a sense of gratitude. Gratitude is the foundation for treating others with respect and for approaching our journey of learning with a sense of optimism. Both help guard against cynicism and allow us to be tough-minded without being hard-hearted.

Lifelong Learning

Where the first two elements focus on spiritual dangers, the last two address our need to keep our minds active and engaged in the kind of searching, seeking process that the Lord outlines in His plan. And this seeking must be lifelong. Thus, the third element of the pattern is a commitment to lifelong learning, especially to rigorous study of the scriptures. Consider this counsel from Hugh Nibley, a legendary Latter-day Saint scholar (the passages in quotation marks are from Joseph Smith):

> Our search for knowledge should be ceaseless, which means that it is open-ended, never resting on laurels, degrees, or past achievements. "If we get puffed up thinking that we have much knowledge, we are apt to get a contentious spirit," and what is the cure? "Correct knowledge is

necessary to cast out that spirit." The cure for inadequate knowledge is "ever more light and knowledge."[10]

Such a commitment to learning throughout our lives is not the traditional pattern we find in modern society. That pattern is one in which education occurs early in life, followed by many years focused on applying that education to earning a living and raising a family, followed by years of retirement in which one may offer some service to the Church or community. This so-called "Learn-Earn-Serve" model of life is now obsolete (there is some question whether it ever had much application to the Latter-day Saints, who serve extensively throughout their lives). One cannot possibly hope to sustain a productive life of work and service on the basis of a few years of education early in one's life. Knowledge simply is increasing so fast that one must plan on a lifetime of learning in order to be effective and productive in the world.

The world, therefore, has now caught up with the Lord. For it has never been the Lord's plan that we would learn a lot in school and then put our minds to rest and work only on applying what we had learned for the rest of our lives. A careful review of the scriptures about study and faith reveals absolutely no time limits, no deadlines, and no calendar constraints on learning. It is to be lifelong. And those Latter-day Saints who are educated and faithful do exactly that, in a variety of ways, including through formal programs, continuing education, reading widely, and so forth. But a litmus test of this element of the pattern is their approach to the scriptures.

For the Latter-day Saints, the scriptures include the Bible (both Old and New Testaments), the Book of Mormon, the Doctrine and Covenants, and the Pearl of Great Price. We also believe in continuing revelation and that when modern prophets speak under the direction of the Spirit of God, what they say is scripture. These records of God's dealings with His children and His revelations to

His prophets can be read at many levels. But educated and faithful Latter-day Saints take seriously the Lord's plan for learning (which applies to all kinds of knowledge), and they study His word rigorously. The Lord commands us not just to read the scriptures, but to "search" them, to "feast" on them (John 5:39; 2 Nephi 31:20). This requires that we use our minds, indeed, every bit of our mental capacity, to study the scriptures deeply and rigorously. Doing so may reveal new patterns, new connections we had never seen before. It may give us new understanding of the context in which revelation has occurred, new insight into the purposes of the Lord's commandments, new ways to think about one's responsibilities.

Of course, the Lord wants us to bring our hearts and our spirits with us on our search. Indeed, studying the scriptures this way helps us to integrate the spirit and the intellect. That is what makes our approach to the scriptures such a powerful litmus test of our adherence to the Lord's plan for learning. Of course, the scriptures are special and come with special promises from God. He provides extra help in teaching His children about His word. But, if Latter-day Saints study the scriptures this way, they develop a capacity for learning—using reason and revelation in an integrated way—that can be used in every context.

Serving the Lord on the Frontier

The final element of the pattern involves service to the Lord. It is connected to humility and to the emphasis on our purpose in the Lord's plan for learning: to prepare for service in the kingdom of God. In the passage from Doctrine and Covenants 88 that I quoted earlier, the Lord makes clear that the purpose of His plan of learning is to prepare the laborers in his kingdom to go out and do His work. It is in the nature of that work that the Lord is always at its frontier. In the early days of the Church, the frontier was always right at hand. There were few "laborers," much to be done, and much that had to be done that had never been done before. The Latter-day Saints of that day were stretched and pushed and challenged almost every day of their lives. And the Lord was always there, because they were at the frontier, where He always works.

Today the Lord's plan of learning and His focus on the frontier are the same, but we face a very different situation. We find ourselves part of a Church with 12 million members worldwide, with a large and capable organization, full of people who know how to do much of what needs to be done. Indeed, there are many, many Latter-day Saints who are so experienced and capable that they can accomplish what they are asked to do without the Lord's help. At least they can when they are not working at the frontier but are back in the more settled parts of the kingdom where things are familiar and comfortable.

There is a frontier today, perhaps not as obvious as the one in 1830, but it is there in the individual lives of God's children (including our own), and in the great work of the Lord occurring all across the world. It is at this frontier that we find the Lord at work, and it is at this frontier that Latter-day Saints can accomplish what must be done only with the Lord's help. That is why service at the frontier of the kingdom is a distinctive element in becoming educated and faithful. It is here, in the unfamiliar territory of the frontier, that one's stock of knowledge and one's intellect and one's spiritual wisdom are inadequate. They are absolutely vital, necessary, but in the end, not enough. One has to turn to the Lord and rely on Him for help. And thus, one has to grow, sometimes spiritually, sometimes intellectually, but always in ways that serve God's children and move His work forward. Thus, service at the frontier adds to one's capacity in the Lord's way.

Conclusion

Commitment to education among the Latter-day Saints is an important aspect of the faith. It is deeply rooted in both the history and the doctrine of the Church. And it shapes in a powerful way the lives of its members. Revelation and commandment link this commitment to religious faith: Among the Latter-day Saints the ideal is to be both educated and faithful. Pursuing that ideal in practice is not just a matter of one's habits of mind, but of the practical pattern of activities that define one's life. In this realm in particular, being an educated, faithful Latter-day Saint is a way of life.

In this chapter I have tried to sketch out a pattern of activities that are characteristic of Latter-day Saints who have successfully pursued education and faith. They cultivate an attitude of humility, take their specific challenges in learning to God in prayer, pursue rigorous study of the scriptures as part of their commitment to life-long learning, and serve the Lord at the frontier. These activities keep them on the Lord's plan for learning and help them avoid the dangers of shallow thinking, cynicism, pride, and greed. Moreover, following this pattern expands their capacity for learning; it also gives meaning and focus to their pursuit of knowledge more generally. We learn in order to be of service to God and because seeking knowledge and intelligence is part of the Lord's great plan of eternal progression for His children. Of course, sometimes we learn because that is part of our plan to get a degree or advance in our profession, so we can build a career and nurture a family. But working at the frontier in serving the Lord, and talking to God every day about our work, helps keep all of this worldly activity in perspective. It guards against cynicism and greed taking root, and it gives righteous motivation to the journey of learning.

Notes

1. Henry Rosovsky, *The University: An Owner's Manual* (New York: W.W. Norton and Co., 1990), 105–7.

2. For a brief review of this history, see David P. Gardner, "Education," in Daniel H. Ludlow, ed., *Encyclopedia of Mormonism* (New York: Macmillan, 1992), 441–46.

3. Gordon B. Hinckley, *Standing for Something* (New York: Times Books, 2000), 59.

4. Hugh Nibley, *Brother Brigham Challenges the Saints*, edited by Don E. Norton and Shirley S. Ricks (Salt Lake City and Provo: Deseret Book and Foundation for Ancient Research and Mormon Studies, 1994), 316–17.

5. *Teachings of the Prophet Joseph Smith*, selected by Joseph Fielding Smith (Salt Lake City: Deseret Book, 1976), 51.

6. Ibid., 137.

7. Hugh Nibley, *Approaching Zion*, edited by Don E. Norton (Salt Lake City and Provo: Deseret Book and Foundation for Ancient Research and Mormon Studies, 1989), 72.

8. David P. Gardner and Jeffrey R. Holland, "Education in Zion: Intellectual Inquiry and Revealed Truth," *Sunstone* (Jan.–Feb. 1981), 59–60, 61.

9. William James, *Writings 1902–1910* (New York: The Library of America, 1987), 491–93.

10. Hugh Nibley, *Approaching Zion* (Salt Lake City: Deseret Book, 1989), 70–71.

Nine Reasons for Learning to Learn

Steven Sharp Nelson

Master of Public Administration, University of Utah

Question:

It was probably about the time my professor began bearing his testimony of capitalism that I began to question the spiritual significance of my "collegiate" experience. He had already marked himself as a man against religion—although he quoted the Bible once, but only as a preface to a statement that the words of the Bible can be beautiful, even if you don't believe it. He went on to testify that capitalism reigned supreme, whether we would admit it or not. We would one day realize that the conspicuous consumption of "stuff" is really all that we are about.

Yes, I think that was about the time I questioned why I was paying for this sort of education—in fact, I questioned why I was even wasting my time when there were much more important things to study and to learn. At length I began to doubt whether or not any classes outside of religion courses amounted to anything but a hill of beans.

They call this *higher* education? I asked myself what this had to do with my eternal destiny. I wanted to raise my hand to ask if my college experiences were going to be on the final exam—the Judgment Day test. What is a college education good for anyway?

My first college degree was in music. I graduated with an A-flat average. It was a default degree—the kind you end up with after trying just about everything else. Looking back, it seems superfluous to think that I could climb a step closer to salvation simply by learning where Haydn was living when he wrote *The London Symphonies*. But then I ask myself, is the knowledge inherent in my degree as important as the *process* by which the knowledge was gained?

What Do I Need a College Education For?

I understand that "if a person gains more knowledge . . . in this life . . . he will have so much the advantage in the world to come," as Joseph Smith said (D&C 130:19). Could it be that a greater proportion of this "advantage" that the Prophet alluded to has less to do with *what* we learned and more to do with *how* we learn, and *how good we are* at learning?

After I started to explore this question, I began to understand an "education" to be more of an acquirable skill than a set of memorized facts, or a "degree." My degree hangs on my wall. I remember the auspicious occasion of hanging it. I stepped back and paused to reflect on what the expensive piece of paper inside the frame really meant. The living prophet told me to get a degree, didn't he? Wait. He told me to get an *education*. Although a degree is an integrally important part of an education and can be essential in a vocational pursuit, an education is much more than a degree, isn't it? Perhaps in the eternal scheme of things, it isn't *what we are* after we graduate (meaning, the label attached to our degree) that is important, but rather *who we are*, and *what we can do*.

This ignites some deeper queries. Is it the *knowledge* we gain that positions us for saving grace, or is it who we are and what we have become *as a result of* the knowledge we have gained?

"Oh Say, What Is Truth?"

I'm a big fan of former general Relief Society president Bonnie Parkin. She once said, "Truth is truth wherever it is found."[1] This is a consolation in the midst of college courses that seem to be dubiously applicable. Truth recognition is part of knowledge acquisition. I have learned that acquiring truth often comes through a process of sifting and separating. My cognizance of this lesson was especially helpful for me in classes that seemed irrelevant to my eternal salvation.

The Prophet Joseph Smith once explained that he recognized eternal principles by how they tasted. He said that truths taste sweet as honey tastes sweet.[2] True principles taste to our soul as honey tastes to our tongue. In college we can enjoy a veritable buffet of knowledge that affords us the opportunity of discarding the bland and the bitter only to seek for seconds on sweet eternal truths—no matter who the professor is, no matter what the subject is.

Is recognizing truth really about becoming like the Savior? Does this mean my college education can actually help me one day more easily recognize the Savior—seeing Him as He is, if I am "like him" in understanding truth from fiction? (1 John 3:2).

How Could the Courses I'm Taking Really Count As "Spiritual Electives"?

Albert Einstein asserted that science was discovering God's methods of governing the universe. Johann Sebastian Bach wrote music in order to praise God. A geologist may very well study the earth in order to understand its spiritual history. But are there subjects that are simply not worth studying at all? Are there subjects that have no chance of glorifying God? Or are all subjects relevant in the end?

How Do I Eventually Graduate with a Degree of "Glory"?

The professor who bore his testimony of capitalism to his class wasn't preaching truth; and maybe my experience in his class generally felt like it was a waste of time and money. I have often wondered, however, whether in his class I was supposed to learn what truth is *not*. I am interested in eventually earning a "degree of glory," and I don't want to take any unnecessary sabbaticals studying something that does not contribute to my progress towards eternal salvation. What is the best way to study relevantly, whether in college or in life? Or should I just focus on the process of knowledge acquisition and learn from whatever comes my way?

* * *

Truman G. Madsen

Professor emeritus of philosophy, Brigham Young University

Answer:

I have never seen a want-ad for a philosopher, which makes me wonder if they are so useful after all. Flying into Los Angeles one weekend I met an executive with U.S. Steel. He had been in Provo for some years and then moved to Pittsburgh. We had an intelligent conversation until he asked the question, "What do you do for a living?"

I stalled by saying, "I do the same thing you do."

"What is that?"

"Pollute the air!"

More seriously, let's take the study of philosophy as an example of pursuit of knowledge that some might consider less than worthwhile—and through that example, answer some of the questions above. There are two parts in this presentation: To begin with I am going to argue briefly that philosophy is highly recommended, that it is in fact commanded, and even that it is unavoidable. Then, second, I am going to speak as if I were talking to a freshman who asks, "What good will it do me?" I will answer him in terms of nine functions, not merely possible or theoretical benefits, but the actual fighting weight of our program, results for which students have come back to thank us.

To begin then, four statements highly recommending the study of philosophy. You may be familiar with these three utterances of the Prophet Joseph Smith. But read them now in terms of the philosophical quest. Here is the first one:

> The things of God are of deep import; and time, and experience, and careful and ponderous and solemn thoughts can only find them out. Thy mind, O man! if thou wilt lead a soul unto salvation, must stretch as high as the utmost heavens, and search into and contemplate the darkest abyss, and the broad expanse of eternity.[3]

Perhaps philosophers generally are too careful, too ponderous, and too solemn. But there needs to be someone.[4]

Second, in the context of saying that other religions and philosophies have some truth, the Prophet said, "We should gather all the good and true principles in the world and treasure them up, or we shall not come out true 'Mormons.'"[5] Third, discoursing on what I reverently call the "theological blockbuster"—the plurality of gods—the Prophet said he despised the idea of being "scared to death" at the idea and added: "When things that are of the greatest importance are passed over by weak-minded men without even a thought, I want to see truth in all its bearings and hug it to my bosom."[6] There could not be a more telling definition of the philosopher's quest or a greater boldness in the adventurer's pursuit of ideas.

A more recent statement from a more recent man. President John Taylor said more than a century ago:

> We [of course he meant the Latter-day Saints] must be philosophers too, and make it appear that our philosophy is better than theirs and then show them that religion is at the bottom of it.[7]

Some people assume that Mormonism is opposed to philosophy. They fail to detect that Mormonism is itself a philosophy and a very comprehensive one at that. Along with being recommended or commended, it is even commanded. Did you know that there is a commandment in the Doctrine and Covenants for you to study philosophy? You hadn't noticed that! I am only half-serious. But in section 88 we find the commandment to teach one another "in theory, in principle, in doctrine." It then goes on to say that we must teach of things "in heaven and in the earth, and under the earth" (D&C 88:78–79; emphasis added). Some might suppose that that refers to astronomy and geology, and perhaps Dante's *Inferno*. But is it not clear that if Mormonism is a philosophy of the "utmost heavens" and the "darkest abyss," then all the things of the earth and under the earth—even supposing them diabolical—must be studied.

But someone will say, "Is philosophy a thing, and more

concretely, is philosophy the kind of thing that is really being recommended in that passage?" Now I have you. Because, you see, even to ask the question, "Is philosophy a thing?" is to ask a philosophical question. And to attempt an answer, even to say, "There is no answer!" is itself to take a philosophical position. Do you consider that argument fraudulent? Reread sometime the whole of Doctrine and Covenants 88.

Mormonism, though it is taught at Brigham Young University and imbues the curriculum there, does not dominate in the sense that Marxism dominates at the University of Moscow or Judaism at Yeshiva University, Catholicism at Woodstock, or certain kinds of secularism elsewhere. For one thing, Mormonism is more inclusive than all of them together. But more to the present point, alternatives are presented here. That is a little different from saying they are advocated; but there is a recognition that every one of the options needs to be understood and taught. So it has been traditionally.[8]

A student once went to Robert K. Thomas, then head of the BYU Honors program, and told him he was dropping my philosophy class.

"Why?"

"Well, he is looking for answers that I already have," he said.

Bob said, "What answers do you mean?"

"Well, we are having a week discussing different theories of truth. Now we know what truth is. It tells us in the Doctrine and Covenants."

"Oh," said Bob. "Where's that?"

The student quoted, of course, the classic statement, "*Truth is knowledge of things as they are, and as they were, and as they are to come*"—a statement, incidentally, that is far more than a truism (D&C 93:24).

Bob said, "Let's stop on that word *things!* Is an idea a thing? Is a contrary-to-fact conditional a thing?"

"What do you mean?"

"Well, take for example, the statement, 'If Hitler had attacked Britain instead of Russia, he would have won the war.' Is that a true statement?"

"Yes, I think so."

"But it isn't a thing. It did not occur."

So, leading the student in a Socratic fashion, Bob Thomas suggested that maybe he could profit a bit from a semantic analysis of the word *truth.* The student returned to class, but too late. He didn't really stick with us long enough.

Of course, as Mormons we have different answers and therefore different questions. But what do these mean in the context of world thought? Is it an advantage to keep that from ourselves and the world?

With that preliminary statement, then, I here offer nine suggested functions of the field—nine ways that philosophical analysis pays off.

1. Gymnastic Value

I begin with the most obvious. It is what William James called the gymnastic value of philosophy. Just as you go into a gymnasium and exercise and thus develop muscle and skill and rhythm, so do you grapple intellectually with the questions and answers and analyses that began with the pre-Socratic philosophers in the Western world and thereby tend to sharpen and muscularize your brain. I grant that there can be evasions here and even corruptions. But by and large, exercise is always good for muscle in the physical realm, as well as in the mental. Thus, when you ask the question, "What good are weights?" the answer is: they provide stress and result in muscle. Philosophers are by that analogy, at least (I do not say at most), smartening dumbbells. The very effort to cope with the field is strengthening. Philosophy has a gymnastic value.

2. Propaganda Resistance

The study of philosophy heightens your propaganda resistance. We live in a time when exposure is universal and unavoidable to all kinds of ideas. You are daily besieged, for example, with approximately four thousand advertisements, and who knows how many thousand *isms* and counsels and arguments and appeals. The notion, by the way, that there is such a thing as immunity or isolation or provincialism in any university in the world, let alone a Mormon one, is itself a most provincial notion. It is impossible to escape the mental weather of our time. To be able to study something of the sources of conviction, to know the basic avenues, the genealogy if you will, of ideas, to study the various techniques of illegitimate persuasion, to develop through practical logic strategies for coping with typical and daily fallacies is great gain. It is to learn a little about the differences between opinion (not yet warranted), knowledge, and certainty, and also to develop enough skill to know that though a man's method may be sneaky, he still may have something.[9] That takes time.

Moreover, philosophers have set us an example, often, of what happens when you take various ideas to extremes. They enable us to make mistakes vicariously. A student can believe in his freshman year at college, for example, that he is not interested in any study except that which changes conduct—"if it makes a difference in my life"—quite unaware that in so saying he is a pragmatist of sorts. If he will study a couple of the pragmatists, for example, Dewey or Mead, he will learn that if he takes that view all the way and defines truth as "what works," he is in serious trouble.[10] He may then be on guard against going that far.

The pervasiveness of philosophy extends not just into the class-room or into the books or the journal articles; philosophy is really being taught in all the fields that you study at any university, and it is even present in your own secret thoughts and conversations. Like nuclear fallout, it is everywhere. It comes as a surprise to some people that philosophy even shows up in our hymn books. There is a hymn that ends, "Truth is the sum of existence"[11]—a correspondence and coherence theory. (That theory is an interesting challenge to those who suppose truth is just a name for what works if you can get away with it.) We have a hymn that sings, "Do what is right, let the consequence follow."[12] That's Kantian formalism as opposed to John Stuart Mill utilitarianism. Everywhere words carry philosophical assumptions.

3. Improved Articulation

The study of philosophy can enable you to be more lucid, cogent, and articulate in thought and expression. Logic has become in this century a remarkable method, a kind of higher mathematics. Set-theory in logic is itself a brilliant discipline. And the study of the forms of valid argument enables you to take what at first may appear to be a congeries of unworkable ideas and carefully trace what is and is not consistent, what is and is not related as argument. It is an important thing just to learn in lecture one in a logic class, for example, that there is a distinction between validity and truth, that an argument may "hold" in some sense but still lead you to a false conclusion. To learn that all language is conventional; that a dictionary is a history book, and an obsolete one at that; that meaning is contextual rather than isolational; that there is a difference between semantics and syntactics and pragmatics—even to come that far is to be better prepared to cope with all other subjects you study and read and talk and write about for the rest of your life.

You ought to take a logic course while at college. And then you can catch people (even yourself) trying to run a round argument through Aristotle's square of opposition.

4. A Mental Framework

Philosophy provides a frame of reference. Aristotle anciently talked about the "categories," and he had several, such as substance and accident, essence and existence, quantity and quality. These were undergirding modes of analysis, cups, as it were, out of which all of existence could be poured. Collingwood, the British philosopher, talked often of "absolute presuppositions," which in his view undergirded a whole culture in a given time. In our own time, Waismann, for one, has traced the root assumptions of scientific method. I take such assumptions (though he does not) as a kind of metaphysics—an implicit theory of reality. Mortimer Adler, with the boy-wonder university professor and president Robert N. Hutchins, some decades ago concluded that because American education has no such undergirding set of categories, no mental framework, we should introduce one, even if we do so arbitrarily. So he recommended that Thomism, the basic assumptions of St. Thomas Aquinas—in a broader scale, scholasticism—be the basis for teaching all subjects at St. John's University. For a period it did so function. He later developed what you have heard about as the "Syntopicon," which revolves around 102 basic ideas and holds that there has been a "continuing conversation" that is grounded in those ideas from Homer to Freud and beyond.

"Philosophy," Descartes once said, "enables one to discourse with an appearance of truth concerning all matters."[13] If that is so, it is because a philosopher has a schema for interrelating ideas that can be very helpful, however tentative or arbitrary it may be at the outset. Now, we are somewhat chary of that enterprise partly because as Latter-day Saints we do not expect forthwith to develop a Thomistic system. Thomas Aquinas and other great system-builders in the history of Western thought, such as Spinoza and Hegel, ended up bagging chimeras. They did not have the final answers, and that has become more and more apparent.

The fact remains that there is something of a unity or coherence of what we have begun to understand. And the so-called great apostasy (T. Edgar Lyon was constantly asked, "What is the finest book on the great apostasy?" He answered, "The New Testament") did not occur because philosophers came on the scene. It occurred, I suggest, mainly because certain major theologians began with faulty premises. One can ask himself, seriously, what might have happened if Clement, Philo, Augustine, Thomas Aquinas, Duns Scotus, Kant, Hegel, and others had begun their hard intellectual analyses with premises derived from Doctrine and Covenants 93 and the King Follett discourse. To say the least, the enterprise would have been more exciting, more comprehensive, and more comprehendible, and would have ended quite differently. In any case, to identify, to classify, to derive ideas is a skill. And having a frame of reference is important. Philosophy can help.

At Brigham Young University we have worked out an amiable and harmonic relationship with all the different "-ologies," and we play into each other's hands. If you take education classes, at some point you have to take a course that deals with the philosophy of education. Occasionally education professors have said, "But you also should take a course in introductory philosophy over there." Students need to have a taste of language philosophy, classic themes, metaphysics, ethics, and so forth. In literary criticism you will eventually confront aesthetics—what Hospers calls "meaning and truth in the arts."[14] Some humanities professors have recommended that their students take a course in aesthetics. In English itself you start spinning off into philology and what makes poetry poetry and prose

prose, and whether there is a grammar of assent, and whether all language is metaphorical. You are again getting into philosophical questions. Physics? They are studying cosmology and ontology, sometimes unawares. The exact sciences? Even in engineering there are certain presuppositions which it is the philosopher's business to bring into the open and analyze. History? What is history if it doesn't include the history of ideas? Psychology? There are as many psychologies as there are philosophies—theories of mind and body and cognitive process and tests for "reality." But all would profit from a course on the philosophy of mind and action theory. What about law? We could talk about the "decision issues" that force one to hand-pan rock-bottom questions. In any case, you benefit by having a framework to interrelate things and push their principles all the way to the roots.

5. Tracing Implications and Applications

The study of philosophy enables you to be sensitive to implications. You see that a certain position leads to certain other positions, that all questions lead eventually to all other questions. That takes some training and mind-stretching—working for the assimilation of many ideas at once. You begin to see how much is implicit, how much is hidden in any posture. Take the question, for example, "Can science and religion be reconciled?" (Depending on which science and which religion, the answer may be no.) And a prior one still: What is science?[15] The question of whether we are doing science when we do this or that raises the question of whether there is a scientific method or many scientific methods. What, then, constitutes an explanation? What constitutes a law? And what is the interrelationship of theory with observation? What is the relationship of exact measurement in formal mathematics to the flux we call "sense experience"? These are all unavoidable philosophical questions. One sees such implications the moment he begins working in the field.

Occasionally, I have toyed with the idea that perhaps Western thought started off on the wrong foot and, what is worse, in the wrong direction, by asking at the beginning what seemed like an innocent question—Plato's "What is ultimate?" Already he presupposes that there can only be one ultimate. He couldn't have asked the question what *are* ultimates, because with his definition of "ultimate" any double ultimate would mean that one or the other would of necessity prevail; Roman Catholic philosophers argue similarly to this hour. But it just happens, as we understand, that we live in a pluriverse where there are many co-ultimates in terms of existence and even in terms of value. Plato began with the other assumption and we have been in serious confusion ever since.

6. Communication

The study of philosophy can enable you to be more communicative. Let us admit that there is a jargon involved in the study of philosophy that many have held makes it impossible to understand anyone, even (especially?) after one has a doctor's degree. "And anyway," they say, "the definitions remain sufficiently ambiguous that all manner of hoodwink can be committed under whatever label." It is fair to say that philosophy is a language. When I am asked occasionally, "What languages have you studied?" I say, "French, German, Latin, and Philosophy." But the terminology used in philosophy is not more difficult to get to and work with than that of any other specialized study. And I am convinced that the advantage of understanding that terminology is not simply that it opens up this or that particular specialty, but that it gives a way of reflecting about all disciplines.

But, the critics may say, "Don't philosophers really tear things apart; don't they paralyze by their analysis?" Some do, but they also strain to synthesize. But, persists the critic, "Name three philosophers who have ever agreed." One reply: "The Father, the Son, and the Holy Ghost." Some say, "We don't have to worry about communicating with other people in terms of their language. That is not our obligation. Let's have them cross over the bridge and learn ours." Well, there is some insight there. If they can cross over the bridge, if they can even hear us so they want to cross over, well enough.

But I submit that we can't even know what we ourselves are saying unless we know what others are hearing. Like it or not, the language frameworks of various philosophical systems do predominate in the world at large—for example, positivism, existentialism, Marxism, and in the Orient, other -isms still—and they control and often control completely the way people hear. When you use words, they hear them in their framework—words like "eternal," "self," "progression," "intelligence," "matter," "soul," "creation"—and you had better know that or you will not be communicating. The distinction between talking with and talking to is precisely at this point. Philosophy at college could therefore be called a second Language Training Mission. We all recognize the need to learn French and German to talk to the French and Germans. We are beginning to recognize that we had better learn French and German culture (which must include philosophy), too, in order to talk with them.

7. Integration

The study of philosophy can enable you to integrate and inter-relate things—things on this campus or any campus, and also things in your own personal philosophy of life. May I here quote a remarkable man? B. H. Roberts was our greatest historian and perhaps in some respects our greatest theologian. Leonard Arrington, a

Church historian, sent out a questionnaire to many educators in the Mormon Church some time ago and asked them to name the greatest intellectuals in Mormon history and to put them in a ranking from one to five. Who would you include? Names were mentioned like Orson Pratt, James E. Talmage, John A. Widtsoe. All respondents felt ambiguous about including Joseph Smith because in one sense he was an intellectual, but he was much more. But except for the Prophet, the man who emerged as the most respected intellectual was this self-taught, immigrant blacksmith named B. H. Roberts. Roberts was excited by the potential for integration that I am here recommending. He wanted to be the Spencer of Mormonism, a synthesizer, one who pulls together the whole thing and makes it coherent. He did not live to do that. But the aspiration throbbed in him:

> My love for the gospel grows out of the partial knowledge [he acknowledged that he didn't have it all. Do any of us? To say that you know the gospel is true may be less impressive when someone asks, "Do you know the gospel?"] I have of the great truths it contains. In it I feel the presence of a marvelous system of truth, a philosophy that gives unity to all history, and proper relationship to all existing things; that fills life with a real meaning, and makes existence desirable. And if I could only intelligently grasp these great truths in the presence of which I feel I am standing when I contemplate "Mormonism," and reduce them to some orderly system which I am sure they are capable of, I would account myself most happy.[16]

Mormonism is continually bursting formulae. It is open at both ends. It has revelations regarding the ages of rocks, but also revelations from the Rock of Ages, and as we reach both up and down our knowledge continues to expand. But even now there are such harmonic insights as enable you to bring all kinds of things together, unifying. And that is what challenged Roberts, as it should us.

Now there is something to be said here about intellectual conversion. We speak frequently of going beyond a merely intellectual assent to something more whole, a religious or total conversion, as if the second replaces the first. I submit to you it *includes* the first. And sometimes the process can work the other way. Listen again to B. H. Roberts. He had been working for some time on a manual for the Seventies. His subject was the Atonement. He comments:

> This late inquiry into that subject has had a wonderful effect upon my own thoughts and state of mind. I have for many years believed in the atonement of Jesus Christ and have accepted its symbols and baptisms and confirmations and have repeatedly renewed my acceptance of that atonement by the sacrament of the Lord's supper. It has been a matter of faith with me and knowledge by the testimony of the spirit of God to my soul, but upon close inquiry, by deeper delving into the subject, my intellect also gives its full and complete assent to the soundness of the philosophy and absolute necessity for the atonement of Jesus Christ, that this atonement, the method and manner of it, is the only way by which there could be brought to pass an at-one-ment, a reuniting of soul of man with soul of God. I account it for myself a new conversion, an intellectual conversion, to the atonement of Jesus Christ and I have been rejoicing in it of late exceedingly.[17]

That's an exciting thing. The intellectual—(I was going to say vitality. I want to say more than that)—the intellectual vigor and power, just the sheer intellectual power, of the ideas that are inherent in Mormonism is underrated, I am afraid most of all, at times, among college-age students. It is treated as old hat. It isn't. It has all kinds of sparkling implications and applications that remain to be mined. And the joy of that kind of discovery and the resultant harmony make all the pain worth it. When I asked David H. Yarn why he would say a student should study philosophy at college, he replied, "It enables you to read the scriptures with greater comprehension and appreciation." He sees things there that maybe some of you don't see—and sees them whole. He sees them because he has been through the options, weighing the alternatives and tracing implications that you don't yourselves recognize as exciting.

Learning isn't ever completely painless. And some people reject the enterprise of a university on the ground that it is hard. I think it is hard. But I want to go on record as saying as a personal testament that the joy of discovery, this kind of discovery, makes all the pain worth it.

8. Of Cyclic Awareness

The study of philosophy enables you to see how our whole culture has become what it is and alerts you to the common but naïve notion that there really is something new under the sun. We talk, for example, in our time about the breaking down of tradition, the "shaking of the foundations," the rise of cultural relativism, new moralities, the abandonment of outworn traditions. But every –ism, however "new," has a counterpart in ancient thought. Every one! Do you think that the notion that all reality comes to nothing, as advocated by certain disciples of Jean–Paul Sartre, is new? Such nihilism is as old as the hills. Is Camus modern in saying, "There is only one problem: suicide"?[18] A man named Hegesias spoke of suicide in similar ways six hundred years before Christ. Philosophy emancipates you from the easy supposition that time automatically brings progress or that being in the twenty-first century means that we don't fall into dead-end patterns and policies of former generations. In fact we are recommitting humanity's accumulated folly daily. Again, it is a profitable thing to know your intellectual pedigree and the things you take for granted. "One who does not know history," Santayana observed, "is condemned to live it over."[19]

9. Of the Tools of Creativity

Now, finally, I think philosophy is to be studied as a tool of creativity. Bertrand Russell is a witness for the defense here. He changed his mind often. That has often been urged against him. It might, in fact, be a recommendation. He had much to say in support of the scientific and naturalistic approach (so, but within limits, do we), and not much good to say about kinds of intellectual rubbish around him (neither do we). At the end of a book on philosophy, Russell says: "Philosophy is to be studied not for the sake of any definite answers to its questions . . ." Now that is numbing to anyone! Why should you study a field if you end up knowing no more than you started with? But listen: " . . . not for the sake of any definite answers to its questions, but rather for the sake of these questions themselves." And then he gives four reasons why entertaining these questions is productive. First, "because they enlarge our conception of what is possible." I suspect that creativity cannot occur unless one develops a certain ability to break loose, to suppose other than routine perspectives, to consider what heretofore you had never considered, to wonder when other people don't wonder. Creativity comes out of freshness. "It enlarges your conception of what is possible." Second, "it enriches your intellectual imagination." Without laboring the "how," such enrichment always enriches life itself. Third, "it diminishes the dogmatic assurance that closes the mind against speculation." Finally—this sounds almost religious, almost mystical in Russell—"Because of the greatness of the universe which philosophy contemplates, the mind itself is rendered great and becomes capable of that union with the universe which constitutes its highest good."[20]

Two qualifications about these statements—otherwise, in spirit, I sympathize:

1. Unlicensed and irresponsible speculation has often been done in the name of philosophy to the detriment of our culture. But I don't know how you know what the limits are until you try to get up to them. I don't know how a man is qualified to say the whole enterprise is futile unless he has made some effort in it.

2. The statement goes against the grain slightly in that we are set (this is built into our heritage) against what are sometimes called "the philosophies of men." We are alerted against falling in love with one's own reason, "Reading by the lamp of our own conceit."[21] We are alerted against pursuing "the mysteries," and occasionally we can write off all philosophy as that identical pursuit. It was Paul who said, "Beware lest any man spoil you through philosophy and vain deceit" (Colossians 2:8). Some problems are 100-percent guaranteed insoluble for now. Many others, though not insoluble, are not of particular interest. But there are some mysteries, which the scriptures call "the mysteries of godliness" (1 Timothy 3:16; D&C 19:10), the deeper things, the richer things; and they are they of which I suspect the Prophet spoke when he said, "I beseech you go forward and search deeper and deeper into the mysteries of Godliness."[22] These are mysteries you are to pursue.

Life itself leads you to the level where you cry out, "Why is there anything at all? Why is there something and not nothing?" You don't hear that question in physics class. But you do in a philosophy class. I submit that there are exciting, if not final, responses to that in your own heritage.

These, then, are nine reasons for learning to learn while at college. They open the door to obtaining a "degree of glory" through intelligence gained in a lifetime study of the ultimate questions.

Notes

1. Bonnie D. Parkin, "Remember Who You Are!" Brigham Young University fireside, 7 March 2004.

2. Stan Larson, "The King Follett Discourse: a Newly Amalgamated Text," in *BYU Studies* 18, no. 2 (Winter 1978). "This is good doctrine. It tastes good. You say honey is sweet and so do I. I can also taste the spirit and principles of eternal life, and so can you. I know it is good and that when I tell you of these words of eternal life that are given to me by the inspiration of the Holy Spirit and the revelations of Jesus Christ, you are bound to receive them as sweet. You taste them and I know you believe them. I rejoice more and more." (See also *The Words of Joseph Smith: The Contemporary Accounts of the Nauvoo Discourses of the Prophet Joseph,* compiled and edited by Andrew F. Ehat and Lyndon W. Cook [Salt Lake City: Deseret Book, 1981], 352.)

3. Joseph Smith, *History of The Church of Jesus Christ of Latter-day Saints,* edited by B. H. Roberts, 2d ed. rev., 7 vols. (Salt Lake City: Deseret Book, 1987), 3:295. The original language of the letter is: "A fanciful and flowely [flowery] and heated immagination be aware of be cause the things of God Are of deep import and time and expeariance and carful and pondurous and solom though[ts] can only find them out. thy mind O Man, if thou wilt lead a soul unto salvation must streach as high as the utmost Heavens, and sear[c]h in to and contemplate the loest <lowest> conside[r]ations of the darkest abyss, and Expand upon the broad considerations of Eternal Expance, he must commune with God. how much more dignifide and noble are the thoughts of God, than the vain immaginations of the human heart, none but fools, will triful, with the souls of men." Joseph Smith, Hyrum Smith, Lyman Wight, Caleb Baldwin, and Alexander McRae to Edward Partridge and the Church, March 20, 1839, Liberty, Missouri. (LDS Church Archives; and Dean Jessee, ed., *Personal Writings of Joseph Smith* [Salt Lake City: Deseret Book, 1984], 388–407.)

4. Mining the gold in these traditions has been encouraged from the

earliest days of the Church. On February 15, 1978, the First Presidency of the Church issued the following declaration: "The great religious leaders of the world such as Mohammed, Confucius, and the Reformers, as well as philosophers including Socrates, Plato, and others, received a portion of God's light. Moral truths were given to them by God to enlighten whole nations and to bring a higher level of understanding to individuals." Daniel H. Ludlow, ed., *Encyclopedia of Mormonism*, 4 vols. (New York: Macmillan, 1992), 2:487.

5. Smith, *History of the Church*, 5:517.

6. Smith, *History of the Church*, 6:477. See also *The Words of Joseph Smith*, 381.

7. John Taylor, *The Gospel Kingdom*, edited by G. Homer Durham (Salt Lake City: Bookcraft, 1987), 33.

8. BYU and its satellite universities are pluri-versities: Religion, science, humanities, the arts, vocational training, law school, pre-med, and continuing research efforts across the board.

9. Consider this syllogism. It is valid and arrives at a true conclusion but has false premises: All gray things have four legs. False. All four-legged creatures are cats. False. All cats have four legs. True.

10. William James defined truth as pragmatic results. But taken all the way, this test can become subjective and arbitrary. "By their fruits ye shall know them" (Matthew 7:20). But fruits may be deceptive or illusory unless grounded in truth.

11. Jean Jaques, "Oh Say, What Is Truth?" *Hymns of The Church of Jesus Christ of Latter-day Saints* (Salt Lake City: The Church of Jesus Christ of Latter-day Saints, 1985), no. 272.

12. Anonymous, "Do What Is Right," *Hymns*, no. 237.

13. René Descartes, *Discourse on Method*, edited by Elizabeth S. Haldane and G. R. T. Ross (Mineola, N.Y.: Dover Publications, c2003), Part 1.

14. John Hospers, *Meaning and Truth in the Arts* (Chapel Hill: University of North Carolina Press, 1946).

15. The assumptions, methods, attitudes, and conclusions of the sciences are somewhat fluid. In my lifetime, a far-reaching attempt to define and inter-relate all the sciences was to culminate in an encyclopedia of unified science. But it failed. If the question is, "Can a prize-winning scientist extend his

truth-seeking into religion and become a saint?" our history furnishes abundant examples.

16. B. H. Roberts, "The Creation of Enthusiasm and Loyalty," *Improvement Era* 9, no. 11 (September 1906): 844. Roberts's account of Spencer can be found in B. H. Roberts, "The Prophet's Generalizations," *Joseph Smith: Prophet-Teacher* (first edition, 1908; Princeton: Deseret Club, 1967), 62–65; also in the summations in volume 4 of B. H. Roberts's *Seventy's Course in Theology*, 5 vols. (Salt Lake City: Deseret News, 1907–1912).

17. B. H. Roberts, Conference Report, April 1911, 59.

18. Albert Camus, *The Myth of Sysyphus and Other Essays* (New York: Vintage International, 2001), 3. The exact quote is "There is but one truly serious philosophical problem and that is suicide." Camus found neither God nor meaning in life and considered suicide. It is still unclear whether he died in an accident or took his own life.

19. George Santayana, *The Life of Reason or The Phases of Human Progress: Reason in Common Sense*, 2d ed. (New York: Charles Scribner's Sons, 1924), ch. 12. "Those who cannot remember the past are condemned to repeat it." A variant reading ends, "they are condemned to repeat their mistakes." Richard Weaver has observed, "It has been well said that the chief trouble with the contemporary generation is that it has not read the minutes of the last meeting." (Richard M. Weaver, *Ideas Have Consequences* [Chicago: University of Chicago Press, 1984], 11.)

20. Bertrand Russell, *Some Problems of Philosophy* (Oxford, England: Oxford University Press, 1959), chapter 15.

21. Joseph F. Smith, *Gospel Doctrine* (Salt Lake City, Deseret Book, 1939), 373.

22. "I advise all to go on to perfection, and search deeper and deeper into the mysteries of Godliness" (*The Words of Joseph Smith*, 366). But Joseph counseled against futile and divisive speculation: "Let mysteries alone lest you be overthrown" (*The Words of Joseph Smith*, 189). He adds: "A man can do nothing for himself unless God direct him in the right way; and the priesthood is for that purpose" (*History of the Church*, 6:363). The context of these remarks is the temple (see D&C 128:7, D&C 76:7), and temple learning requires more than abstract reflection. We are taught: "These revelations, which are reserved for and taught only to the faithful Church members in sacred temples,

constitute what are called the 'mysteries of Godliness.' The Lord said He had given to Joseph 'the keys of the mysteries, and the revelations which are sealed.' (D&C 28:7.) As a reward to the faithful, the Lord promised: 'And to them will I reveal all mysteries, yea, all the hidden mysteries of my kingdom from days of old' (D&C 76:7)." (Harold B. Lee, *The Teachings of Harold B. Lee,* edited by Clyde J. Williams [Salt Lake City: Bookcraft, 1996], 575.)

Diverging Roads

Kimberlee James

Master of Social Work, University of Utah

Question:

Today is your day.
You're off to Great Places! You're off and away!
You have brains in your head.
You have feet in your shoes.
You can steer yourself
any direction you choose.
You're on your own. And you know what you know.
And *YOU* are the guy [or gal] who'll decide where to go.[1]

I used this passage from the wise words of Dr. Seuss in his book *Oh, the Places You'll Go!* in a speech I gave at my seminary graduation in high school. It was an exciting time. I was ready for the adventure called life. I felt as though I had the whole world before me. The adventure began with my declaration of independence, signified by moving out of my parents' home and then going away to college. I just didn't know at that time what kind of responsibilities would fall upon me in my new independent state.

I know that God has given us the gift of agency in order for us to grow and become more like Him. Sometimes answers seem obvious when I need to make decisions between right and wrong. In those cases, it is easy to see what the best use of my agency would be, even if following through is hard at times. But what about deciding between two good choices? Sometimes these decisions can affect the pathway of my life drastically, even determining who I will become.

The opening words to *Oh, the Places You'll Go!* made the life before me seem so exciting. Once I entered college and took on more responsibility, I found myself constantly faced with troublesome decisions between two goods. Now I had to ask myself questions like "What should I major in?"; "Should I go on a mission or should I marry this nice guy?"; "Once I graduate from college should I go to graduate school?"; "Whom should I marry?"; "What job should I take?"

Sometimes I find myself growing dizzy from my own indecisiveness. Each road has different people to meet and different experiences to be had; these things shape who I ultimately will become. I find myself becoming unduly anxious to make the right choice between two great options; of course, what I really want to do is the Lord's will. Sometimes it seems the importance of the question has little correlation with the clarity of His answer.

The decisions between two goods are hard, and I have constantly inquired of the Lord for guidance. With some decisions, however, there have been no "bolts of lightning." With these decisions I have tried to be guided by the peace that I felt. Sometimes I have simply had to start down one of the possible paths, hoping for the best. This has not always proven successful, resulting in self-doubt and fear with respect to later decision-making efforts.

Why does the Lord give stronger answers to some questions than others? Are there circumstances when the Lord really doesn't care what I choose to do? How much does He leave up to me? What is the Lord's role in my agency?

* * *

Virginia H. Pearce

Master of Social Work, Utah State University;
Former Counselor in General Young Women Presidency

Answer:

The Road Not Taken

Two roads diverged in a yellow wood,
And sorry I could not travel both
And be one traveler, long I stood
And looked down one as far as I could
To where it bent in the undergrowth;

Then took the other, as just as fair,
And having perhaps the better claim,
Because it was grassy and wanted wear;
Though as for that the passing there
Had worn them really about the same,

And both that morning equally lay
In leaves no step had trodden black.
Oh, I kept the first for another day!
Yet knowing how way leads on to way,
I doubted if I should ever come back.

I shall be telling this with a sigh
Somewhere ages and ages hence:
Two roads diverged in a wood, and I—
I took the one less traveled by,
And that has made all the difference.
—Robert Frost[2]

Time after time each of us is that traveler approaching divergent roads. A decision is required. Sometimes the choice is made without so much as a moment's reflection. Our feet hardly hesitate as they turn slightly to the left or right and come down on the new path. But other times, we stand in agony straining to look into the future as far as possible, "until it bends in the undergrowth." Then, shifting to the other foot, we examine the other choice, or choices—comparing, weighing, wondering, asking—all the time knowing that this particular decision could, in fact, make "all the difference." Studying, praying, and stalling as long as possible or tolerable, to our dismay we are sometimes still unable to see with clarity. We cannot describe a burning confirmation or a stupor of thought, just a jumble and a growing list of "pros and cons."

Sometimes decisions are between good and evil. Given our easy access to scripture and latter-day prophets, those decisions are fairly straightforward. They may not be easy to make. Temptations are cunningly devised and we are mortal. But, if approached prayerfully and with righteous desires, the preferred decision is clear, even though it may be difficult to execute and even harder to stay the course. The consequences of decisions involving basic honesty, sexual morality, the Word of Wisdom, and so on, are fairly clear to see if we honestly stop to look down the path of the future.

I don't believe that these are the kinds of decisions Robert Frost is describing in "The Road Not Taken." In fact, at first he thinks that the road he is choosing to take is "more grassy and wants wear," but on closer examination they both seem to be worn about the same. They both seem desirable and good to the traveler, and though he hopes to take the other on another day, he knows it is unlikely to be available in the future, precisely because of today's choice.

And so we wish to examine the dilemma of making decisions when the choices are between two or more seemingly good roads. However, because of the choice we make we will experience different scenery and adventures, encounter different traveling companions, and arrive at different destinations, having become ourselves different travelers. Yes,

> I shall be telling this with a sigh
> Somewhere ages and ages hence:
> Two roads diverged in a wood, and I—
> I took the one less traveled by,
> And that has made all the difference.

There are some foundational doctrines, big-picture givens, that help us understand important concepts about our day after day mortal adventure in decision-making. I wish to present them simply and briefly and then be more specific about my own experience as I have watched and participated in the struggles inherent in "deciding."

The grand purpose of our mortal experience is to become like our Father in Heaven and His Son. Therefore, *personal, individual growth toward godhood is the business of life.*

In order to facilitate this growth, God gave us *agency* and required that we be individually accountable for its exercise. Agency is the vehicle by which we can grow and become like Him, because its wise use is the way we mature, the way we develop wisdom, judgment, discernment, and all of the other attributes of God. He will not and cannot simply hand us these qualities. That is why, in the beginning, God gave us our agency (Moses 4:3). It is the fundamental reason Lucifer's plan was rejected. Godlike attributes come from experience in making choices and answering individually for those choices. Those around us must also make choices—choices that often determine our own next set of choices. It all becomes rather complicated until we realize that at every point we must answer only for ourselves, not for others.

The plan for our life on earth also requires *faith*. We have to believe in Christ and follow Him to become like Him. Therefore, faith becomes fundamental to our returning home. Our faith can become much more than just believing that He exists; it can develop into a complete confidence and trust in Him and His Plan—not only the Big Plan, but His plan for us individually. Elder Neal A. Maxwell taught:

> Our faith and trust in our Heavenly Father, so far as this mortal experience is concerned, consists not simply of faith and gladness that He exists, but is also a faith and trust that if we are humble, He will tutor us, aiding our acquisition of needed attributes and experiences while we are in mortality. We trust not only the Designer but also His design of life itself, including our portion thereof![3]

When discussing faith as a foundational doctrine in decision-making, it is helpful to recognize that the antithesis of faith is fear.

Faith indicates that we have the opportunity of believing in God—trusting Him and His word—with our very lives. Our faith tells us that because of His great wisdom and love, we will have *just* the right mix of experiences and support during our mortal lives to create individual growth.

Believing and trusting are not easy when we are separated from God by a veil of forgetfulness. Learning to trust is a lifelong enterprise. "Coming to put our trust in the living God is not the work of a day or a season. Instead, this mortal school continues to the very end, when the final school bell rings for each of us."[4] Faith feeds our growth toward godhood when we *choose* to do what it takes to develop a relationship with Him. In other words, as we keep our covenants and become true followers of Jesus Christ, we will each someday see him as he really is, because "we shall be like him" (Moroni 7:48).

So we have *individual growth, agency,* and *faith* in place. We have, in shorthand form, the destination (godhood) and the vehicles (agency and faith) to reach that destination.

Now look at the process of facing and making decisions in light of these doctrines. It's perfect. It is nowhere near the jumble it sometimes seems to be. Or perhaps it is better said that it will always *seem* to be a jumble, for it is precisely the complexities and ambiguities that push us to rely on faith, exercise agency, and grow.

Whom to marry, what course to pursue in school, job and career decisions, questions about financial matters, and geographic and housing decisions are just a few of the jumbles we find ourselves in regularly. Is there a formula? No, I don't believe so, but there are components or things you can think about that might help.

Keep your covenants and pray continually for the companionship and direction of the Spirit.

Pay attention to your own desires.

Gather information and use common sense.

Understand that the Lord can turn any righteous and prayerfully made decision to your good.

My husband, Jim, loves science—everything about it. As a young boy, he and a friend set up a little chemistry lab in his basement. They gathered supplies and would race home from school to pore over a chemistry book and perform experiments. He loves the idea that there are rules to science, that 2 plus 2 equals 4 and always will. As he took classes at the university, he couldn't think of another way he wanted to go, but within that broad field of science were a multiplicity of majors and careers. And so the jumble began. He prayed. He registered for classes, studied hard, and prayed some more. He paid attention to other people in his classes. What were they majoring in; what were their career goals? He sought counsel and took a battery of tests at the career guidance department at his university, wanting to know if there might be limitations on his ambitions. He read and reread his patriarchal blessing. Time passed, as it always does. Every time a decision *had* to be made, he made it, but the path he was choosing didn't particularly feel like a "calling." Way led onto way, and he began taking premed classes. He applied to medical schools; while he was waiting to hear, he started graduate school in molecular and genetic biology. He was thoroughly enjoying his studies when he was accepted to a medical school. Should he go or should he continue to pursue a PhD? He talked to others, gathering information; he tried to see where each path would lead; he tried to read his own heart; he tried to weigh possible lifestyle differences; he tried to know the Father's will for him. With no particular witness, the day of decision came and he chose to go to medical school, thinking at the time that he would pursue the same research he had begun in graduate school after receiving an M.D. degree, "saving the first for another day . . ."

It has been more than forty years since Jim stood where those paths diverged. So many more decisions have been made. If he were to go back to that one: to go to medical school or graduate school, would our lives have been different? Of course! Where we lived, what he did all day long every day, whom he worked with, the adversities, the opportunities—all of those things and many more would have been decidedly different. But so much is just the same. He is still in his heart a scientist. But a clinical career in internal medicine has helped him to develop a tremendous appetite for service—a joy in relieving suffering. Could he have developed that love for service as a scientist in a laboratory? Of course. The Lord has the wondrous ability to take our circumstances and consecrate them to the "welfare of our souls" (2 Nephi 32:9) *if* we live prayerfully, performing whatever we do to Him and His glory.

Yes, the Lord can turn *any* righteously motivated decision to our good. Brigham Young's words assure us of this: "If I ask him to give me wisdom concerning any requirement in life, or in regard to my own course, or that of my friends, my children or those that I preside over, and get no answer from him, and then do the very best that my judgment will teach me, He is bound to own and honor that transaction, and He will do so to all intents and purposes."[5]

In the summer of 1836 one of Joseph Smith's great concerns was the financial situation of the leaders of the Church. They were in great debt. We, of course, assume that Joseph was keeping his covenants and prayerfully seeking guidance on this particular matter. During this time he heard of buried Spanish treasure in Salem, Massachusetts. He, along with Sidney Rigdon, Oliver Cowdery, and Hyrum Smith, made a decision. They traveled to Salem, set up residence and began investigating, only to find that the rumor of treasure was ill-founded. No relief for their financial ills. Wrong decision? Doctrine and Covenants 111 is the Lord's response to them. It begins, "I, the Lord your God, am not displeased with your coming this journey, notwithstanding your follies" (D&C 111:1). In His tender kindness, the Lord recognizes Joseph's good intentions, if not his perfect judgment. He reassures Joseph that he will help him solve the debt problem in another way, then tells him that he will turn his decision to good, "for there are more treasures than one for you in this city" (verse 10). Joseph and his companions stayed in Salem for over a month, "teaching the people from house to house, and preaching publicly, as opportunity presented; visiting occasionally, sections of the surrounding country, which are rich in the history of the Pilgrim Fathers of New England, in Indian warfare, religious superstition, bigotry, persecution, and learned ignorance."[6]

This is a charming instance of the Lord's ability and willingness to turn a foolish decision to good. It is also a wonderful example of how even a prophet is allowed to use his agency and make mistakes. I particularly love the gentle lesson with the great promise given in the final verse of section 111: "Therefore, be ye as wise as serpents and yet without sin; and I will order all things for your good, as fast as ye are able to receive them. Amen" (verse 11).

Now, you are saying that some decisions have more power to destroy our happiness than others. Careers and paying off debt are one thing, but choosing a marriage partner is another. I cannot diminish the importance of that choice. Personal happiness and the good of future children are at stake. However, look again at the doctrinal premises. Life isn't just about happiness; it is about developing godlike attributes. And it always includes agency—our own and others'.

You and I know more than a few people who approach marriage righteously. They live prayerfully, keep covenants, and seek the Spirit as they begin marriage. They pay attention to their own desires—their natural compatibility and the easiness with which they grow to care deeply for one another before deciding to marry. They gather information and use common sense. They may even feel strong confirmations as they make their marriage covenants in holy temples with proper priesthood authority.

And yet, years later the marriage dissolves, often due to sin on the part of one of the marriage partners. The "wronged" spouse may look back in dismay. Did I make the wrong decision? We, who look on, wonder the same. In fact, many young adults looking on may be fearful to make marriage decisions of their own, concluding that because happy marriages cannot be guaranteed, it is better to remain unmarried.

Remember our foundational doctrines? Faith, not fear, must rule as we make decisions. We must believe, really believe that even if the unrighteous choices of others result in unhappiness for us, God can still pour out his blessings upon us, consecrating our suffering to our welfare—and yes, to our ultimate happiness.

You and I know those who have gone through the suffering of divorce and still hold fast to God and His promises. They tell us that they, in fact, did make a marriage choice based on common sense, righteous personal desires, and confirmations of the Spirit. They tell us that this does not guarantee future decisions made by each of the partners—and yet, how can they look back with despair when they experience the joy of children from that union and when they realize their own increase in godly attributes due to the fiery furnace of experience? Francis Webster of the ill-fated Martin Handcart Company said what many have learned about suffering: "The price we paid to become acquainted with God was a privilege to pay and I am thankful that I was privileged to come in the Martin Handcart Company."[7] Elder Orson F. Whitney has added this encouraging testimony:

> No pain that we suffer, no trial that we experience is wasted. It ministers to our education, to the development of such qualities as patience, faith, fortitude and humility. All that we suffer and all that we endure, especially when we endure it patiently, builds up our characters, purifies our hearts, expands our souls, and makes us more tender and charitable, more worthy to be called the children of God . . . and it is through sorrow and suffering, toil and tribulation, that we gain the education that we come here to

acquire and which will make us more like our Father and Mother in heaven.[8]

Brother Webster's and Elder Whitney's words are just another way of saying that God will, in fact, turn even our sufferings to our eternal good. As we respond to those sufferings in a godly way, we can become like Him.

This God-given right and responsibility to make decisions for our lives is one of our greatest blessings. We can exercise our agency joyfully and out of confidence in His willingness to pour out blessings, even greater than we are able to ask. And through this jumble of making decision after decision, we can come "to know the love of Christ, which passeth knowledge, . . . [and] be filled with all the fullness of God . . . [for he] is able to do exceeding abundantly above all that we ask or think, according to the power that worketh in us" (Ephesians 3:19–20).

It is my personal experience that, in fact, God expects us to be wise and righteous, and that when we endeavor to be so, He will, indeed, "order all things for our good, as fast as [we] are able to receive them" (D&C 111:11). I also believe that somewhere, ages hence, we will look back, seeing clearly *all* of the diverging roads, and come to know that there was far more guidance and direction than we can possibly conceive of now, for we will have learned precisely the things we need to know and become precisely the people He alone knew we could become. And we will kneel in gratitude for His wisdom and great love.

Notes

1. Dr. Seuss, *Oh, the Places You'll Go!* (New York: Random House, 1990), 1–2; used by permission.

2. Robert Frost, *The Poetry of Robert Frost: The Collected Poems,* edited by Edward Connery Lathem (New York: Henry Holt & Co., 1969), 105.

3. Neal A. Maxwell, *We Will Prove Them Herewith* (Salt Lake City: Deseret Book, 1982), 12.

4. Neal A. Maxwell, *That Ye May Believe* (Salt Lake City: Bookcraft, 1992), 33.

5. Brigham Young, in *Journal of Discourses,* 26 vols. (London: Latter-day Saints' Book Depot, 1854–86), 3:205.

6. Joseph Smith, *History of The Church of Jesus Christ of Latter-day Saints,* edited by B. H. Roberts, 7 vols. (Salt Lake City: Deseret News Press, 1902), 2:464.

7. Andrew Olsen, in *The Price We Paid: The Extraordinary Story of the Willie and Martin Handcart Pioneers* (Salt Lake City: Deseret Book, 2006), 3.

8. Orson F. Whitney, in Spencer W. Kimball, *Faith Precedes the Miracle* (Salt Lake City: Deseret Book, 1972), 98.

10 Commandments for Balancing the Life of the Mind and Spirit on Campus

Lorin Pace

Bachelor of Arts in Economic Sociology, Stanford University;
Master of Business Administration, Harvard University

Question:

The case-teaching method at Harvard Business School is unique: the professors ask the questions and the students provide the answers. Following an effective case, participants depart with more questions than answers. The chief assumption underlying the case method is that asking the right questions is more challenging than producing acceptable answers. This may be true in the business world, but when I find myself troubled with spiritual questions, answers can seem incredibly elusive.

I have come to realize that I feel neglected not for lack of correct answers but rather due to my inability to accept and commit to one of many right answers. Success is possible only when we are willing to take the first step down a good path, even when we are not completely sure it is the best path. This is the natural predicament of a faithful Saint, at once guided by the Spirit but required to exercise autonomy. There are simply too many good causes in which we can be "anxiously engaged" (D&C 58:27) for us to have only one right answer to every question.

Certain transcendent truths are particularly helpful not only in guiding us to the right questions, but also in auditing our array of hypothetically acceptable answers. One true principle has particularly influenced my scholastic experience: "For unto whomsoever much is given, of him shall be much required" (Luke 12:48).

This truth harmonizes perfectly with one of the fundamental tenets of neoclassical economics. Neoclassicists assert that human beings are rational creatures who seek to maximize the "utility" or value that they can achieve within a given set of constraints. While we may not be able to measure spiritual activity such as charity in terms of utility, the concept of "economic rationality" is no less useful as a construct for holistic self-evaluation. We succeed to the degree in which we take full advantage of our opportunities, both secular and religious.

Asking the right questions, accepting the imperative to act despite ambiguity, and referencing sublime truths to adjust one's course make up a model that will help with key decisions. But as the collegiate barrage of ideas and impressions intensifies, tradeoffs become opaque. The intuition required to thrive amidst this chaos must be forged in the confluence of the mind and the spirit. How does one cultivate balance between the intellectual and the spiritual?

* * *

Philip Barlow

Professor of Theological Studies at Hanover College (Hanover, Indiana)

Answer:

People enroll in college with diverse and mixed motives. Some go for sheer love of learning. Others go to find themselves or to open doors on the universe and society. Some go to stall, to look or feel respectable while they cast about for direction or until they find a job. Some go to party or to court, pleased at the freedom offered on campus and by large numbers of eligible and attractive others.

There are those who enroll to get a degree—literally. The credential they pursue will, they believe, widen their chances for obtaining a better paying job. Because graduation is their primary goal, they approach it in the most efficient way they can envision: taking the fewest and easiest courses they can get by with, or taking implausible overloads during several terms (while working considerable hours for pay) to shorten the process. They seek a certificate, not an education, and they value grades more than wisdom. Such "students" are not really "in" but merely "at" college. They will have little interest in the essay that follows.

Another class of students enters school more earnestly. Like the credential-seekers, they think of college primarily as a stepping stone to a career, but they are serious about acquiring the specific skills they will need to do their jobs well. They may study business, engineering, or education, accounting or pre-law or pre-med. While their leading motivation is pre-professional training, many of them are hardworking by nature and thus do their best in each class. Some may attend a vocational school in which most of their courses focus on immediately practical skills such as would sustain a future welder, nurse, or computer technician. But if they attend a college or university, they will encounter, at least briefly, a wider world. No matter what their focus, they will be required to take courses touching upon the basics of science and social science. They will be introduced to the world of humanistic ideas, formal logic, the study of other cultures and languages—the ways and minds of people quite foreign to the world and beliefs with which they are familiar.

A final type of student comes to understand that colleges have other purposes beyond job training. These purposes point toward implied (though often unspoken) questions: What does it mean to be human? How have individuals and civilizations gone about it, and how shall we? What is the nature of the universe we inhabit? These are questions about which the gospel has things to say, of course, but from angles of vision, intent, detail, and method apart from (not necessarily incompatible with) those of the academy. Often trivialized by the term "general education," courses of study looking at aspects of these questions have emerged from specialized disciplines invented to pursue them. At least brief exposure is required of all who would graduate.

Some students become more thoroughly engaged than others in these issues and disciplines. Hence they may "major" in physics or geology, psychology or political science, history or philosophy. They are aware of the eventual need to find jobs, and some will retain their pre-professional majors; they may also have interest in dating; their aspirations are composite. But when they come to care about critical thinking, evidence, and the nature of "knowing" not simply for job skills but also for what Socrates called "the examined life,"[1] they are going to have questions—and they should have questions—about how all this relates to what they have learned at home and in church.

Some of these questions may be by-products of study not focused on religion. For example, how shall I respond when I encounter overwhelming scientific evidence pointing to the evolving nature of the physical and biological universe over millions of years if this seems at odds with my understanding of scripture or what I was taught in seminary? What should I do if historical study of even such restricted topics as Stalinist Russia, Nazi Germany, or twentieth-century Cambodia or Ethiopia conjures haunting images and prompts questions about faith in a God who could allow such terror and death to millions of innocent children and adults? What if anthropological or historical study of the world's varied cultures makes me wonder about the plausibility of "one true church"? Sometimes religion as such may be treated with condescension or derision.

There may even be times, especially if one enters college where there are many Latter-day Saints, when the Church itself comes directly under fire. When I returned from my mission and entered Weber State College in northern Utah, I enrolled in a certain philosophy class for which only six students had signed up. Even by professorial standards, Professor Olson was a distinctively learned man, a sensation on campus and in some circles in Utah. He may have possessed something of a photographic memory; at least he seemed able regularly to recite the library's call numbers of many books to which he called my attention in our later conversations. On the first day of class the professor, who had a reputation as a threat to students' faith, offered comments that seemed to disdain the Church. As this continued, I at last raised my hand. He and I then began an exchange (with Professor Olson doing most of the talking) that lasted three weeks. On the second day of class, to my discomfort, the professor arrived carrying a formidable armful of books, pressed up against the bottom of his chin and spanning a vertical line downwards to his hands, extended below his waist. He placed them ceremoniously on the table before us, and I noticed the Book of Mormon among the titles, as well as *Teachings of the*

Prophet Joseph Smith, Doctrines of Salvation by Joseph Fielding Smith, works by other modern authorities of the Church, and many titles I did not recognize. It seemed the teacher's central concern was to promote honesty, enlightened critical thinking, and a regard for scholarship. These he was convinced the Church did not foster. He presented many issues with which I was unfamiliar: principles of epistemology; alternate accounts of Joseph Smith's First Vision; bigoted published defenses of priesthood policy; and ecclesiastical denigration of credible and loyal Latter-day Saint scholars, such as Juanita Brooks, who had published on important but sensitive topics.

I later became a teacher myself, a formal student of religion. In subsequent years I have watched, counseled, taught, learned from, and corresponded with students who have ignored or engaged such issues as these. Some of them have lost—and some of them have retained or found—their faith through encounters in college. Because I believe the loss of the foundations of faith to be unnecessary and tragic, I have fashioned Ten Commandments for LDS students attempting to balance faith and learning while at college.

My "commandments," of course, represent my own understanding; they have authority only for me. For interested others, they amount to suggestions: an approach to formal learning, in the context of faith, to be adopted only as you may be prayerfully and thoughtfully persuaded. You may disagree with aspects of my commandments. If so, I hope you are stimulated to fashion your own. It should go without saying that other commandments—those we hold to have a divine source—ought not be discarded on account of anything I say here. The reader will also do well to be suspicious of the convenient number "ten"; the list could of course grow long. Finally, I stress that the principles behind the "commandments" are interactive and connected. They must be applied in relation to one another. Failure to do so will distort their meaning and their effect.

1. Seek truth, seek good, and bind them together.

I regularly encounter students (Latter-day Saints, Baptists, Muslims, atheists—students of all sorts) who are so determined to shield their faith and their perspectives that they seem closed to fundamental discovery. They believe it their job to hold onto their secular or religious faith as if holding their breath, no matter what they experience. Some avoid, fight, or tip-toe through certain courses, not really engaging them, afraid or angry that they may confront a topic or a fact that threatens their understanding. The threat they perceive has various potential sources. The subject may be biology or geology, philosophy or history or religion; or it may have less to do with a subject than with a particular professor or peer.

Faith is a necessary and precious thing, the first principle of the gospel. I sympathize with this impulse to protect it at any cost. However, spiritual and mental tragedy can come not only through loss of faith, but also through inauthenticity, ignorance, and fear.

Faith does not exist in a vacuum, and not all faith is healthy or righteous. After all, terrorists, on the basis of faith, fly airplanes into tall buildings filled with innocent people. What is wanted is not the rigid, uninformed, closed, and cocksure faith-assertions of the fanatic, but a thoughtful and open trust, an organic and living faith, born of love and welcoming of growth, inquiry, new perspectives, and adjustment.

In this light, it helps to remember that our Father in Heaven is the Lord of Truth. "Yea, Lord, I know that thou speakest the truth, for thou art a God of truth, and canst not lie" (Ether 3:12). God's "Word" is "the way, the truth, and the life" (John 1:1; 14:6). My faith in the Lord of Truth is prompted not only by scriptural proclamation, but by something deep within me. This sense would thrive even if scripture did not declare it. For if our God were not a God of truth, He would, as the Book of Mormon puts it in another context, "cease to be God." Even if powerful, such a god would be worthy of neither our trust nor our worship. "But God ceaseth not to be God" (Alma 42:23). Among other things, this means that God is unafraid of truth, including any human truths we might encounter in our study.

Of course, alleged facts can be dangerous for inexperienced minds lacking sufficient context and means of testing and explaining them. It is essential to realize that what we take to be facts are properly contested in the academy. One purpose of an education, indeed, is to deepen the ability for informed and critical thought that is increasingly able to discern the credibility of arguments, alleged facts, and their proper contexts. Moreover, to accept something as "fact" is not the same as assigning that fact a meaning. "So what?" is an excellent question. We should be wary of our own and others' (including our teachers') perceptions, weaknesses, tendencies to leap to conclusions, or sneering or condescending attitudes that may cast a false pale over even legitimate facts. But the proper response to all this is further study, conversation, testing, experience, thought, discipline, and prayer—not avoidance. The ongoing pursuit of truth—rather than an expressed or unstated boast that we already possess and comprehend it in its fullness—can and should be at one with hungering and thirsting after righteousness. God and truth are perfectly aligned.

Joseph Smith taught that our Heavenly Father invites us to become whom we should and can become in relation to Him, to each other, and to the universe in which He has placed us. We ought, then, to study what we can of Him, of each other, and of our world and universe. Doing so in the formal and relatively demanding setting of college is not the only way to progress, of course.

Family, the Church, and the privately bended knee exist for a purpose. But higher education can be an enormous boost if its resources are rightly engaged.

In the university we may find ourselves uncomfortable with some or another new truth we encounter—as do many children when they discover how humans come into the world, when they confront the nature of Santa Claus, or when they glimpse the reality of suffering and death. But such truths do not embarrass the Lord of Truth. We are threatened by them only in relation to our own understandings, which are subject to change, correction, and growth. Dedication to reality (and the perpetual, faithful, and critical exploration and amendment of our internal maps of reality) is basic to mental and spiritual health and growth. To avoid the work, pain, challenge, and adjustment demanded by this process tends to result in damnation (the blocking of spiritual and mental progress) or emotional, spiritual, and mental illness (which, as imperfect people, we have all tasted at least in mild forms). Our perceptions and capacities should evolve in a great upward spiral. There is no truth one will encounter at the university that is unknown to God. What, then, shall we fear? Adult naiveté is not generally a virtue. The scriptural mandate (Matthew 10:16) is that we "be wise as serpents, and harmless as doves"—not harmless as doves and just as dumb.

One difficulty with this quest for truth is that what we mean by "truth" and how we obtain it is not always obvious or uncontested. While we should try to shed our defensiveness and remain open to new truth and growth through experience, study, and prayer, it helps also to remember that "truth," like "knowledge," is always partial, always situated in a context informed by competing values, always presented in one of many possible frameworks of interpretation. This is readily apparent in the study of politics, religion, history, or philosophy. In some respects it is true even of scientifically established knowledge, as academic debate in recent decades has made more evident. An impressive comparative objectivity exists in the sciences, but humans seeking knowledge are not objects. Despite the welcome advances in scientific method and results in recent centuries, values and contests are at work in the fabric of the enterprise, even in the types of questions that are shaped and followed. No human knowledge is pursued without context. This is not the place for a technical discussion of such issues, which can be explored on any college campus. It is, though, an invitation to consider the relation of "truth" and "goodness"; failure to do so in the academy can seduce rather than bless us.

One of history's great writers, Fyodor Dostoevsky, implied a provocative understanding of this relation in a private 1858 letter to a friend, Mme. Natalya Fonvizina. Writing about his faith from an agonized exile in Siberia, where he experienced cruelty and evil and witnessed much death, Dostoevsky wrote that "if someone proved to me that Christ were outside the truth, and in reality the truth were outside of Christ, then I should prefer to remain with Christ rather than with the truth."[2] At first hearing, that statement may disappoint; it seems an act of cowardice, an instance of Freud's assertion that all religion is wish-fulfillment. Scrutiny of Dostoevsky's life, character, and mind, however, make such an assumption problematic. This genius, who could have avoided Siberia by surrendering his conscience, was no coward.

While we must include truth among our deepest values, its pursuit in the abstract must exist in relation to an even more pressing—and unavoidable—concern: How shall I live in this moment, this day? What I think Dostoevsky was getting at was this: there is a point at which it is not merely "truth" that defines all other reality, ethics, and wisdom. Instead, there is a point at which something even more fundamental brings "truth" into being, gives it its nature and meaning. For Dostoevsky, that "something" was Christ—what

Christ represented and embodied. Irrespective of people's historical, metaphysical, and ontological claims and perceptions about Christ, the quality or character of what Christ existentially was, as Dostoevsky experienced him, gave meaning to what was "good," "true," and "beautiful." In the realms of values, quality of soul, the making of meaning, and how to place oneself in the world, this "quality" defined "truth," rather than the other way around. I believe, said Dostoevsky, that "nothing is more beautiful, profound, sympathetic, reasonable, [courageous], and more perfect than Christ; and I tell myself with a jealous love not only that there is nothing, but that there cannot be anything higher."[3] For Dostoevsky, Christ is truer than "truth," not in the sense of some metaphysical or doctrinal fact, but because "truth" gains its meaning in relation to the quality of being that was Christ as experienced in Dostoevsky's spiritual life.

All this could, of course, involve us in a complex conversation. For a full, persuasive, and enjoyable exploration of the idea that "quality" defines "truth" even apart from religious contexts, I invite you to examine or reexamine Robert Pirsig's classic novel, *Zen and the Art of Motorcycle Maintenance.* A related and briefer thrust, however, is offered by Moroni as he brings to a close the records we call the Book of Mormon. Immediately following his famous exhortation to future readers to pray concerning the truth of the records in his custody (Moroni 10:4), the prophet seems virtually to equate the quality of goodness with the concept of truth: "And whatsoever thing is good is just and true" (Moroni 10:6). As with Dostoevsky, this has nothing to do with "lying for a good cause," any more than does trying to represent a three-dimensional object by a two-dimensional drawing. That which is genuinely good . . . is true.

Let us be unafraid of truth, but let us also distinguish truth from mere fact. Let us think carefully about alleged implications of both truth and fact. And let us tether our quest for "truth" to the quest for "good." The one will help disclose the other.

2. Do not disparage the intellect.

We Latter-day Saints hold spiritual matters as precious. We believe in inspiration and revelation. Of course, these realities, like any good thing, can be abused. And the realities have counterfeits. Even authentic inspiration has to be received by human beings, and everything filtered through human beings has limitations. In our stage of things, as Paul observed, "we know in part, and we prophesy in part." In a future realm, he says, "when that which is perfect is come," it will not be so. "For now we see through a glass, darkly; but then face to face: now I know in part; but then shall I know even as also I am known" (1 Corinthians 13: 9, 10, 12). Latter-day Saints remain unashamed and grateful, nonetheless, to believe there is such a thing as authentic contact with the divine. As a people and in many cases as individuals, we believe we have experienced this contact.

Unfortunately, because of such blessings and loyalties and the consciousness they spawn, we sometimes make the mistake of trying to elevate the spiritual by denigrating the intellect. Indeed, the word "intellectual" seems to carry a largely negative connotation in popular LDS discourse. Perhaps, however, we confuse "intellect" or "intellectual" with other difficulties.

Several problems attach to this confusion. I will mention three. First, our own scriptures instruct us that "to be learned is good if [we] hearken unto the counsels of God" (2 Nephi 9:29). Some learned people fail to heed God, of course, just as some unlearned people fail to heed God. The problem, however, is not in learning itself, but in growing spiritually inert while learning, or in selective laziness. Perhaps it lies in insufficient wisdom. Often its roots are nourished by pride (2 Nephi 9:28).

All manner of things—including beauty, wealth, talent, reputation, power, and authority—can, if our response to them goes awry, sponsor pride. As the Prophet Joseph said, "We have learned by sad experience that it is the nature and disposition of almost all men, as soon as they get a little authority, as they suppose, they will immediately begin to exercise unrighteous dominion" (D&C 121:39). The problem, though, rests not in authority as such, nor in beauty, wealth, talent, learning, or a keen intelligence, but in a misunderstanding and distortion of their nature, limits, source, and proper ends. Although beauty can lead one astray, a handsome young man or woman does not draw inherently closer to God by seeking to become unattractive. We must be wary of vanity, but we ought not confuse vanity with beauty. Just so, a good mind by nature aspires to become a better mind—and college can help. This remains true despite the fact that one can go astray by mutating into an intellectual peacock rather than flourishing as a wise, humble, and knowledgeable servant of God and humanity.

Another problem with disparaging the intellect is that we are, in our essential natures, intellects (intelligences) fully as much as we are spirits. According to the Prophet Joseph, our Father in Heaven also is an intelligence—more intelligent than all the intelligences that were organized by Him before this world was created. Joseph taught that intelligence cleaves unto intelligence, that it cannot be created or destroyed but only organized and developed, that it constitutes the glory of God, that whatever principle of intelligence we gain in this life will rise with us in the hereafter (D&C 88:40; 93:29, 36; 130:18; Abraham 3). To disparage the intellect or intellectuals (those who are intellectually accomplished or who have high regard for the intellect) is to show contempt for our own natures, created in the image of God, and to disparage those who have most fully developed themselves in this regard as God commands. To attack the intellect constitutes an indirect form of blasphemy. Intellectual progress is an essential dimension of eternal progress. The mandate upon us is to love the Lord with all our heart, soul, *mind,* and strength (Mark 12:30). Intellectual sloth is no more admirable than any other kind.

A third motive for honoring rather than demeaning the intellect is that the spirit and the mind are entwined. One may suffer from spiritual insensitivity, just as one may fail to develop one's mind, but where both mind and spirit are robust, they are inseparable. Study, pondering, and prayer are linked, and frequently so in the scriptures. Joseph taught that his revelatory experiences often consisted of receiving "sudden strokes of ideas" from the Spirit and that the "Holy Ghost has no other effect than pure intelligence."[4] If one is spiritually healthy, one is mentally healthy. If one is mentally ill (disregarding its physiological components), one is spiritually ill. "Let us," as President McKay urged, "seek to live intellectually."[5]

3. Understand that reason is not the only avenue to truth.

Because the academy specializes in, excels at, and rewards the important realm of rational thought, it can intentionally or inadvertently foster the illusion that this is the only source of enlightenment. While we must seek truth, however, it is a mistake—an intellectual as well as a spiritual mistake—to misunderstand human reason (much less formal Western logic, empiricism, and science) as the sole avenue to truth. "Life, divided by reason, leaves a remainder,"[6] as the German writer Goethe observed.

One cannot think too well. Yet one can think too much, as does an athlete or singer who, under pressure, remains too deliberate, too conscious, too rational, failing to release their bodies and unconscious selves to other kinds of knowing. One cannot in general know too much, but one can confuse knowledge with wisdom and fact with understanding. One cannot reason too keenly, but one can by injudicious and relentless abstraction deter the Spirit, obscure intuition, stifle imagination, and unhinge the heart. One can persuade in debate while failing to discern deeper realities. One can be an impressive lawyer and a poor judge, a dazzling scholar and an inept lover. One can, as the scripture says, be "ever learning, and never able to come to the knowledge of the truth" (2 Timothy 3:7).

That rational calculation is neither the sole nor sufficient path to the kind of truth required for successful living is evident in everyday experience. We do not learn to swim or to ride a bike without gaining a feel for the task—a "feel" that transcends reason. We do not produce art worthy of the name through mere rationality. We do not experience faith and the "knowing" of friendship and love merely through scientific experiment and empirical scrutiny. Our physical senses are not our only senses. No one has ever seen a feeling; no one has seen a thought. Yet our feelings and thoughts are where we fundamentally live.[7] Instincts, intuitions, and promptings of the Spirit are in a similar category. These invisible realities are not to be dismissed merely because science is not prepared to deal with them. Reason absorbs no dishonor by a recognition of its limits, and belief in inspiration need not be an embarrassment on campus.

If our radar is fully functional, we can experience inspiration directly, thus requiring no exterior proof of its dimensions. When I was in college, I began to pay close attention to "ordinary, everyday life" as not so ordinary, as full of clues about how I should live most meaningfully. In that state of mind, the following incident left an impression. It is not its drama but rather its apparent simplicity that captured my attention, for it helped me see that inspiration could work through the ordinary course of everyday living. One Sunday morning, my roommate and lifelong close friend, who was also the man to whom I served as counselor in the elders quorum presidency, unexpectedly stood in the middle of a quorum meeting, in our college ward, to speak. I was seated next to him. As he rose, he leaned toward me, shook his head, and whispered under his breath, "I don't know why I'm doing this." He then proceeded to ask the quorum if there was an "Adult Aaronic" brother present who would like to participate in an ordinance we were about to perform. A young man about our age, near the back of the room, promptly stood and came forward. For some reason he had been waiting that morning for just such an invitation—something that would suggest that the Lord was aware of him and would encourage his impulse to come back to church and get involved. I was subsequently assigned as a home teaching companion to this brother, whom I came to know reasonably well. His life was turned in a new direction, cultivated by the gentle bit of inspiration that came to my roommate.

I have no urge to use the story as proof for skeptics. This is not the sort of thing that proves anything to anyone else, and the episode could of course be assigned a naturalistic explanation. But as I witnessed and participated in it, this gentle encounter with grace left an imprint. It anticipated, for me, a pattern of later experiences which keep my spiritual antenna up. I work as hard as I am able at disciplined, critical thought; I am also satisfied through direct experience that we have access to resources beyond the rational intellect. Unbelievers and believers alike can readily access at least some forms of this through, for instance, dreams and other manifestations of the unconscious mind. It is not at all uncommon for me to wrestle with this or that problem, often under severe time constraint—and then to awake in the night or morning with solutions or ideas for approaches that my rational self was not successfully addressing.

Other kinds of encounters also remind us of the limits of rationality when accounting for things we can come to know. The celebrated psychiatrist Scott Peck, before he submitted to a Christian baptism, wrote of such an instance:

> Having arrived after dark on a vacation in Singapore for the first time, my wife and I left our hotel for a stroll. We soon came to a large open space at the far end of which, two or three blocks away, we could just make out in the darkness the vague shape of a sizable building. "I wonder what that building is," my wife said. I immediately answered with casual and total certainty, "Oh, that's the Singapore Cricket Club." The words had popped out of my mouth with utter spontaneity. Almost immediately I regretted them. I had no basis whatever for saying them. I had not only never been in Singapore before, I had never seen a cricket club before—in daylight, much less in darkness. Yet to my amazement, as we walked on and came to the other side of the building, which was its front, there by the entrance was a brass plaque reading *Singapore Cricket Club*.[8]

How did Peck know that which he could not know? He implicitly rejects this explanation, but perhaps he had glimpsed a picture of the place at some earlier point, had permanently forgotten doing so, while the label of the building came unconsciously to mind at the moment he describes. Perhaps it was an instance of what the French call *déjà vu*, or a matter of what the Hindus understand as reincarnation. Maybe it was what we Latter-day Saints would be comfortable calling a spiritual prompting—for some purpose yet unknown to Peck. Peck's own conjecture is that he may have been affected by what psychiatrist Carl Jung called "the collective unconscious," in which we inherit the wisdom of the experience of our ancestors without personally having had the experience. (Peck links this collective with God.) It is not for me to declare the source or explanation of Peck's experience. My point is only that humans are not restricted to rational processes in their authentic knowing, and that this is easy to forget when one is immersed in the academy. There need be nothing embarrassing about the idea of revelation or inspiration. A belief in inspiration, as part of nonrational knowing, is not a silly notion.

Of course, one can use alleged inspiration—or even the idea of inspiration—illegitimately. One can indulge in superstition. Or, in the teeth of a difficult intellectual challenge, one can repeatedly assert one's faith and reject the hard mental work required of growth in understanding. While this may be appropriate in certain situations, since faith can precede and outrank knowledge, the problem with resting permanently and frequently in such unthoughtful confidence is that this is a common posture for con-tradictory religious and secular purposes of all stripes, including those by apparently sincere critics who bear "testimony" against The Church of Jesus Christ of Latter-day Saints. What some people take as spiritual promptings, indeed, sometimes seem to seasoned outsiders as perhaps projections of inner hopes or fears. For example, a beautiful, earnest, and spiritually sensitive young Latter-day Saint woman once confided to me, with considerable confusion and unease, that she had had multiple suitors each declare his assurance that the Lord had designated her as his eternal mate. Beyond this, it is not difficult to point to episodes where people have committed heinous acts justified by a sense of personal reve-lation. Ron and Dan Lafferty's gruesome 1984 murder of their sister-in-law, Brenda, and her fifteen-month-old daughter, in the Utah town of American Fork, is one such instance.

None of this negates the importance of legitimate faith born of spiritual promptings. Receptivity of spirit, heart, and mind is at the core of authentic living. But we do well to remember, especially in an academic setting, that an informed and thoughtful faith is best sustained by a healthy and balanced input for our faith, including checks and balances. What might these checks and balances look like?

The Book of Mormon prophet Moroni offers a much-cited promise: that "by the power of the Holy Ghost ye may know the truth of all things" (Moroni 10:5). Just how the Holy Spirit will do this is not spelled out by Moroni, nor is everything that may be required of some of us to receive and sustain this blessing. The passage does indicate that we must read, ponder, and ask of God with sincerity. Other scriptures suggest additional elements for faith. Alma 32 proposes an "experiment," with "the word" (in which one is to have faith) sprouting as a nurtured seed whose goodness and life can take organic root in, and thus become self-evident to, one's heart, soul, and understanding. In addition, we should carefully observe those who allege truth, for "by their fruits ye shall know them" (Matthew 7:15–20). We should participate in and thereby test such principles as are proclaimed to us (John 7:17: "If any man will do his will, he shall know of the doctrine, whether it be of God, or whether I speak of myself"). We must give away our sins. We must yearn "to be called [God's] people"; "to bear one another's burdens"; "to mourn with those that mourn," "comfort those that stand in need of comfort," and "stand as witnesses of God at all times and in all things, and in all places" (Mosiah 18:8–9). By these and other elements—prayer, study, pondering, experiment, following the counsel of wise leaders, repentance, observation, participation, and active service—we may come to know the truth of all requisite things. Our growing faith will then not remain a tissue of gossamer, vulnerable to the next intimidating professor, book, acquaintance, or troubling discovery potentially around each corner. Instead, a resilient and flexible fabric will comprise our faith, one that is welcoming to growth and truth of all kinds.

4. Realize that the Church has always consisted of human beings—flawed and wondrous—who are trying to respond to the divine with which they have been touched.

If you are authentically enmeshed in your work at college, you are going to engage conceptual thickets. You are going to learn new ways of thinking. Where your study impinges on faith and your understanding of reality, you are going to encounter facts and alleged facts—or interpretations and seeming implications of real or alleged facts and events—that are new to you. Apparent or genuine problems may surface directly or indirectly, from conversation and reading inside or outside of the classroom. In some circumstances, you are apt to run into questions directly involving The Church of Jesus Christ of Latter-day Saints.

Such questions may range widely: What of the dark stain of the massacre that occurred at Mountain Meadows in southern Utah in 1857? Does the Church have a racist past or present? Did it not, and does it not, fully respect the separation of church and state? Was not polygamy a licentious affair, or at least an uneven and sexist one damaging to the lives of women, children, and men? Does Latter-day Saint culture confuse authority with authoritarianism? Is the Church not naive about modern methods of scriptural study? Does it fully respect freedom and intellectual rigor? Is it honest in its study of its past and in all its dealings? Is it authentically Christian? What of past and present uses of the Church's vast financial resources? Does not the Book of Mormon show evidence of nineteenth-century authorship? Do angels delivering gold plates and divine messages to a teenage boy constitute a plausible basis for religious adherence? Why was I not told this or that in Sunday School, seminary, or institute? Varieties of these and additional questions may beset an earnest student.

Often enough such questions, posed by others, are informed by ill-will or personal hang-ups rather than a desire to understand;

this should prompt in us love, faith, prayer, and patience more than intellectual engagement. Sometimes the questioners are ill-informed or conceptually ill-equipped; this should invite a similar response of love and patience, as well as the gentle use of better factual and conceptual information readily available to most Church members. But there may be times at college where potentially more substantive questions and problems arise, ones not easily dismissed. As always, this requires love, faith, prayer, and patience, but it also may demand acquired knowledge and wisdom. Such questions warrant real responses, not ones that avoid the issues. Toward such circumstances as these, this book suggests an array of constructive and faithful options.

The principle under immediate consideration is simple, but crucial—and frequently not fathomed: to apprehend that the Church on earth consists of human beings. Church leaders and Church members are human beings, with all that that entails. They are human beings who are trying to respond to revelation, to a call to something higher and better, to an authority and a responsibility to foster eternal life, to comfort the sick and the weary, to build faith, invite repentance, live healthily, turn the hearts of the children to their forebears, build Zion, and promote love and mercy. This is a sacred enterprise, one to be proud of. Those who serve and lead its cause in diverse and complex contexts deserve our deep respect, our loyalty, our readiness to serve, and our openness to counsel.

This vast and holy project also deserves our prayerful thoughtfulness. To forget that it is humans (rather than flawless Saints of our imagination) who are attempting to respond to this divine call risks a diluted idolatry and makes for a brittle faith, subject to the next discovery of historical, philosophical, or scientific difficulty. For the historical record holds no shortage of human traits and failings, just as the records of ancient Israel do. And we need honestly to study, be informed by, be inspired by, but also be chastened by and generally to learn from this historical record. Not to do so is to court amnesia, to detach our vision from its context, to see falsely.

If we fully apprehend, however, that it is we humans who comprise the Church, we will not be surprised by foibles, and we will not be lured to a judgmental posture. If we apprehend our own humanity, we will be better positioned to take weakness for granted and then to marvel at the inspiration that touches the Church, at the immense resources for edification and service and care that it constantly enacts. We ought not allow imperfection to drive us away from a cause so great as Joseph Smith envisioned.

If we are to be humble before the Lord, we as a people need to be self-critical, forgiving, authentic, and eager to sense how we can improve. We must study and learn from the past. All of us, from prophets to the newest converts, are humans trying to respond to the divine with which we have been touched. As one thoughtful Saint puts it: "The Church I believe in is not an ascending hierarchy of the holy. It is millions of ordinary people calling one another 'brother' and 'sister' and trying to make it true."[9]

5. Know that character affects I.Q.

Joseph Smith taught that "a man is saved no faster than he gets knowledge."[10] This is a striking doctrine, surprising to other Christians. It connects with several commandments offered here, especially the first two. By inverting the Prophet's phrase, however, prominent Latter-day Saint historian Richard Bushman once offered a complementary truth: "A man gains knowledge no faster than he is saved."[11] Bushman was conversing with historians, but I will borrow his phrase for my own purposes here. What I mean is this: *Just as knowledge affects character, character affects knowledge— and even intelligence.*

Knowledge affects our character at the most basic level. Most people, for example, admire courage, kindness, and honesty. As abstractions, who wouldn't? Yet knowledge—what we believe we know—colors what courage, kindness, and honesty actually mean to us in practice. Two sets of parents are "loving" and "kind" in their intentions. With contrasting "knowledge," however, one set manifests this love by readily giving their child everything the child demands. The result is a spoiled child, retarded in development by indulgence masquerading as "love"—a pseudo-love based on errant "knowledge." Thus knowledge conditions our character—who we are—because it determines how we interpret what we experience and thus, in part, how we respond to it.

A less obvious truth is that our character conditions what we know. In fact, our character is a lens that filters our awareness as a whole. Let me offer an example. *When I am grateful, I am smarter than when I am not grateful.* It is not simply that being grateful is a good thing because it is "nicer," true as that may be. It is also that my grateful mental state lets in a different view of reality than is otherwise possible. *Grateful* comes from the same verbal root as *graceful.* When I am grate-ful, I am grace-full: full of grace; fully aware of the "grace" or "giftedness" of each breath I take, the gift-edness of my life and your life and everything about us (Mosiah 2:20–21). And when I am thus conscious of my life and the world as a gift, I am less preoccupied with self. My attention focuses else-where. I am more alert to other people's needs and virtues. I find my wonder awakened by just about everything: the engineering behind the physique of a cricket or a fly, for instance, or the beauty in even a pebble. In other words, when I am grateful, I tend toward a higher mental (and spiritual) state. I take things—people, order, air, roundness, everything—less for granted. Hence I notice things otherwise invisible to me. It is as if I have a sixth sense, taking in more context, more reality. If my temporary taste of gratitude becomes a disciplined habit, an ongoing attitude and state of mind,

I am "smarter," more aware, than if this were not so. To the extent that I become a habitually grateful person, I engage a different and richer reality than the "me" who is less grateful.

Courage works similarly. Courage does not mean "fearless"; many threats exist that we would be foolish not to fear. Courage, rather, is a *response* to fear, a willingness to absorb and address fear. Unchecked fear paralyzes, constricting my awareness as I shrink from real or perceived threats. Courage in the face of my fears, by contrast, opens me to the world and extends the radar by which I navigate reality. If the university presents me with new theories and knowledge and paradigms that seem threatening to my map of reality, courage enables me to think critically and imaginatively about this purported new knowledge. Striving for this trait works better for me than assuming that I already possess all necessary truth merely because I have a testimony. It works better than adopting the heads-down posture of the ostrich—and misconstruing this cowardice for faith.

Humility is another example. When you learn things in college, humility may be undermined. You may be tempted to think you know more than you know and that you are subtly better than those around you who have not learned what you have.

It is practically always the case that we know less than we think we do. However, if your knowledge actually does grow deep in some particular specialty, such as medicine or history or literature, you may, in Church settings, genuinely understand some problems, facts, and concepts that are invisible to the faithful around you. With restraint, care, wisdom, modesty, and love, you may be able at points to draw on some of this understanding constructively to enliven your own mind and spirit or the minds and spirits of those about you. You may be tempted to think yourself superior when in conversation, Church classes, and worship, as academics and others are sometimes tempted to do whenever they engage in subjects in which they have training. Remember that God's project entails an invitation to the divine, which leaves little room for preening, artifice, self-promotion, inert or arrogant intellectualism, or one-upsmanship. Understand that you are always surrounded by people, even when they appear simple, who are better at some things than you are—often without conceit. Some of them are expert at fixing the engine of your car, at removing your tonsils, at growing or preparing food, at making music; in none of their superiorities is aloofness or condescension appealing, admirable, or helpful. Many Saints with whom you attend church or among whom you live are expert at disciplined, courageous, intelligent (or innocent) loving, which generally matters more than whatever academic perspectives you bring. Moreover, as with a lack of gratitude, conceit is not merely off-putting; it actually constricts your consciousness—inhibits your radar for learning surprising things from surprising sources. So it is that the quality of our characters and souls helps define the caliber of our minds. Such traits as humility, courage, and gratitude make us smarter and wiser. That is a good thing in college, as in life.

6. Claim a wise mentor and good conversation partners.

If you are studying seriously and considering the things that matter most, you will generate questions and challenges to your understanding. If you do not, you are not growing. Questions are not cause for alarm. Issues exist whether or not we discover them, and an authentic grapple with them is one avenue toward growth. No matter how bright, well-grounded, independent, and faithful you deem yourself, however, you would do well to be in ongoing conversation with thoughtful and wise conversation partners who are encountering or who have encountered similar issues. It is easy to get lost in complex terrain, and sometimes we get lost without knowing it.

The give and take of verbalized exploration can give better form to vague concerns and can yield concrete questions to address, as well as provide specific ideas about how to approach them and who might be able to help you. Cultivate, share, and exchange with at least one or two friends—make new friends as needed—who are working in the realms you are. Such people do exist, even if finding them takes imaginative effort.

Above all, in the midst of your learning and stretching and questioning, find a mentor whose mind, character, and spirituality you thoroughly trust. Ask around. The mentor should be one with whom you can grow comfortable posing *any* question and sharing any anxiety. Much faith is unnecessarily undermined because candor is aborted for fear of disapproval. At least one such mentor should be a Latter-day Saint who is knowledgeable about areas that concern you and who has succeeded in relating his or her field to a constructive, deep, and honest faith. This does not necessarily mean, of course, that your ultimate answers will at last align wholly with those of your mentors. But God deserves a faith and a devotion from you that is schooled by the best thinking and best examples we have to offer. Even if your questions are about God, you yourself deserve the best thinking and counsel. Although it may surprise you, few of your questions concerning the great issues will be new. This means there are always mentors and conversation partners to be found, including those who have left record from years and ages past.

7. Do not forsake the wisdom of the thirteenth Article of Faith.

When I went to Cambridge, far from my Utah home, to study religious history in graduate school, I grew more conscious of a fact that should have dawned on me earlier. I found myself surrounded by people (from history and in the present) who seemed inspiringly good, astoundingly bright, and who often were more informed and experienced in the world than I. Yet these people were happily committed to religious traditions apart from my LDS faith.

In some ways I was pleased and fascinated—drenched in opportunity for learning and exhilarated by edifying diversity. Yet some part of me also found this unsettling. How was it that I belonged to "the one true church" and yet lived, studied, and worked among people who had so much to teach me, people whose spiritual, moral, mental, and social inferiority I could less and less discern? I know that many students, Latter-day Saints and others, similarly encounter in college a world of learning that introduces them both to difficulties among their own people, ideas, and history, as well as to ennobling dimensions of lives and notions toward which they had earlier condescended or remained oblivious.

Humbled by my encounter in Cambridge, I grew quickly more sensitive to parts of the scriptures and the gospel I had earlier ignored. I continued to sense the divine within passages of modern scripture that moved me. I remained grateful for the marvelous work and wonder, the light and love and service and faith that unfold through the mechanism of the Church. I could still appreciate Joseph Smith's vision of Zion and the religious confusion and hypocrisy that he experienced at the time of his initial vision. What I could no longer do was to prop up my perspectives with caricatures of people and traditions of which I had been so ignorant.

I discovered and rediscovered, indeed, that a cluster of prophets forbade my chauvinism. Both experience and scripture taught me that we Saints, in possession of treasured and distinctive truths, have no monopoly on truth itself. God is God to all of His children, as the Book of Mormon insists. Through Nephi, for example, the Lord condemns a self-satisfied attitude too constricted to value

God's word wherever it takes form. "Know ye not that there are more nations than one?" He asks.

> Know ye not that I, the Lord your God, have created all men, and that I remember those who are upon the isles of the sea; and that I rule in the heavens above and in the earth beneath; and I bring forth my word unto the children of men, yea, even upon all the nations of the earth? . . . I command all men, both in the east and in the west, and in the north, and in the south, and in the islands of the sea, that they shall write the words which I speak. . . . I shall speak unto the Jews . . . and I shall also speak unto the Nephites . . . and I shall also speak unto the other tribes of the house of Israel . . . and I shall also speak unto all nations of the earth (2 Nephi 29:7, 11–12).

Alma similarly decries religious conceit:

> Now the place was called by [the Zoramites] Rame-umptom, which, being interpreted, is the holy stand. Now, from this stand they did offer up, every man, the self-same prayer. . . . We thank thee, O God, for we are a chosen people unto thee, while others shall perish (Alma 31:21–22, 28).

Standing against this narcissistic Zoramite arrogance, I love this declaration by the Prophet Joseph, who adapted the language of Paul while couching what we now call the thirteenth Article of Faith: "If there is anything virtuous, lovely, or of good report or praiseworthy, we seek after these things." Later prophets elaborated similar themes: that which is good, virtuous, noble, and beautiful is to be sought out. Rather than being a threat to gospel truth, such things are to be embraced as a part of our religion, whatever their immediate source.

We have much to share with the world; we have much to take from the world and its people of diverse persuasions. Who can fail to be inspired by a Gandhi or a Galileo, a Mother Teresa, a Martin Luther King, an Einstein? To see and be edified by truth and nobility within and outside our Latter-day Saint tradition is not an erosion of faith. It is humility before the Lord of all creation.

8. Serve, pray, and remain active in the Church while you study and search.

Some years ago a widely-regarded historian, David Brion Davis, reviewed for an academic journal a landmark in scholarship: the three-volume *Encyclopedia of the American Religious Experience*. Davis praised the overall accomplishment, the most formidable summary of American religious scholarship to date. He was vexed, however, that believers among the scholars who had written the work had cloaked their own religiosity. Most contributors had so thoroughly distanced themselves from partisanship that religion, in their rendition, seemed either colorfully eccentric or inert and cold. Davis could scarcely trace among the authors much sense of the sacred, of spirituality, of the mystery of life and being. Given this rift between the one hundred contributing scholars and the subject they so coolly analyzed, the reviewer contemplated the *Encyclopedia*'s most likely readers: religious people. A startling analogy then took shape as an image in Davis's mind: the specter of "countless numbers of married couples consulting one hundred celibate monks and nuns for their wisdom on the American sexual experience."[12]

An equally silly image emerges when I picture times in my life when I have fancied myself intellectually clever and have been critical of something in the Church—while failing to magnify my calling, failing to take the practical and tangible steps to transcend the trivial, the routine, or the errant, failing to transform what seemed busywork or wrongheaded conceptions into the fostering of Zion and assisting as I can "to bring to pass the . . . eternal life of man" (Moses 1:39). My failure, I now recognize, was a failure of my own imagination and dedication. Such a failure, if sustained, is a recipe for losing one's sense of proportion, losing one's way, losing generosity, losing the Spirit.

I suggested earlier that it is impossible to think too well. I reiterate that it is, nonetheless, possible to deliberate too much. It is similarly possible to think too abstractly, or at least disproportionately abstractly, with too little hands-on involvement and "gut feeling" for one's subject. When the subject under scrutiny is my very self and faith and life, it is crucial that I complement my abstract thought and my book learning with active loving and giving to my brothers and sisters, and also with prayer, wherein my deepest yearnings reach out to the Lord. Short of this, I literally "lose touch." I need to experience in my cells a kind of "body knowing" and, in my heart and mind and soul, a "spirit knowing" that derives naturally from *doing*, from active participation and giving. Short of this, my rejection of faith or activity in the Church will be a rejection of something I have either forgotten or have never known in the scriptural sense of the term. To the ancient Hebrews, the word we commonly translate as "know" in the English Bible entailed more than "to comprehend." It meant "to experience."

When one is authentically blessing other lives through teaching the Beehives or Scouts or some other form of service, one needs little exterior verification that this is good and true. The verification is direct, intrinsic to the activity; one feels, experiences, and lives the truth. If I am ineffectual as a home teacher to those who will at least receive me, if the experience collapses to a form of role playing, it is apt to be me who is in part at fault, unable to create a bridge to friendship. If I do not trivialize but, instead, magnify my calling, I "taste," "feel," and "know" the truth by direct intuition and experience. If I find myself struggling in a calling that does not induce this spiritual awareness, conviction, and satisfaction, it may be that I should discuss things with my bishop so that I can serve in ways to which I am genuinely committed. There have been times when I have struggled with how to relate to routinized public prayer, socially scripted class discussions, unrestful and meeting-laden Sabbaths, and assumptions of those about me that I did not share. In the long run I have found that if I look inward and prayerfully renew my efforts, I can see that my lack of faith and spiritual satisfaction in my calling is apt to be at least in part a product of my own laziness, lack of imagination in making things relevant, or poorly arranged priorities. School is a good place to explore questions; my ward is a good place to practice mercy, humility, spiritual self-scrutiny, and service.

To analyze and critique other people—their lives, their practices, their beliefs and institutions—is a fairly easy exercise. Anyone can do it of almost anyone and anything. To do so seems much easier if one remains remote, free of a genuine and participating feel for the life-pulse of the people and all their struggles and the amazing workshop for love that constitutes the Church. The problem is—if one's goal is an active faith rather than an academic exercise—analyzing from afar is like a tone-deaf instructor teaching me to sing or like a coach, who has not played the game successfully himself, who yet confidently and urgently berates his team to better play and conquer. There is something missing here, namely a "feel" for that which is distinct from and more than a merely intellectual knowledge.

Along with your acquisition of the important knowledge that derives from books and thought and abstraction, it is essential that you not surrender this other, more basic kind of knowing, this feel for the ongoing life of faith. To lose this feel is automatically to distort. Be with people; serve them; join the institute of religion; keep physically active; stay *alive*—not merely bookish. "If any man will do his will, he shall know of the doctrine, whether it be of God, or whether I speak of myself" (John 7:17).

9. Think of boredom as a sin; cultivate an attitude of faithful inquiry.

Speaking through the Prophet Joseph Smith, and explicitly refusing to distinguish much between "sacred" and "temporal" commandments, the Lord challenged His people into an education:

> Teach one another the doctrine of the kingdom. Teach ye diligently and my grace shall attend you, that you may be instructed more perfectly in theory, in principle, in doctrine, in the law of the gospel, in all things that pertain unto the kingdom of God, that are expedient for you to understand.

He then laid out the breathtaking scope of the things "that pertain unto the kingdom" and "are expedient for [us] to understand":

> Of things both in heaven and in the earth, and under the earth; things which have been, things which are, things which must shortly come to pass; things which are at home, things which are abroad; the wars and the perplexities of the nations, and the judgments which are on the land; and a knowledge also of countries and of kingdoms—That ye may be prepared in all things when I shall send you again to magnify the calling whereunto I have called you, and the mission with which I have commissioned you (D&C 88:77–80).

If we are to be prepared to serve the Lord in the world at our highest capacity, we have our work in learning cut out for us!

In light of that injunction, one can imagine that, in the modern world, a formal college education might help to equip us. What obstacles to such an education present themselves? Insufficient funds? Ill-equipped teachers? The inaccessibility of a good college or university? In our affluent society, these are not insurmountable problems. A more common barrier is internal: laziness, a lack of passion, and a premature lust for practical security. Often the problem is, in fact, a form of overt or disguised boredom. We are "not interested" in this topic; we do not like that teacher; "I don't see how I will ever use this."

It is a spiritual and intellectual mistake to be bored. Like everyone else, I have encountered what I thought was a dull book, an uninspiring teacher, a tedious task. But I cannot recall the last time I was bored. This is a relief because boredom is a failure of imagination, a passive indulgence in self-pity, an abdication of responsibility, a willingness to let our development and experience depend on happenstance, such as the personality of a teacher. I am tempted even to construe boredom as a sin, because it is a kind of blockage: a damming (or damning) of what should be eternal progress in probing, learning, service, and growth. This harsh judgment may not apply to all peoples in all conditions, for life under political oppression or material deprivation can be onerous. But it may be true for a person so privileged as to be in college in a country where freedom of expression is a constitutional right.

Two principles have essentially dissolved for me the experience of boredom. The first is to recognize that while there are boring approaches to subjects, practically no subject is intrinsically boring. If the teacher is failing, I may need to bring some creative extra work to the task. The second principle is that if I feel trapped in circumstances that threaten to bore—if I am bagging potatoes on a production line, for instance, as I did each morning before my classes in high school—I have an entire universe to contemplate and people all around me about whom I might imagine ways to help. That is, my interior life need not remain hostage to my physical surroundings. I am not wholly responsible for encountering boring circumstances; I *am* accountable for my response to them. Even the very concept of "boredom" is interesting to work through when necessary, as is the attempt to understand and love any person or subject that strikes me as bored or boring.

Never did it occur to me while in college to study such a subject as geography; this evidently seemed too obviously tiresome and irrelevant to consider. I now see, however, that it is not geography that was by nature boring. Instead, the "boringness" was in me: in my ignorance, in my presumption, in my lack of initiative even to explore why such a field had come into being. By contrast, I now see that competing understandings of "space" and "place" condition our consciousness. In the realm of religion, for instance (let alone politics, law, history, art, and many other domains), geography controls much. One does not understand the Bible without grasping the covenantal foundation of the promised land. One does not know Islam without meditation on the role of pilgrimage to sacred ground or of facing Mecca five times each day in prayer. One does not know Christian history without wrestling with the geographical basis for Eastern Orthodoxy and Roman (Western) Catholicism, nor Hinduism nor Judaism without grappling with the richness of zones of meaning in and of cities like Benares or Jerusalem. Traditional Native American religion would unravel entirely apart from its understanding of the land. Latter-day Saint history would be a different thing were it not for the nineteenth-century geographical commandment to "gather," the sacred space of the temple, the Church's Utah homeland, its original American context, and its shifting international consciousness. The Book of

Mormon itself is in one sense an edited tract arguing the Lord's intent for America. Within the religions of the world, "chosen people, promised lands, sanctified cities, sacred rivers, taboo forests, holy mountains, hallowed directions—all suggest an intricate mesh of religion and 'interpreted space.'"[13] This sort of surprising importance for what many presume to be a dull and secondary discipline applies, as I keep learning, to every field I encounter.

A fundamental culprit allowing boredom to squelch our incentive may be a stunted sense of curiosity. If one's curiosity is sufficiently healthy and passionate, I fancy that one can overcome even fear: the fear of hard work, of looking foolish, of self-exploration, of change. When in my classes I encounter a person whose dwarfed curiosity fails them, someone who has come to my classroom for some reason other than an education, I observe them and wonder, "How did this happen to you?" After all, curiosity is native to children; it is prominent before they can walk or talk.

When I was very young, I often found myself "lost" in the color—the "orangeness"—of even a Wheaties box that faced me at the breakfast table, let alone the more compelling colors of nature or the more common experience of losing myself in the odd feel and appearance of tree bark, or in the fact that grass seemed to grow "up" instead of sideways, or in the peculiar beauty I discovered in the human face. That there could *be* such a thing as orangeness (or texture or direction or beauty) astonished and delighted me.

Perhaps the process of anesthetizing this God-given curiosity involves something basic. For instance, I recall taking my nephew David, age one, out for walks in the forest that lay behind our family home in Utah. Together we took pleasure in implausible wonders: November air crisp as an apple; red ants and black ants resolving some dispute that was no doubt the result of ethnic prejudice; three distinct trees somehow grown together as one; blue-brown beetles visually more formidable, up close, than any dinosaur. As we walked, we named. I would say "robin" or "lily" or "dirt"; David would approximate the sound. I cheered and hugged—David was reinforced. He learned language.

But in time I noticed a change. The focal point of his attention, fostered by my cheering, subtly shifted *from* the bird itself or the flight of the bird *to* David's own ability to attach conventional sounds to the bird—to name it. Now acquiring language seems to me a good idea, but in the process of becoming himself in this way, David diluted—distorted?—another part of himself: his unvarnished sense of relation with the world. Over time, alas, we may come to care less about experiencing and understanding the universe and more about getting A's in school.

What forces like this constrict our curiosity? Socialization? Pain? False confidence? Punishment, arrogance, stupidity, routine, resentment, insecurity, comfort, bad teachers, cheap distractions, lack of nurture, hormones? Who-knows-what? As for my own children and my own students, I hope everything in the universe seems partly strange, bulging with events, dynamics, people, and phenomena that beg exploration. The Lord has placed us in a peculiar, fascinating world. Whatever else college teaches us, it ought to teach us disciplined wonder. And disciplined wonder is fostered through asking questions.

In the realm of faith and the Church, fundamental questions can be misconstrued as a disloyal act. Of course, questions can indeed be wrongheaded if laced with cynicism, anger, or conceit. And there is a time and a place for different types of questions, and that place is not always in church meetings. However, it is an error to militate against authentic and probing inquiry as such—a truth suggested by the ancient story of Job, which is rich and layered with meaning and truths that transcend its simple plot. The Lord does not chastise Job for asking authentic questions, but for pressing accusations against God in the guise of rhetorical questions. For this the Lord puts Job in his place—for four long chapters (Job 38–41). Yet in the end God esteems Job above his friends, even though, on the surface, the friends' words seem pious and faithful. These friends defend God's justice but ask no questions of God or of themselves. Rather than inquire, they pronounce. In smug self-righteousness they are sure—and they are wrong—that they know God's ways and intent. "The Lord said to Eliphaz the Temanite, My wrath is kindled against thee, and against thy two friends: for ye have not spoken of me the thing that is right, as my [now repentant] servant Job hath" (Job 42:7).

In the academy, one will grapple with a more complex, problematic, and suffering world than one was aware of without the experience. Neither Job's angry accusations against God nor the dubious certainty of Job's friends are apt to serve Latter-day Saints well on campus. Nor, as we have already suggested, is the morally detached perspective of science sufficient. The fundamental attitude I recommend for a Saint in the academy is one of "faithful inquiry." "Faithful" ought not to be confused with zeal or with mere intellectual belief. "Inquiry" must be earnest, persistent, and humble. Both aspects of the admonition to "faithful inquiry" should be informed by others of our "ten commandments." The resulting orientation may have something in common with what the medieval writer Anselm meant when he described his intellectual quest as "faith seeking understanding."[14]

10. Remember the point.

President Gordon B. Hinckley has correctly noted, when speaking to the young people of the Church, that we

> are moving into the most competitive age the world has ever known. All around you is competition. You need all the education you can get. Sacrifice a car; sacrifice anything

that is needed to be sacrificed to qualify yourselves to do the work of the world. That world will in large measure pay you what it thinks you are worth, and your worth will increase as you gain education and proficiency in your chosen field.[15]

Becoming professionally competitive is one important reason for entering college, and it is not one that tends to be lost on students and on the families that support them.

A contributing element to this practical success that college tends to promote is also an element with far wider applications and implications than being a good provider to self and family. Proper training at a good college develops critical thought, clear expression, the art of discovering and weighing evidence, a hunger for knowledge, and the ability to solve problems. These are skills that help in almost any profession, and they are skills that come into play in one's life as a whole.

If your education has been successful, then it has just begun. Because of it, you will better have learned how to learn. You will think differently than before you entered college. You will better distinguish the permanent from the transient. You will see things differently, in new and wider contexts, and you will see issues, dynamics, and relations that formerly were invisible. When you see differently in these respects, you judge and respond differently; you become a different person than you otherwise would be. When you achieve an authentic liberal education, you are better equipped to function as a free and responsible citizen, in negotiation with the world, with enhanced angles of vision, theory, and context for weighing not only good and evil, but good and bad quality generally.

The personal stakes in this educational enterprise thus are high.

They are high for you, they are high for those who may come under your influence, and they are high for the Lord who loves you.

Conclusion

These, then, are ten commandments—ten words of counsel for balancing the life of the mind and the spirit in an academic setting. As noted earlier, one should not invest too seriously in the number ten; other principles warrant attention, including social ones. But these at present serve as my "top ten" suggestions for those students to whom serious questions arise in the course of their studies. If we will honestly seek truth and appreciate its relation to goodness and "quality"; respect the intellect; know the limits of reason, the situated nature of all knowledge, and the reality of the Spirit and other supra-rational ways of knowing; remember that the Church on earth consists of humans who are imperfectly trying to respond to the divine; understand that our character affects how smart we are and filters what we can know; find a wise and faithful mentor and good conversation partners; embrace truth and virtue from whatever source; remain active in prayer, service, and the Church while magnifying our callings and experiencing directly the goodness and fulfillment this brings; cultivate an attitude of faithful inquiry; and remember that the point of college eclipses professional preparation—then the hard work of education may promote spiritual as well as mental growth. Reality and opportunity are apt never to look quite the same and quite as small as they did before. The adventure of college may become, in the end, a cause of celebration.

Notes

1. Socrates's phrase recorded in Plato, *Apology* 38a, in *Plato in Twelve Volumes*, vol. 1, translated by Harold North Fowler (Cambridge, MA: Harvard University Press, 1966).

2. *New York Times Review of Books,* January 1, 1984, 33.

3. Ibid.

4. Joseph Smith, *History of The Church of Jesus Christ of Latter-day Saints* (Salt Lake City: Deseret Book, 1967), 3:380, 381.

5. David O. McKay, in Conference Report, October 1920, 42.

6. A paraphrase of an insight Goethe's fictive narrator proffers in book IV, chapter XVIII, stanza 5, of *Wilhelm Meister's Apprenticeship* (New York: The Harvard Classics Shelf of Fiction, 1917), 274.

7. See Houston Smith, *The Soul of Christianity* (San Francisco: Harper/San Francisco, 2005).

8. M. Scott Peck, *The Road Less Traveled: A New Psychology of Love, Traditional Values, and Spiritual Growth* (New York: Touchstone, 1980), 251–52.

9. Laurel Thatcher Ulrich, "Lusterware," in Philip Barlow, ed., *A Thoughtful Faith* (Centerville, UT: Cannon Press, 1986), 200; originally published in *Exponent II* (Spring 1985).

10. Joseph Smith, *History of The Church of Jesus Christ of Latter-day Saints,* edited by B. H. Roberts, 7 vols. (Salt Lake City: Deseret News Press, 1902), 4:588. The core thought is expressed variously by several scribes who recorded Joseph Smith's King Follett sermon.

11. Richard Bushman, "Faithful History," *Dialogue: A Journal of Mormon Thought,* 4, no. 4 (Winter 1969): 25.

12. David Brion Davis, "Review Essay," *Religion and American Culture* 1 (Winter 1991): 119–27.

13. Edwin Gaustad and Philip Barlow, *New Historical Atlas of Religion in America* (New York: Oxford, 2002), xxi.

14. "Faith Seeking Understanding" was the original title of Anselm's famous *Proslogion.*

15. Gordon B. Hinckley, "A Prophet's Counsel and Prayer for Youth," *New Era,* January 2001, 8.

Honest in Heart and Mind

Elizabeth Vincent

Bachelor of Arts in English, University of Utah

Question:

Honestly, I can't say that I've had many life-altering moments—a single instant when my perspective was forever changed. More often than not, truths come upon me gradually, which is a lucky thing, considering that many of my epiphanic moments have brought some pretty hard truths.

Take, for instance, Santa Claus. My believing heart was crushed to hear he wasn't really making a list and checking it twice. Or, on my baptism day, when I realized I was no longer perfect because I'd argued with my sister—already. Or when I realized, too late, that my first kiss was going to be stolen by a boy I was not remotely interested in.

Trivial examples, I know. But, small as they are, these hard truths have opened the door to greater truths: the reality of the Savior's birth, of His atonement, and of trusting the Spirit. The removal of illusions, innocence, and naiveté necessitated the search for higher truths and allowed me a new perspective with which to find them.

I remember another such moment. I don't recall who was speaking, where I was, or even specifically when I heard it, but I was listening to a story about young Gordon B. Hinckley. He had been excited to be part of the initiatory seventh-grade class at Roosevelt Junior High. But as the school year began, Gordon was disappointed to learn he'd have to spend another year at his elementary because the junior high was overcrowded. He felt he'd paid the price to attend a junior high school and so, the following day, he went on strike. When he returned to school the next day, he and his friends found the principal waiting for them at the front door. The principal informed them that they would be readmitted only with a letter of explanation from their parents. Gordon was stung by his mother's note, which read, "Dear Mr. Stearns, Please excuse Gordon's absence yesterday. His action was simply an impulse to follow the crowd."

That's when it hit me; I was not as honest as President Hinckley had been as a boy. The importance of honesty was not the speaker's point, but while I was listening to the story, I realized I was scheming in my head to think of ways I would avoid telling my mother if I were in the same scenario. I would have eventually resigned myself to the fact that I'd have to get a note from my mother, but my heart wouldn't be in it—it would have been done begrudgingly. And I wanted to be honest in heart.

So I began to build a solid foundation. But it's not always that simple. From politicians to mechanics to those with elaborate double lives making the news, sometimes it's hard to find good examples. And in college, the pressure can become especially intense. A recent survey revealed that 100 percent of dating couples surveyed lied to each other in about a third of their conversations. College students lie in 50 percent of their conversations with their mothers. Ninety-five percent of participating college students surveyed were willing to tell at least one lie to a potential employer to win a job—and 41 percent had already done so.[1] Dr. Charles Ford of the University of Alabama suggests that the average person lies about seven times an hour, if you include all the times people lie to themselves. So what are the real consequences of all this? What does it take to really become, and remain, honest in heart?

$$* * *$$

James S. Jardine

Managing Director and Trial Lawyer, Ray Quinney and Nebeker, a Salt Lake City Law Firm

Answer:

We speak of the "honest in heart." Indeed, we pray that our missionaries may be led to those who are honest in heart (Luke 8:15). We believe that those who are truly honest in heart will be receptive to the truth and will have the courage to change their lives for that truth. Less often do we ourselves focus on becoming honest in heart, although it is a condition of being accepted by God (D&C 97:8).

The ideal of becoming honest in heart involves more than personal resolutions about honesty and lying. It also requires an awareness of *external* influences that favor convenience or advantage over fidelity, as well as a constant *internal* introspection of our own conduct and character. It requires courage, because honesty frequently has personal cost.

Our search for truth and our full embrace of honesty as a personal virtue are the endeavors of a lifetime. But it is particularly important that college students, who are laying lifelong foundations and who face special pressures, learn to love honesty.

There is a relationship between Truth and Honesty. Truth exists independently (D&C 93:30). Truth is knowledge of things as they really are (D&C 93:24). Honesty is the attitude that we develop about Truth. "The moral domain of intended truthfulness and deception [is only a part] of the much vaster domain of truth and falsity in general."[2] The honest in heart seek Truth, and they know that daily honesty is a kind of search engine.

Being honest in heart has two separate aspects—a heartfelt desire to know the truth, and a heartfelt commitment to speak the truth, the whole truth, and nothing but the truth. I hope in this essay to explore the realities of the day-to-day pressures on our personal honesty, the interplay of our personal honesty in the context of several kinds of relationships, and some specific steps we can take to prepare our hearts to love truth.

One starting place is to recognize that our secular environment is not encouraging of honesty. Not more than a few decades ago, honesty was a preeminent societal value. Although we still hear media reports of some remarkable acts of honesty, such as returning lost money, those stories now contain a strong sense of astonishment. We no longer can count on our secular institutions or social mores to help to prepare honest hearts or to support us in that effort.

Indeed, the decline of honesty as an overriding virtue in the world is quite apparent. So many prominent individuals have been caught in lies of one kind or another that we no longer expect to be told the truth. From falsified corporate financial reports to exaggerated resumes, stories of deception abound. People seem more interested in beating the system than in keeping their word. The divided public reaction to the lying of a president just a few years ago illustrates this fact. Contrast that with the country's view of two revered earlier presidents. No story about George Washington is more often told than his purported youthful response to his father, "I cannot tell a lie." And the country's affectionate nickname for President Lincoln, Honest Abe, reflects something very valued about him.

Church members are not immune to this societal drift, this increased casualness towards personal honesty. Some Church members make personal copies on office copy machines without recording it or take off work without permission or penalty to do Church work. Some faithful Church members in Utah buy boats and license them in Oregon to avoid property tax. Questionable tax avoidance schemes abound. We hear reports of students cheating in school and adults cheating on expense-account reports. A few may even exaggerate their monthly home teaching visits. This occurs even though, as Church members, we must answer in a sacred setting whether we are honest in our dealings with others.

In counseling people in difficulty, I have repeatedly seen that dishonesty is at the core of all sin. In my experience, lying is inextricably linked to sin—lying to ourselves, lying to others, lying to God. Some form of dishonesty is always a companion to sin. As Oliver Wendell Holmes observed, "Sin has many tools, but a lie is the handle which fits them all."[3] In the most obvious sense, we cover up our sins with lies, and the domino effect of those lies begins—one lie begetting another lie begetting another lie. As has been observed over the years, it is easy to tell a lie but hard to tell just one.

We know from the scriptures that Satan is the "father of all lies" (2 Nephi 2:18; Ether 8:25; John 8:44). That description seems both figurative and literal—that he is not just the symbolic father of lies but that he begets falsehood in a real sense. We are told in 2 Nephi that Satan entices men to become liars (2 Nephi 28:8). How does he do that? By the deceit that there "is no harm" in such falsehoods (D&C 10:25). Why does he do that? Because Satan "seeketh that all men might be miserable like unto himself" (2 Nephi 2:27). Satan desires that we enter the prison of sin and misery, a prison kept locked by the bar of our own falsehood. Almost any lie will be imprisoning.

By contrast, the truth will set us free (John 8:32). Truth is the key that unlocks the prison of misery and sin.

Dishonesty is also devastating to personal spirituality. Jesus said, "I am the way, the truth, and the life" (John 14:6). We are told in the book of Jacob that "the Spirit speaketh the truth and lieth not" (Jacob 4:13). If the Spirit is with us, it directs us to speak truth and lie not. Indeed, God is "a God of truth, and canst not lie" (Ether 3:12). So if we are to become like God, we must be people who not only will not lie, but who cannot lie. It is our hearts more than our heads that make us incapable of lying. If we are truly honest in heart, our hearts will not fail us but will hold us firm to the truth.

Thus, a serious discussion of personal honesty is relevant to active Latter-day Saints—because the societal pressures are great, because personal honesty is so crucial, and because even minor dishonesties will become corrosive. We always underestimate the effect of our dishonesties; we rationalize them away. We suppose there "is no harm." But dishonesty, even on relatively inconsequential matters, is like a cancer cell and will metastasize within us.

We know the account of Thomas Marsh's wife taking the cream from the top of the neighborhood milk bucket. But it wasn't the theft of the cream, it was her inability to admit the wrong to her neighbors—the continuing lie—that produced the Marshes' slide out of the Church.

I know this from personal experience. I love sports and have coached both my sons in youth basketball leagues. Several summers ago I took my youngest son to a basketball camp. He was eleven years old at the time. Boys twelve or older could play with the more advanced group. I wanted him to play with the older group, so I told the officials he was twelve. Afterwards, I began to reflect back on that moment. Even though on one level it seemed harmless, my son had seen his father lie for personal advantage. I went to him and asked for his forgiveness. I went back to the camp the next day, informed the officials he was really only eleven, and apologized. I have come to see such seemingly small matters as of great consequence. There is no such thing as an inconsequential dishonesty in terms of our own hearts or in its potential impact on others.

The importance of personal honesty can be seen in several different contexts. I would like to focus on three of those: our personal health and happiness, our relationship with others, and our relationship with God.

Honesty and Personal Mental Health

Honesty is essential to our personal health and happiness. Personal mental health depends on an honest comprehension of ourselves and of our environment. In *The Road Less Traveled*, M. Scott Peck writes: "The tendency to avoid problems and the emotional suffering inherent in them is the primary basis of all human mental illness."[4] Avoiding personal problems, denying reality, is a form of personal dishonesty. Looking at ourselves accurately, to see who we are and what we are doing in the world, to really see ourselves, is the essence of mental health. It is also the foundation of personal progress. In the book of Jacob we are told that the Spirit helps us to see "things as they really are" (Jacob 4:13).

The inability to see things as they really are—to distort our world—may lead to mental illness. John taught that "if we say that we have no sin, we deceive ourselves, and the truth is not in us" (1 John 1:8). This doctrine is true for all. Some Latter-day Saints may feel they are committing no material sins. This sense of well-being is dangerous. We ignore our small sins. In assessing ourselves, in an accounting sense, we round up to our own benefit. When we look at ourselves and say there is no real sin in us, we deceive ourselves in harmful ways. We see no need to change or repent. We see no personal failure and, therefore, see no need for the Atonement. Self-deception is thus spiritually debilitating because it blinds us to our need for the Savior.

Self-deception is personally harmful because it brings us into the realm of Satan, the father of lies. Satan tells us what we *want* to hear, but God tells us what we *need* to hear. In our own lives there are some people who tell us what we need to hear (friends) and others who tell us what we want to hear (flatterers). What makes us susceptible to such flattery is that most people, to borrow a phrase, would rather be ruined by praise than saved by criticism. Thus, praise and flattery are tools of Satan (2 Nephi 28:22) and help promote self-deception.

This self-deception manifests itself in a number of ways. As a stake president in a family student stake at the university, I did a great deal of marriage counseling. One night a young couple came to see me. They had not been married long, but they were struggling. It took only five minutes of visiting for me to realize that the root of the problem in their relationship was the husband's complete self-absorption. He defined his world entirely in terms of how things and people affected him; he could not see past his own wants and needs. This made a healthy relationship with his wife—or anyone else, for that matter—difficult. After visiting with him for a while, I suggested he read *The Road Less Traveled.* If you have read that book, you will know the point I intended for him to learn. In that book, Scott Peck defines love as willing ourselves to nurture the spiritual growth of another. I thought the book would be helpful for him to read, that it might give him some insight to himself. We scheduled a follow-up meeting a week later. When we met, he said, "I've read the whole book." I was surprised because it was unusual for a person to actually read the book that quickly. He said, "It was one of the best books I have ever read. I am so grateful you gave it to me. I just loved it. You have such insight. I do not know how you knew that it's just what my wife needs." This story would be humorous if it wasn't true. This young man simply could not see himself at all; the truth was not in him. And his self-deception was debilitating to him personally, to his capacity for love.

Self-deception is also self-limiting. Our biases paralyze us. William James said that "most people think they are thinking when they are merely rearranging their prejudices."[5] That insight rings true. Knowing the truth, seeing the truth about ourselves, not only allows us to change but empowers us to change. President Brigham Young made this point in his talk, "The Wilderness Was Kinder to Us Than Thou":

> Sometimes I think that the worst thing that can happen to a man is to grow old. His experience becomes like a solid wall around him and he grows blind trying to look through that and he takes his own memories for the facts of the new changing world around him. And then if the spirit comes to reveal the truth of life to him, he tries to reconcile it with his own opinions and that is living death. It tells in their faces, their manners and their voices. Nothing keeps a man young and up to his times like being open to the inspiration of the spirit.[6]

Among other things, this powerful insight explains President Hinckley's youthful ninety-plus years.

Dishonesty is demoralizing and depressing. It is truly darkness. Vaclav Havel, the first elected president of Czechoslovakia, said the following:

A person who has been seduced by the consumer value system, whose identity is dissolved in an amalgam of the accoutrements of mass civilization, and who has no roots in the order of being, no sense of responsibility for anything other than his or her own personal survival, is a demoralized person. The system depends on this demoralization, deepens it, is in fact a projection of it into society.[7]

Being demoralized means being deprived of a moral foundation. Our dishonesty deprives us of a moral foundation, and we become demoralized or depressed.

The power of honesty gives us strength; it gives us confidence; it gives us a sense of peace. We are free from fear of discovery, free from internal conflicts, free from the depression of dishonesty. We can put on the armor of truth as a shield to the various assaults of the world.

If personal honesty is hardwired into our self-image—if we are truly honest in heart—it will lift us in powerful ways. I believe Abraham Lincoln cultivated his nickname in part because it was a way to reinforce his own consciously adopted self-image. And that self-image clearly was empowering to him.

In Robert Bolt's play, *A Man for All Seasons,* King Henry VIII wants Sir Thomas More to take an oath of allegiance to the Crown to signify his agreement with the king's divorce. But that position is contrary to More's Catholic faith, and More will not take the oath. As a lawyer, More knows that if he does not take the oath and is silent on the reasons why, he cannot be convicted under the law. The law will hold him accountable only for what he does say. On this point, because of his stature in England, his silence is deafening. The king imprisons him in an effort to force him to take the oath. Eventually the king allows More's family to see him in prison in an attempt to get him to capitulate. His daughter, proposing the device of mental reservation, says to him, "Father, take the oath." He replies he cannot. She then argues, "Speak the oath with your lips but in your heart think otherwise."

More replies, "What is an oath, Meg, but words we speak to God." And then he adds, "When a man takes an oath, he's holding his own self in his own hands [like water]. And if he opens his fingers then, he needn't hope to find himself again."[8]

It is a powerful image, and true. Our honesty is at our core; it holds our souls together. If we lose our personal honesty, we may not find ourselves again.

Honesty and Our Relationship with Others

Honesty and its companion, trust, are essential to our relationship with others. Dishonesty is the most destructive and corrosive influence on love and trust. This is so because honesty and trust are linked together. We are honest with those we trust, and we trust those we have found to be honest.

When we are dishonest with a spouse, a wall goes up. We begin to compartmentalize, to hide off a part of ourselves. We are then not a whole person, loving another whole person; we are mismatched at a fundamental level. We withhold a part of ourselves from the relationship because we do not want that part to be discovered. This truth operates in dating as well. We may want to impress so much that we present ourselves falsely.

A friend once told me that when he ordered clothes from a catalog, he had them sent to his work rather than to his home because he did not want his wife to find out how much money he was spending. An alarm went off in my mind. A few years later, they ended up divorced. Even though that dishonesty in buying clothes may have seemed a small thing, it was a hidden wedge in that relationship.

One of the most pernicious forms of dishonesty in marriage occurs with indulgence in pornography. If men are addicted in any way to pornography, they begin to lead a separate, secret life. They necessarily lie to their spouses on that issue, which can then lead to lying on other matters, such as finances. That dishonesty is absolutely destructive to relationships. The scriptures explain why this is the case. In Proverbs 26:28, we learn that "a lying tongue hateth those that are afflicted by it." It is true that we come to hate those who are injured by our lying, such as our spouse. Those we would love we ultimately hate if we lie to them. This is in part because we know on some level that we are injuring them, even though they are unaware of the falsity. We begin to feel guilty about them; then we resent them for the guilt we feel. The psychology of this process is real.

We cannot insulate our children from our dishonesty. In the novel *The Winter of Our Discontent*, John Steinbeck tells the story of a man who is morally bankrupt. He betrays his employer; he lies on his expense account; he cheats on his wife. The only redeeming thing in his life is his son—a teenager whom he loves completely. That son is the one ray of light in his otherwise dark world. In his love for this son, in that one relationship, we can glimpse some humanity in the man. In the novel, the son wins a national essay contest and is invited to Washington, D.C., to receive the award. As the book concludes, it is discovered that the son has plagiarized his essay. In that moment the father realizes that he has not been able to shield his son from his own dishonesty. He could not really compartmentalize his life. His own dishonesty has infected his son. It is a poignant and powerful story.

Our personal dishonesty is a toxin in the environment for our children. That is why it was important for me to go back to the basketball camp with my son to correct the lie about his age. His trust in my fidelity to the truth was more important than any athletic experience he could ever have.

We must create an environment where those we love feel empowered to be honest with us, where forgiveness and understanding are present. Our children, who know our hearts, must find honesty there. If honesty rules in our homes and if family members feel empowered by it, then their confidence in the triumph of truth will trump fear and insecurity. If our children come and confess something to us, we will value their honesty. It will be a firm foundation upon which we deal with them. Trust as well as truth will prevail.

Honesty and Personal Spirituality

Honesty is essential to our most important relationship—the relationship with God our Eternal, Heavenly Father. If we are not honest with God there can be no true relationship with Him. When we fail to address falsehoods in our lives, we avoid the God of Truth. When sin persists, there develops a falseness to our professions of faith. Our religion becomes all ritual and no reality. Prayer is lost to us if we are not honest with God because the last person in the world we want to talk with is He who knows all things. In Huck Finn's famous words, we cannot pray a lie. When we tell a lie in this world, it is not just a failure of faith; it is an affirmative expression of disbelief because it connotes that we care more about some gain in this world than the God of this world and of the world to come.

Some years ago, I met with parents whose son had just phoned from the missionary training center to say that he needed to come home. We talked for a few minutes, and it was obvious that they were in real distress. After expressing my love for this young man, I became direct. I said, "Let me understand this. Your son has just decided that what God thinks about him is more important than what you think about him and what your neighbors think about him. I know that you wish this hadn't happened, and I wish it hadn't. But your son has just made a decision that is going to make every decision for the rest of his life easy, because he has chosen to be honest with God in this most critical moment."

We must treasure up the truth in our hearts as part of our worship and as an act of spiritual self-preservation. "If our heart condemn us not, then have we confidence toward God" (1 John 3:21).

Suggestions on Becoming Honest in Heart

I would like to offer some suggestions on how we become honest in heart, with particular focus on some challenges to college students.

First, to become honest in heart, we must love honesty. It cannot be just a matter of intellectual conviction; there must, at our deepest emotional levels, be an exhilaration in the truth. We are told by the Apostle Paul that love "rejoiceth in the truth" (1 Corinthians 13:6). We should pray to hunger and thirst after honesty. We must become passionate about truth, so that our emotions, and not just a sense of duty, compel our honesty. Like Lincoln, we must be unable to sit still while a mistaken overpayment has been made or some other falsehood remains uncorrected. This standard of honesty applies to all our daily activities, including writing papers, taking tests, building resumes.

Second, we become honest in heart by preparing our hearts in private, deciding in advance to be honest in later "moments of truth." Stephen Covey has noted that prayer is our private battlefield where we pray over the conflicts and pressures and hard choices that are to come. We ground and root ourselves in prayer so that when we enter onto the public battlefields of life, we are not indecisive or vulnerable to the winds that blow. We can also make advance decisions on truthfulness in discussions and commitments with our spouse and children.

My wife was in the parking lot at the university a few years ago, driving our Suburban. As she backed out, she scraped an unoccupied car. She wrote her name and contact information on a note and left it on the windshield. The owner of the other car later called with particular gratitude. We talked over with our children the temptation to leave and how important it is to be honest for our own sake, even if no one else sees or knows.

In the book *All the President's Men,* about the Watergate affair, the two investigative reporters are trying to trace money at issue in their inquiry and go to the home of the treasurer for the Committee to Re-elect the President. When they arrive at his house, his wife will not let them talk to her husband. But as they are leaving, she fixes them in her gaze and says, "I want you to know that this is an honest house."[9] Shortly thereafter her husband discloses to the reporters what he knows to be the truth.

Wouldn't it be strengthening if we said to each other every day that ours is an "honest house"?

Third, to be honest in heart, we must be prepared to live with the consequences. As a young man, I watched the 1968 Masters Golf Tournament where a golfer named Roberto De Vicenzo tied for the lowest score, but then signed an inaccurate scorecard. He reported this error and, under the rules of golf, was disqualified. It is an inspiring story, except that there is no fairy-tale ending. He was headed for a playoff but was denied the opportunity because of his mistake. He received no trophy. Nevertheless, he had the personal integrity to do the right thing. He had prepared himself to live with the consequences of being honest, and he held firm under pressure. We must have an internal priority system that tells us that being honest is more important than any other reward or honor the world can confer.

Fourth, we should take concrete steps immediately to make an honesty "to do" list. Paul counsels us to "[renounce] the hidden things of dishonesty" (2 Corinthians 4:2). The things of dishonesty are by definition, almost always hidden. The first step on such a "to do" list is to shine a light on those hidden things and begin to correct them. When I got home from my mission, I went to the Highland Drive-In Movie Theater and gave them $75 for the times in high school I had sneaked in. I needed to renounce that hidden dishonesty.

We must firmly desire and seek honest feedback—even if it is sometimes painful. One reason I love my wife is that she gives me such honest feedback. When I give a talk, she will tell me what worked and did not work. I know that she cares enough to give her very best, and most honest, views. We do not want to be like the rich young man who did not really want the feedback that Jesus had to give him (Matthew 19:16–22). For that reason, we should prize friends who will tell us what we may not want to hear. These people do not become our enemies when they tell us the truth (Galatians 4:16).

In a world that increasingly prizes personal accomplishment, we must avoid personal exaggeration. College students often face the temptation to inflate resumes. When I was a senior in high school I was cut from the basketball team. I love basketball with a passion and have continued to play most of my adult life. Since then, one of my challenges has been to be honest about my experience as a senior. When people have asked if I played basketball in high school, I could say "Yes," because I did play some years. But a perfectly honest answer is "Yes, but not my senior year." We must be scrupulously honest about our own record.

Be careful about attribution. This is a more sophisticated issue than the evil of plagiarism, made easier today by the Internet. If you are borrowing somebody's ideas, be clear about it. It takes nothing away from you to recognize someone else's work. It honors them—and they often learn about your recognition of them (or failure to do so). I have been in meetings where points I had made in earlier talks were used by others without attribution. Some unworthy feelings of resentment went through me. Unfortunately, it was my own pride, not my concern about their failure to attribute, that I felt. Nevertheless, if we borrow ideas from others, they should be recognized.

We must not gossip. This is a constant challenge because we may get momentary credit with some for passing on "secrets" or "inside information." In that sense, we are promoting ourselves at the expense of others. Our responsibility is to speak truth. It is not sufficient to pass on a rumor with the caveat that we do not know ourselves whether it is accurate. When we pass some rumor on, we affirm it by repeating it, notwithstanding any disclaimer. It is dishonest to repeat information the truth of which we do not know. We do double harm—to our own hearts and to the subjects of our gossip. We simply cannot rationalize gossip on any ground.

Keep confidences. If you want to be a servant to others, they must have trust in you. Keeping confidences is another way of saying we should keep promises. Breaking such promises means we have lied to those who trusted us.

Pay taxes honestly—and start when you are young, even if your income is meager. Will Rogers said the biggest cause of lying since the invention of golf is the tax return. This can be a challenge for college students whose earnings (such as tips) are not reported by employers and are therefore left to them to report.

Finally, we should constantly make the condition of our hearts a matter of prayer. Ask for God's help. You have heard the marriage advice, "Don't go to bed angry." I believe our life advice should be, "Don't go to bed dishonest with God." He knows we need His help.

Prayer is the tool to pierce through our self-delusions, to identify our deceptions, to focus on our falsities (Ether 12:27).

Let me conclude with another story. When I was a freshman at the University of Utah, I finished the winter quarter and received my mission call. When I went to look up my final grade for one class, an "Incomplete" was posted on the grade sheet. I went to see the professor and asked why the incomplete. He said that he had irrefutable proof that I had cheated on the final examination. He said that not only would I get an incomplete for the class but that I would be expelled from the university. In fact, I had not cheated. But you can imagine the feelings I had.

I went to see another professor I knew and asked how I should deal with it. For two or three days I was in utter turmoil. Although I had my mission call and was set to leave, I did not see how I could leave under that cloud. Finally, it turned out that an acquaintance who sat next to me in that class had without my knowledge copied off my exam. He went to that teacher and explained what had happened. I received an apology and a final grade.

In those several days of distress, I swore an oath to God and to myself that I would never again put myself in such a position of vulnerability. I had a sense then—as I do even better now—how critical honesty is to my own spirituality, how important it was to my peace and my personal security, to my ability to go forth and serve God.

There will be no greater goal for each of us than that those looking for the honest in heart may find us so to be.

Notes

1. "The Truth about Lying," *Psychology Today*, 30 (May/June 1997): 53.

2. Sissela Bok, *Lying* (New York: Vintage Books, 1989), 6.

3. Oliver Wendell Holmes, *The Autocrat of the Breakfast-table* (Boston: Ticknor and Fields, 1865), np.

4. M. Scott Peck, *The Road Less Traveled* (New York: Simon and Schuster, 1978), 17.

5. William James, in Clifton Fodiman, *American Treasury, 1455–1955* (New York: Harper, 1955), 719.

6. *The Essential Brigham Young* (Salt Lake City: Signature Books, 1992), 240–41.

7. Vaclav Havel, in *First Things,* 55 (August/September 1995): 41.

8. Robert Bolt, *A Man for All Seasons* (New York: Vintage Books, 1962), 81.

9. Carl Bernstein and Bob Woodward, *All the President's Men* (New York: Warner Books, 1974), 83.

On the Strength of Learning by Faith

Eric Sorte

Master of Physics, Columbia University

Question:

As a student of science and a rationalist, religion has always posed a philosophical dilemma for me. I deeply fear becoming a moral hypocrite—on the outside, telling people that I possess the ultimate truth and urging them to follow on the one hand; but inside, too timid to question seriously my own beliefs out of fear of societal and familial repercussions. My ecumenical studies dating back to early childhood have attempted to impress upon me a certain approach to epistemology—an approach given to *a priori* knowledge, divine edict, and the validation of the role of feeling and impression in the search for truth. This approach to the problem of knowledge seems to directly contradict the Aristotelian methods of inquiry taught by my professors, which generally rejects the acceptance of feeling, revelation, or any other spiritual method of obtaining knowledge, allowing only externally verifiable means derived directly from the five senses, augmented by logical deduction. My religion, conversely, suggests I regard my human intellect and logical powers as nice, but ultimately superfluous, and encourages me to focus instead on my feelings, impressions, and on trying to "lean not unto [my] own understanding" (Proverbs 3:5).

So where does that leave those of us who demand the best and most rational within ourselves and who remain ambivalent about the seemingly unverifiable assertions of Sunday School? Could God really be asking me to suspend my reason and mind to accept what many may say amounts to a stock of unbelievable stories substantiated only by theocratic dictate? Could God really be commanding me to follow blindly and *not to think* as religion makes seemingly implausible claims about supernatural visitations; divine healings; and new, proprietary apostolic authority? Wouldn't our God of boundless reason and immeasurable intelligence want me to follow the advice of my teachers and educated authors, withholding judgment on faith-based and unsubstantiated beliefs until they can be tangibly verified? Wouldn't a God who continually exhorts me to "study [problems] out in [my] mind," who tells me that "knowledge . . . shall greatly enlarge [my] soul" (see D&C 9:8; 121:42)—wouldn't He tell me that until I can formulate logical arguments to validate what I profess to "know" (the same way I know everything else) that I cannot be honest in saying that I know it? Is a witness from the Holy Ghost really the evidence needed to say, "I know"?

I do not wish to accept ideas that are not true simply because they are culturally fashionable. Neither do I wish to fall prey to the trap of accepting the fallacious philosophies of men (Colossians 2:8), such men as Paul warned of, who wander about trying to obtain knowledge, "ever learning, and never able to come to the knowledge of the truth" (2 Timothy 3:7). My studies reveal disturbing and thought-provoking opinions of those like Karl Marx, who allege that "religion is an opiate of the masses"[1] and a tool of repression to wield arbitrary control over the uniformed and uneducated, which make me question my reasons for believing; and yet

I likewise shrink from second-guessing an All-Wise God who must have reasons for asking for my trust, faith, and patience.

These questions can be answered from either side of the aisle, but always with a directional bias. In my perspective, religion resolves the conflict by telling me to abandon as youthful hubris the wish to have an immediate, logic-based foundation for my ideology; science tells me to abandon faith and feeling and to be consistent in my methodology of establishing truthful premises—that is, to use the same heuristic in establishing the existence of God as I would use to establish the existence of a table. Can I be entirely consistent in myself by unconditionally accepting revealed religious truth, while continually seeking for a rational and scientific explanation for all that I am being taught? Or am I destined to be the eternal incarnation of a divided soul unable to accept transcendental truth because of my inability to articulate the appropriate arguments, yet always yearning to believe what so many find easy and natural to accept—the unmistakable truth of the divine?

* * *

William Hayes Pingree

Visiting Professor of International Studies and Political Thought at the University of Utah

Answer:

Understanding how individuals come to know things is a fascinating and uniquely human endeavor. Comprehension and knowledge of the world in which we live strikes a balance; on the one hand, it is an encounter only with what is in some manner understood, and on the other, it is mystery. The resolution of this balance, the desire to produce certitude with respect to absolute understanding, requires exertion in a mysterious world and has often become an effort to abate mystery rather than to achieve definitive understanding. The study of the human condition has long been fascinating to both the natural sciences and the humanities. Both disciplines have produced countless essays on this subject, using a variety of epistemological methods in which mankind's nature has been probed, researched, and catalogued with respect to how human beings process information and how this information shapes our understanding of our own world.

These studies have tended, in recent years, to focus on the scientific method, with emphasis on being able to reproduce experiments and thus prove, in a scientific way, the premise under investigation. Universities have been the repositories of these accumulative efforts, and countless journals have detailed the development of our understanding of both human behavior and human conduct. As a result of these empirical inquiries, it is clear that the world has become one in which technological information on the human condition is readily available and abundant.

Normal science in which human beings are the subject is a puzzle-solving undertaking and consequently is a highly cumulative enterprise, eminently successful in its aim, by which the steady extension of the scope and precision of scientific knowledge regarding behavior is extended. In this process, as each study builds on the previous one, new and unsuspected phenomena are repeatedly uncovered by scientific research, and radical new theories have again and again been invented by scientists to explain the human condition. History even suggests that the scientific enterprise has developed a uniquely powerful technique for producing surprises of this sort. With the invention of the Internet, science has linked together experiments regarding human behavior, and a seamless web of greater and greater scientific knowledge tends to overwhelm other realms of inquiry, such as reason and the pursuit of *a priori* knowledge, or knowledge beyond the senses. This realm of inquiry, a rational or reasoned approach to discover knowledge that is not apprehendable by the senses, is transcendental and is called the process of thought approach. If the epistemological characteristic of science, the object of sense, is to be reconciled with a parallel discipline, the process of thought, then research under each paradigm must be particularly sensitive to the claims of the other. One must not be sacrificed in pursuit of the other.

Members of The Church of Jesus Christ of Latter-day Saints are in a unique position to pursue both paradigms. President David O. McKay taught, "The Church of Jesus Christ of Latter-day Saints makes an appeal to all men to seek the higher life, *intellectual* and *spiritual,* and to incite them to a greater intelligence in striving for the abundant life."[2] As an undergraduate student many years ago, I had the opportunity of attending a debate held at the institute of religion. The topic to be discussed was the relevance of "creationism" as it was positioned against "scientific evolution." As I listened, it seemed as if those devoted to science and those devoted to scripture talked past each other. Each side made assumptions that the other did not accept. The debate clearly was about how we come to know things: the creationists were relying heavily on *a priori* knowledge and the processes of reason and thought, while those devoted to scientific evolution apprehended truth only by the object of sense. The debate was resolved in favor of science because the members of that team "proved," by the use of then extant genetic theory, that a gene pool created by two people was insufficient to produce the entire human species with all its variations. Imagine my surprise when some twenty years later, on the cover of a national magazine, it was announced that science, through DNA research, had concluded that a female individual who lived ten thousand years ago, code-named "Lucy," was the genetic type whose DNA was now contained in all individuals of the human family.

As I read the article, my thoughts reflected back on the debate. I realized that a scientific inquiry into the human condition was indeed a rendezvous with phenomena only partially understood in time and that "facts," which had delved into the mystery of creation clearly deduced by an empiricist epistemology twenty years ago, were only valid for a short period of time and certainly were not absolute.

This event prompted reflection and further review. The Lord has clearly told us in Doctrine and Covenants 9 that His method of coming to know things involves both study and prayer. He states in verses seven and eight:

> Behold, you have not understood; you have supposed that I would give it unto you, when you took no thought save it was to ask me. But, behold, I say unto you, that you must study it out in your mind; then you must ask me if it be right, and if it is right I will cause that your bosom shall burn within you; therefore, you shall feel that it is right.

The above verse has been become platitudinal and is quoted repeatedly to tell us how we come to discover truth in a spiritual sense. The ability to have this "burning in the bosom" has become an indication, even a litmus test, of the magnitude of our own spirituality; the ability to "feel" truth has become a measure not only of our commitment to the gospel of Jesus Christ but also of our standing before the Lord. This verse has caused great confusion and some difficulty with Latter-day Saints who are familiar with both methods of understanding truth, namely, the empirical object-of-sense method and the transcendental method, or the process of rational thought. Many devotees of the empirical method, when hearing of another's conviction based on the "burning in the bosom" phenomenon, may caustically remark, "That sounds like angina to me." Others, who eschew the scientific method as a total repudiation of faith, are taken in a sense of "blind obedience" to such truth without any reflection, and thus disciples of both regimens talk past each other just like the creationists and the evolutionists did decades ago.

In considering these two methods, however, there can be little doubt that *a priori* knowledge, produced by direct revelation, if true, produces a certitude that is beyond question. For example, knowledge produced by direct revelation, such as the knowledge Joseph Smith took with him from the First Vision, becomes absolute for Joseph, who received such direct knowledge. Notwithstanding Joseph's experience, there needs to be a means or methodology whereby those who did not likewise receive such a vision can come to know that such knowledge is true. This can be an epistemology that relies on the use of sense, which in the case of revelation is never completely satisfying; or conversely, and perhaps in connection with using our senses, it can be an epistemology that relies on the process of thought, study, and prayer to come to know if the revelation is true. The Lord stated in Doctrine and Covenants 88:118: "As all have not faith, seek ye diligently and teach one another words of wisdom; . . . seek learning, even by study and also by faith."

And further, in Doctrine and Covenants 46:13–14: "To some it is given by the Holy Ghost to know that Jesus Christ is the Son of God, and that he was crucified for the sins of the world. To others it is given to believe on their words, that they also might have eternal life if they continue faithful."

It is clear that for those who receive direct revelation and declare such to the world, the issue of certitude is resolved; however, for the majority who do not have such direct experiences, even for prophets, the need to find certitude by a means of inquiry that will enable them to apprehend such knowledge as is produced by unique experience still remains. The prerequisite of such a method is an ability to seek certitude by means of acquiring *a priori* knowledge on our own, "even by study and . . . faith," so that we can believe the words of those who have the direct *a priori* experiences that also produce certitude.

Thus the debate, the quest of how to learn truth, is fundamental to Latter-day Saints and is age old. Contrasting views on how to come to know the truth were established by the central epistemological approaches of Plato and Aristotle many years ago. Plato was convinced that absolute knowledge was discovered by transcendental means, by argument, thought, and reason, while Aristotle, the world's consummate biologist until the 1850s and the advent of Charles Darwin, believed that absolute truth was discovered by observation of phenomena, further study to form a hypothesis of truth, testing said hypothesis, and proving the postulate by an experiment that relied on the senses. In this age of scientific discovery, this second method, the method of sense, the one followed by Aristotle, has become the preferred way to prove all things; indeed, it was used by those debaters devoted to evolution to "prove" their point.

However, as time inexorably marched on, in many instances, the point "proved" so long ago was "unproved" as scientific inquiry matured. As methodology expanded the realm of truth available to scientific examination, knowledge fell within the grasp of science that was previously unattainable. So the conclusions drawn so many years ago, in light of new evidence, became hollow and were shown to be contingent. To those who prefer the other method, the method of thought and feeling, it might be tempting to blindly jump to the "burning in the bosom" phenomenon and state, "If those scientists back then had simply prayed about it, with faith, they would know that their conclusions were wrong." This kind of jump is fraught with great danger. It leads those who would advocate such a view to ensnare themselves in a pit of contingent relativism. Those who advocate this jump trap themselves into the belief that the canon of scripture, the process of continuing revelation, has also been closed. How often has the Lord given us further light and knowledge on subjects we thought were forever tenets of our faith? The manifesto of Wilford Woodruff changed our view on plural marriage; the revelation of Spencer W. Kimball that gave the priesthood to all worthy males suggests that revelation, the supreme transcendental method of capturing truth, is conditional as well. Our understanding of the revelations of God develops and matures with further study, prayer, and revelation. It would thus be folly to make such a jump.

A Bridge between Two Approaches

Michael Oakeshott suggests an approach that is beneficial to both realms of inquiry and provides a middle ground, a bridge between the two. Oakeshott examines a familiar analogy from Plato's *Republic*. Plato uses prisoners in a cave to explain an important principle relative to comprehending truth. In his analogy, Plato explains that these prisoners use shadows on the walls of the cave to explain their world, little realizing that the source of light that comes from the entrance to the cave, if explored, will change the reality of the truth examined in shadows.

In his analysis of Plato's "Analogy of the Cave," found in Plato's *Republic*, Oakeshott explains:

> The cave-dwellers, who inhabit a "hollow in the earth," occupy a platform of conditional understanding. They recognize their world in terms of identified and named

occurrences understood as compositions of characteristics. It is, thus far, a world of intelligibles and they move within it confidently. . . . And the more intelligent among them are admired by the rest, and sometimes rewarded with small prizes for the reliable information they have acquired and are able to impart about the connections and correlations of at least some of these occurrences, and for their ability to forecast their appearance upon the scene.

This platform of understanding is, however, a "prison." Its inhabitants are "prisoners,'" not merely because they are wholly ignorant of its conditions but because the level of their understanding excludes even the recognition that it is conditional. In short, in Socrates' phrase, they are "like our- selves," only more so than Plato will allow. Distracted by his exclusive concern with the engagement of theoretical understanding and with the manifest shortcomings of this platform of understanding, the intelligibility of the cave- dwellers world seems to him at once so complete and so minimal. . . . This, I think, is a mistake. It is a conditional understanding of the world, valuable as far as it goes, and indispensable in the engagements of practical life, but not fully in command of itself because it is unaware of its conditionality.[3]

Oakeshott points out that all knowledge, in any larger sense, arrived at by any epistemological method brings us to a platform of understanding that is wholly conditional. Time is needed to "sea- son" knowledge on its "platform of understanding" and bring it into context with other knowledge contingent to it. As time passes, events will lead us to a greater awareness of the fact that the knowl- edge on our "platform" remains conditional; or time moves our knowledge closer to a contingent, unconditional state that is either refuted by additional new knowledge or, through experience (transcendental or empirical), moved closer to certitude. Such is the nature of the "prison" of conditionality, and so it is with all knowledge arrived at by both methods. The cave-dwellers were able to measure their world and apprehend truth by their senses. They were also able to reason from a position beyond their senses and draw conclusions about their environment based upon the experience of their senses, as well as upon their ability to think and reason. What they did not realize was that their entire knowledge of their world, whether derived from either the method sense or of thought, was completely conditional, dependent upon their existence in the cave.

My experience with the evolutionary debate dealt with the scientific method, an object of sense, and was resolved by scientific evidence that, at the time, was not refutable. However, as time passed, it became clear that the debate was indeed not "resolved" in any absolute sense. It was the "best synthesis" available at the time, but over time, it was clearly shown to be a conditional synthesis. The scientists were confident then that this answer, if not the entire solution, would be part of the foundation for further research; they certainly did not expect that research to refute their claim. It was considered "the answer," a conclusion drawn as a result of the object of sense. However, at the time, as Oakeshott pointed out, all of us were unaware of its conditionality. Likewise, with the process of thought and with matters informed by revelation and *a priori* knowledge, it is evident there is a conditional component.

At the end of the nineteenth century, Wilford Woodruff announced the end of plural marriage. Before, it was considered an absolute tenet of our faith. Celestial marriage was interpreted to mean plural marriage even though a minority of members lived the new and everlasting covenant of plural marriage. Those that entered into the practice of plural marriage have given abundant testimonies of its divine sanction; similarly, there are testimonies of many pioneer women whose hearts were broken by its observance. President George Q. Cannon observed the following concerning the practice of plural marriage in the 1890s:

> I know (I speak it almost with a feeling of shame) that there have been serious abuses of that doctrine [plural marriage]. I believe that both men and women have been guilty of many things that are offensive in the sight of God. I have said that if there were no other reason than this, it would be sufficient, to my mind, for the Lord inspiring His servant to give that manifesto. But there were other reasons for this, and as a people we should be prepared by the assistance and testimony of the Spirit of God that the manifesto should be given.[4]

President Cannon, a practitioner of plural marriage, knew that circumstances had changed and that the introduction of plural marriage in the 1840s by the Prophet, later interpreted by Brigham Young and John Taylor, had brought the Church to a crossroads. The Lord revealed to President Woodruff the consequences to the Church of the continuing practice of plural marriage and he acted upon that further light and knowledge. In our zeal to defend plural marriage, the membership of the Church had overlooked the Book of Mormon's counsel regarding this practice. Upon careful examination of Jacob 2:24, 27–28, 30, we see that the Lord himself explained that plural marriage was a conditional commandment. Jacob explains:

> Behold, David and Solomon truly had many wives and concubines, which thing was abominable before me, saith the Lord. . . . Wherefore, my brethren, hear me, and hearken to the word of the Lord: For there shall not any

man among you have save it be one wife; and concubines he shall have none; for I, the Lord God, delight in the chastity of women. And whoredoms are an abomination before me; thus saith the Lord of Hosts. . . . For if I will, saith the Lord of Hosts, raise up seed unto me, I will command my people; otherwise they shall hearken unto these things.

The Lord shows us that the rule of heaven with respect to the plurality of wives, at the time of Jacob and indeed at the time of the Prophet Joseph Smith, was one man and one wife. However, He further explained that if He desired to raise up seed unto Himself, He would command otherwise. The Lord did command Joseph to introduce plural marriage, and then He commanded Wilford to pull it back. Both men were great prophets and both had followed the practice outlined in Doctrine and Covenants 9 and 46. Both had followed the Lord's admonition to "study it out in their minds" and then put the matter to the Lord. Both prophets had received the "correct answer" as a product of the process of thought. They had received *a priori* knowledge from the Lord that was both times conditional. The historical record shows that plural marriage is indeed conditional. The Lord sanctioned the plural wives of Abraham and Israel, as well as those of Moses and Job. These prophets were conspicuously omitted from Jacob's condemnation of plural marriage. Yet they belong to the times when the Lord explicitly commanded His people to "raise up seed" to himself.

There are those yet today who regard plural marriage as an essential gospel tenet, one that might once again be reintroduced. The conditional nature of plural marriage and its status as an eternal doctrine of the Church were clearly established by James E. Talmage shortly after President Woodruff's manifesto. In the 1901 October general conference of the Church, Elder Talmage

explained that plural marriage was never a vital tenet of salvation.
He stated:

> The Latter-day Saints were long regarded as a polyga-
> mous people. That plural marriage has been practiced by a
> limited proportion of the people, under sanction of Church
> ordinance, has never since the introduction of the system
> been denied. But, that plural marriage is a vital tenet of The
> Church is not true. What the Latter-day Saints call celestial
> marriage is characteristic of the Church, and is in very gen-
> eral practice; but of celestial marriage, plurality of wives
> was an incident, never an essential. Yet the two have never
> been segregated in the popular mind. . . . As the Church had
> adopted the practice under what was believed to be divine
> approval, they suspended it when they were justified in so
> doing.[5]

Elder Bruce R. McConkie put it even more succinctly when he
wrote, "Plural marriage is not essential to salvation or exaltation."[6]

In an interesting footnote, President Gordon B. Hinckley supported Elder Talmage and further showed the conditionality of plural marriage when he answered a question regarding its exercise in
the Church. He referred to plural marriage as a practice of the
nineteenth century when asked about it during his first interview
with Larry King, an interview that aired on national television on
CNN, September 8, 1998. He did not call plural marriage a doctrine, which would imply its immutability. This reference caused
some consternation among the members of the Church and
prompted many to write to President Hinckley concerning his
remarks. During the subsequent semiannual conference of the
Church, in October 1998, at general priesthood meeting, President
Hinckley told the brethren he had received many letters about his

comments and informed us that he knew the doctrine of the Church and his comments were not in conflict with that doctrine.[7]

As it has been illustrated, both methods of inquiry—the object of sense and the process of thought—initially produce conditional results. In light of these observations, a question naturally arises concerning each method. Does each of these methods provide a degree of certitude with respect to the knowledge acquired by each method? Our society has answered this question in the affirmative for those who use solely the object of sense to acquire truth. The empiricist apprehends knowledge through experience by creating repeatable and verifiable tests, which thereby produce conclusions upon which we can, apparently with a great degree of certainty, rely. Books of science are filled with experiments that have produced the laws of science and that have been verified through measurement, observation, and through our other senses. In the modern world, as has already been noted, this method of exploration has become the preferred method, almost to the exclusion of the other. Truth obtained through the object of sense is proclaimed with certitude to be absolute, even though it has been established that this claim is always, in the beginning, conditional.

On the other hand, those who come to know things by the process of thought, while not rejecting truth comprehended by the object of sense, discover *a priori* knowledge that is deduced by discussion and reason. Our modern world is filled with the alleged certitude of science, and there seems to be little room and certainly less appreciation for those who come to know truth by the process of thought. Yet there is a considerable amount of truth that science has perceived through the process of thought that has no empirical basis. This is best illustrated by a question Albert Einstein answered in a press conference held shortly before his death in 1955. He was asked how he had "discovered" the theory of relativity. Science would have expected Dr. Einstein to have illuminated

206 / William Hayes Pingree

several previously tested theories as a basis for his new theory. Science would have expected this new theory to have risen out of experiments previously conducted. Dr. Einstein simply stated, "It came to me as I boarded a bus in Zurich in 1905."[8] It is clear that the direction of Einstein's research was "revealed" to him from an *a priori* source. He did not question this enlightenment, nor did he reject it on the grounds that he could not prove its origin as an object of sense; on the contrary, he accepted it and used it as the basis to complete his theory of relativity. This theory moved physics in an opposite direction to the well-known and well-tested Newtonian laws of physics still used today. What, then, are the boundaries of each domain, and how do they enhance and complement each other?

An answer to this question is given by David Hume:

> Nothing is more usual than for writers, even on moral, political, or physical subjects, to distinguish between reason and experience, and to suppose, that these species of argumentation are entirely different from one another. The former are taken for the mere result of our intellectual faculties, which, by considering *a priori* the nature of things, and examining the effects, that must follow from their operation, establishing particular principles of science and philosophy. The latter are supposed to be derived entirely from sense and observation, by which we learn what has actually resulted from the operation of particular objects, and are thence able to infer, what will, for the future result from them. . . . The same distinction between reason and experience is maintained in all our deliberations concerning the conduct of life. . . . Though it be allowed, that reason may form very plausible conjectures with regard to the consequences of such a particular conduct, it is still, supposed

to be imperfect, without the assistance of experience, which is alone able to give stability and certainty to the maxims derived from study and reflection.[9]

Hume strikes a balance between *a priori* knowledge, ascertained through the process of thought, and knowledge that is discovered as an object of science. He explains that information obtained by both methods needs to be subjected to the test of experience, which alone will give such knowledge permanence and certitude.

However, with respect to science and empirical analysis, Hume reasons that there are specific bounds to truth obtained as an object of sense. He argues as follows:

> It follows then, that all reasonings concerning cause and effect are founded on experience, and supposition that the course of nature will continue uniformly the same. We conclude that like causes, in like circumstances, will always produce like effects. It may now be worthwhile to consider what determines us to form a conclusion of such infinite consequence. It is evident that Adam, with all his science, would never have been able to demonstrate that the course of nature must continue uniformly the same, and that the future must be conformable to the past. . . . All probable arguments are built on the supposition that there is conformity betwixt the future and the past, and if it must be proved, will admit of no proof but from experience. But our experience in the past can be a proof of nothing for the future, but upon supposition that there is a resemblance betwixt them.[10]

Hume's resolution concerning the experience of science shows that continued experiments conducted by the scientific method verify those conducted in the past. These verifications confirm the data so gathered, and the conclusions thus presumed seem to confer an absolute quality to the knowledge thus deduced. Hume warns us that in fact knowledge arrived at in such a manner, and repeatedly tested, really only confirms a greater and greater *probability* of truth and not a certitude regarding either the causes of such observations nor the reason for such. Hence, Hume confirms Oakeshott's view that all truth, especially scientific truth (particularly in the discovery stage), is conditional. Science does not confer certitude in any absolute sense, but only a greater and greater probability that the truth so arrived at is unconditional. In fact, with greater repetition of experiments, certitude is assumed but never proven.

Truth that is confirmed by the object-of-sense method is restricted by this method of inquiry largely due to its own methodology. In order to provide a value-free verity, this method removes all normative elements from its analysis. Normative elements are the biases and values of the tester. Truth so discovered—by the very method of object of sense—is not prejudiced by preconceived ideas about what the results ought to be. While this approach provides the truth-seeker with a great service, it also constricts the field of experience so that some truth inevitably escapes its examination. The value-free analysis thus blocks an avenue to certitude and confirms Oakeshott's original premise that any knowledge arrived at by any method of inquiry produces a "prison," a platform of understanding that has produced conditional knowledge. In truth, the scientific method is designed not only to remove values, but also to avoid the fooling of the senses, which would lead to unwarranted conclusions. Even with the efforts of the scientific method of investigating truth, René Descartes shows that this can be dangerous. Descartes was a great proponent not only of mathematics and scientific investigation but also of rationalist thought, which underscores the likelihood that senses can be deceived. In his "Sixth Meditation" on philosophy, Descartes states:

> Later on, however, I had many experiences which grad-
> ually undermined all the faith I had in the senses.
> Sometimes towers which had looked round from a distance
> appeared square from close up; and enormous statues
> standing on their pediments did not seem large when
> observed from the ground. In these and countless other
> such cases, I found that the judgements of the external
> senses were mistaken. And this applied not just to the exter-
> nal senses but to the internal senses as well. For what can be
> more internal than pain? And yet, I had heard that those
> who had had a leg or an arm amputated sometimes still
> seemed to feel pain intermittently in the missing part of
> the body.
> [A] reason for doubt was that since I did not yet know
> the author of my being (or at least was pretending not to), I
> saw nothing to rule out the possibility that my natural con-
> stitution made me prone to error even in matters which
> seemed to me most true. . . . But now, when I am beginning
> to achieve a better knowledge of myself and the author of
> my being . . . everything I seem to have acquired from the
> senses . . . should be called into doubt.[11]

The scientific method, as an expression of the object of sense, produces a prison of conditional knowledge, which prison sets a boundary that is not overcome in any systematic way by the object-of-sense method. Descartes even raises the possibility that knowl-edge discovered as an object of sense can be shown to be an illusion, a fooling of the senses into a condition of a false certitude that is later, upon future inquiry, refuted. The use of the senses as the only epistemological method dooms truth so obtained to be placed in a realm where the boundaries and limitations of such knowledge cannot be overcome. This is indeed what happened to me in the evolutionary debate discussed earlier in this essay. In fact, the conditionality of such conclusions is only confirmed by their inability to transcend the methodology used to produce knowledge. Therefore, the scope of truth found through the value-free scientific approach is relegated to establishing only a greater and greater *probability* of absolute truth, which probability is racked with doubt and with the possibility that the senses can be deceived. As such, the object-of-sense method never achieves the promise of certitude so touted by its advocates.

This doubt, this lack of being able to overcome the conditionality of knowledge established by the Oakeshottian prison of conditionality, presents a challenge to truth apprehended by the process of thought as well. Knowledge captured by the object-of-sense method has clearly been shown to be conditional, and the bounds of that conditionality, due to the methodology inherent in the scientific method, are not overcome. Does knowledge produced by the process of thought, the transcendental method, also suffer from a similar methodology, one that does not allow the boundary or prison of conditionality to be overcome? The answer to this question is that it does not. It has been clearly shown that the scientific method is extremely useful and necessary in discovering truth. It suffers from a methodological limitation, however. In removing the biases and prejudices of the testor, the scope and vision of this method surrenders certitude to the methodology. Truth-seekers gain greater and greater probabilities, but in the name of avoiding the duping of the senses, the truth-seeker is permanently disabled in the quest to discover absolute truth. Scientific examination, in order to remove values and clarify any possible duping of the senses, surrenders certitude to skepticism and leaves the truth-seeker permanently disabled in the quest to discover absolute truth. As the Apostle Paul said of those who exclusively use the object-of-sense method, they are "ever learning, and never able to come to the knowledge of the truth" (2 Timothy 3:7). The pursuit of truth by the process-of-thought method seeks to overcome this difficulty.

Truth As the Subject

There must be another way to comprehend absolute truth, a new method of inquiry that will provide an escape from the Oakeshottian prison of conditionality. As new ontological views have been forthcoming in the twentieth century, even such modern existential thinkers as Soren Kierkegaard realize that new epistemological approaches must either be revived or created in the search to produce certitude. Kierkegaard, in his Christian existential approach, requires a "leap of faith" to transcend the prison walls imposed by the methodology of science. For Kierkegaard, this leap is not rational; in fact, he calls it absurd, for in science, truth is always an *object* of effort, never the *subject*. He explains his "leap of faith" in the following manner:

> The subjective reflection turns its attention inwardly to the subject and desires in this intensification of inwardness to realize the truth. And it proceeds in such fashion that, just as in the preceding objective reflection, when the objectivity had come into being, the subjectivity had vanished, so here the subjectivity of the subject becomes the final stage, and objectivity a vanishing factor. Not for a single moment is it forgotten that the subject is an existing individual, and that existence is a process of [that individual] and therefore the notion of the truth as identity of thought and being is a chimera of abstraction. . . .

If an existing individual were really able to transcend himself, the truth would be for him something final and complete, but where is the point at which he is outside himself?[12]

Hume offers insight to Kierkegaard's question. For Hume, it became very clear that the scientific epistemological approach, or the approach to truth apprehended as an object of sense, is just that, an object. This condition is a universal one, especially given the fact that the senses can be deceived. The truth so perceived must be one that is discovered through or confirmed by the senses and accordingly must be objective. There are many great thinkers who objectify truth. But Kierkegaard points to a new path, one where truth is obtained as the subject and not the object. Philosophers of the Enlightenment such as Locke, Kant, and John Stuart Mill drew heavily on reason to dispel the mystery and superstition rampant in the Middle Ages. In so doing, however, limits on other methods of exploration that long produced *a priori* truth were ignored. Hence, it is not possible to transcend oneself by the object-of-sense method, as Kierkegaard asks. There needs to be another path of inquiry that enables this to happen.

With the process of thought, truth can be grasped not only objectively, but also subjectively, transcendentally, and indeed personally in ways that escape the boundaries placed by scientific inquiry. Kierkegaard's "leap of faith" permits the breaching of the prison walls of objective conditionality and allows the other domains of truth to be explored. The method of the process of thought does not return the truth-seeker to a conundrum of myth but allows for truth that can be *a priori*. Max Weber, a father of sociology, explains that the use of the processes of thought leads the truth-seeker to a greater and greater level of understanding ("verstehen") that is clearly not medievalism.[13] Weber allows us to build on Oakeshott's analogy of the platforms of understanding and the conditionality of knowledge and shows that the process of thought can actually transcend the prison boundaries established by the platforms of understanding. The process of thought, in contrast to the methodology produced by the repeated testing of science, which only confirms the probability that the senses may not have been deceived, leads to a path of transcendental escape from the Oakeshottian prison. This path is highlighted by Supreme Court Justice Potter Stewart's understanding of pornography when he said, "I shall not attempt further to define the kinds of material [pornography]. . . . And perhaps I could never succeed in intelligibly doing so. But, I know it when I see it."[14]

The process of thought allows for an equally valid method of inquiry that further defines us as human beings. Such a method allows us to transcend the world of determinism and recognizes the fact that humans can find truth apart from discovery as an object of science and sense grasped only by empirical analysis. Charles Taylor clarifies Weber's concept of understanding ("verstehen") and strengthens the Weberian insight into the additional superstructure that is built on Michael Oakeshott's foundational bridge between the two realms of inquiry. Taylor shows that this superstructure also provides the truth-seeker a ladder over the prison walls of conditionality established by science when he also revisits Plato's "Analogy of the Cave, as a prelude to his analysis:

> In terms set out above, Plato offers us a view of moral sources. He tells us where we can go to accede to a higher moral state. And we might say that the site he shows us is the domain of thought. . . . What we gain through thought or reason is self-mastery. The good man is "master of himself." Plato sees the absurdity of this expression unless one adds to it a distinction between higher and lower parts of

the soul. To be master of oneself is to have the higher part of the soul rule over the lower, which means reason over the desires.

And so, we become good when reason comes to rule, and we are no longer run by our desires. But the shift in hegemony is not just a matter of one's set of goals taking over the priority from another. When reason rules, a quite different kind of order reigns in the soul. Indeed, we can say that order reigns there for the first time. By contrast, the realm of desire is that of chaos.[15]

Taylor explains that reason has allowed humankind to accede to the higher moral state of self-mastery, which leads the truth-seeker to a new domain, the domain of thought. Descartes began to point in this direction when he noted, in his second reason for doubt in truth obtained through the senses, that he needed a better knowledge of himself and the author of his being if he hoped to be able to come to certitude. This knowledge of self is indeed a key element in our ability to find certitude. Socrates said, "The unexamined life is not worth living."[16] It is the knowledge of self that permits a hierarchical ordering of knowledge, or an establishment of the fact that all truth is not of equal value. The hierarchical ordering of knowledge organizes it in such a way that permits knowledge to be valued; such information can then produce the understanding discussed by Weber. Taylor uses this discovery of the ordering of the soul into a higher moral state of self-mastery to escape the boundaries of conditionality, which binds inquiry by the object of sense to the conditionality of being only an object.

He then makes the following observation regarding Plato's "Analogy of the Cave":

And Plato does turn to an image of this kind at the culmination of his great allegory of the Cave. Some people think, he says, that education is a matter of putting true knowledge into a soul that does not have it. The model here would be the virtues and capacities of the body, which Plato agrees should be seen as things we acquire by habit and practice. We incorporate them in us, as it were, and put them where they didn't exist before. But specific virtue of thought doesn't come to be in this way. Rather we should see ourselves as having something like a capacity of vision which is forever unimpaired, and the move from illusion to wisdom is to be likened to our turning the soul's eye around to face in the right direction. Some people, the lovers of sights and sounds and beautiful spectacles, are focused entirely on the bodily and the changing. Making those people wise is a matter of turning the soul's gaze from the darkness to the brightness of true being. But just as swiveling the whole body can only turn the physical eye, so the whole soul must be turned to attain wisdom.[17]

Truth can thus be apprehended as a subject as well as an object, because there is now a capacity for vision that can move beyond an illusion—that the only reality is the one confined and measured within the cave—to a wisdom that transcends the probability produced by measuring shadows. It is accomplished by facing the source of light, and thus the gaze of the soul is changed from looking within the confined prison boundary of the objective search for truth to the brilliance of light that comes from a source that lies beyond experience. The soul, the self, becomes the vehicle of transmission of this light, and thereby this kind of truth no longer is objectified but becomes the subject in which this *a priori* truth is contained. Einstein's experience of having his theory of relativity "come to him" as he boarded that bus in Zurich so long ago attests to the fact that he himself was able to transcend the boundaries of Newtonian physics and become the subject capable of both receiving and transmitting the light of truth, which light was appre-hended by a source outside the grasp of the senses. No one would call Einstein a mystic. He used both methods, the object-of-sense and the process-of-thought methods, to discover truth. He had replicated numerous experiments and was satisfied that the truth so discovered, which was the object of these experiments, displayed a greater and greater probability of certitude with respect to Newtonian physics. However, within himself, he felt that there was yet an undetected direction that would further explain phenomena not yet grasped by these experiments. He needed to place himself in a position to receive truth by becoming the subject, the vehicle itself that would both receive and transmit this *a priori* truth not yet discovered precisely because it lay outside the prison boundaries of the Oakeshottian walls.

The prerequisite conditions to being able to become the subject—the vanishing objectivity that Kierkegaard suggests, the vehicle for both receiving and conducting this truth—involve order-ing the soul. Both Plato and Taylor suggest that chaos, which seems to be present at first in the process-of-thought approach, is over-come by ordering the soul and attuning it to the "higher part." This ordering conditions the individual and allows the self the strength to transcend the Oakeshottian walls of conditionality. Taylor's con-tribution is to acknowledge Oakeshott's prison of conditionality and to suggest a way by which this conditionality can be overcome. By becoming the subject of truth and not only the object, the truth-seeker finally finds certitude with respect to truth within his reach and his grasp.

"I Am the Truth"

As Latter-day Saints, we see clearly in Christ the example of how to become the subject of truth. The central mission of Jesus

Christ and His atonement become the core doctrine by which all absolute truth is measured. The Lord realized this when he told his disciples:

> Then said Jesus to those Jews which believed on him, If ye continue in my word, then are ye my disciples indeed; and ye shall know the truth, and the truth shall make you free. . . . If the Son therefore shall make you free, ye shall be free indeed (John 8:31–32, 36).

Later, He explained that He was the subject and He was the truth. He said, "I am the way, the truth, and the life" (John 14:6). The Lord has pushed away the objective query of discovery, "Is it the truth?" and replaced it with the subjective declaration, "I am the truth." By so doing, He has become the primary subject of *a priori* truth and, as such, has transcended the bounds of the Oakeshottian prison of conditionality—and He likewise invites us also to transcend those boundaries. As part of His example, He has told truth-seekers that it is not possible for them to do this on their own. As it has been shown, when truth is pursued as an object, all truth is then conditional, even transcendental truth. But the Savior, by making Himself the subject, has given humankind a great key to certitude: He is the truth. Elder Neal A. Maxwell taught the importance of recognizing this key when he explained:

> So many other people openly hunger, soulfully and deeply, for an understanding of how things really are and really will be, for purposes that outlast the moment. They are kept from the truth only because they "know not where to find it" (see Doctrine and Covenants 123:12). This search for meaning is the search for an explanation of self and of life, and for the underlying purposes of the universe. This deep craving for truth is expressed in many ways by

many mortals, often directly, other times indirectly; sometimes foolishly, other times wisely. Blessed are those who
have found *the* truth and have, thereby, been made free,
and who have learned that there is both eternal and personal purpose![18]

This point was earlier made when Jesus, as Jehovah, spoke to
Moses at the burning bush:

And Moses said unto God, Behold, when I come unto
the children of Israel, and shall say unto them, The God of
your fathers hath sent me unto you; and they shall say to
me, What is his name? what shall I say unto them? And
God said unto Moses, I AM THAT I AM: and he said, Thus
shall thou say unto the children of Israel, I AM hath sent me
unto you (Exodus 3:13–14).

The great I AM is indeed the subject in the truth-seeker's search
for certitude and, as such, He sets him or her free from the prison
walls of conditionality: "Ye shall know the truth, and the truth shall
make you free" (John 8:32). Kierkegaard's question regarding
when one transcends oneself is answered as the moment
approaches when the truth-seeker realizes the overwhelming presence of "The Truth," the transcendental fact that Jesus is both the
subject and the transmitter of *a priori* truth. It is He and only He
that can produce certitude. The search for truth now has a powerful partner that empowers the truth-seeker both to use objective
inquiries to satisfy the desire for consistency and value-free knowledge and to transcend oneself in an abrupt discovery of *a priori*
truth. At the same time, this partnership frees individuals from the
prison walls of conditionality. By His confronting presence, complete with values and vision of a perfect being, the Savior not only
declares Himself to be the truth, but He invites us to become like

Him. In 3 Nephi the Lord challenged us to receive absolute truth as we receive Him:

> And know ye that ye shall be judges of this people, according to the judgment which I shall give unto you, which shall be just. Therefore, what manner of men ought ye to be? Verily I say unto you, even as I am [or importantly, as I AM]. And now I go unto the Father. And verily I say unto you, whatsoever things ye shall ask the Father in my name shall be given unto you. Therefore, ask, and ye shall receive; knock, and it shall be opened unto you; for he that asketh, receiveth; and unto him that knocketh, it shall be opened (3 Nephi 27:27–29).

This means that His values and His views are hierarchically more important than our views and values. As He is embraced, and as men and women knock on the door of the Father, in His name, absolute truth will be given to them. The requirements of Taylor to order the soul to "higher morals" are a precondition to receive this truth. The skepticism of Descartes, which caused him to conclude that enlightened truth, truth that would not deceive his senses, would perhaps be discovered if he could but "know himself and the author of his being" a little better, is resolved by encountering Jesus. The process-of-thought method has led the truth-seeker from the value-free exercise so merited by science—which rids the truth-seeker of imposed agendas and values—to the companion path of confronting the Lord. By so doing, they transcend their thoughts and frequent prejudices and replace them with His values and vision. They are indeed set free by this encounter. Truly the Lord declared through Isaiah, "For my thoughts are not your thoughts, neither are your ways my ways, saith the Lord" (Isaiah 55:8).

The impact of this cognizance cannot be overstated. Again, Elder Neal A. Maxwell emphasized the relevance of this realization:

Jesus taught us that life consists not in the abundance of the things we possess, but in how rich we are "toward God." (Luke 12:15 and 21). Keeping the commandments is vital in our progress toward God—and so is working on each thing that is lacking—as in the case of the good, rich, and noble young man who inquired of Jesus. (See Matthew 19:21.) We too may shrink from such confronting moments, but they will come, and what we lack will be made plainly and painfully clear. We will not be able to say we were not shown and reminded repeatedly. Therefore, as we search the scriptures, our focus should be upon that which will tell us what we must do (to become as He is) and upon that which will stir us so to do. And the very word "search" means from the beginning to the latest unfolding of Holy Writ.[19]

In their own search for truth, Latter-day Saints can now realize the primary reason the Lord wants us to be obedient to His commandments. It is so that we may encounter Him. The Calvinistic quest for rewards so often offered as reasons for obedience is supplanted by the desire to transcend the prison walls of conditional knowledge to the supernal unconditional platform of knowledge produced by the reality of our Savior and His "infinite and eternal" certitude (see Alma 34:10). This discovery—that the Savior is the subject and the source of certitude—is transcendental, *a priori* knowledge acquired by the process of thought. A methodology now must be implemented which will lead the truth-seeker to find certitude in Christ, since all who seek this truth do not receive it by direct revelation from Him. While it is true that such confrontation does not usually come by penetrating the veil and entering into His presence—an event the truth-seeker hopes one day to achieve—such confrontation does produce the realization that for now, he or she must find the transcendental methodology, the process of thought and prayer that will satisfy Taylor's condition of building a ladder to escape the Oakeshottian prison walls of conditionality. By so doing, this absolute truth (attained by the process of thought) can be accessed. Taylor suggested that "order must reign in the soul" as a precondition to constructing the ladder of escape, which order and focus come by encountering the reality of Jesus, but other building materials must also be found to complete the process.

In confronting Christ and His values and vision, the transcendental methodology of ladder building suggests that instead of being invited into His presence, the truth-seeker is invited instead to take his yoke. In Matthew the Lord says:

> Come unto me, all ye that labour and are heavy laden, and I will give you rest. Take my yoke upon you, and learn of me; for I am meek and lowly in heart: and ye shall find rest unto your souls. For my yoke is easy, and my burden is light (Matthew 11:28–30).

By taking the yoke of our Lord, other building materials of the ladder of transcendence appear before us. Along with the yoke, we receive the admonition to "learn of me" because He is meek and lowly. The primary material by which the ladder is fashioned, then, is a meek and lowly heart. To learn from the Lord, to be able to access this *a priori* source of absolute knowledge, requires as the first and most fundamental principle a broken heart and a contrite spirit. This is the first and most important of the building materials. Nephi said succinctly,

> Behold, he offereth himself a sacrifice for sin, to answer the ends of the law, unto all those who have a broken heart

and a contrite spirit; and unto none else can the ends of the law be answered (2 Nephi 2:7).

The necessity of a broken heart and a contrite spirit in order for the soul to transcend itself, as Taylor and Kierkegaard require, is often overlooked. In the truth-seeker's zeal for knowledge, this important requirement is pushed aside in favor of "checklists of obedience," "self-centered service," and "self-righteousness," all undertaken so as to validate our meritorious request for the Savior to recognize our righteousness and thus qualify us to receive absolute truth; however, these are only recipes for failure in the quest for certitude. For the ladder to be successful, it must be fashioned with a broken heart and a contrite spirit. King David realized this when he exclaimed to the Lord,

> For thou desirest not sacrifice; else would I give it: thou delightest not in burnt offering. The sacrifices of God are a broken spirit: a broken and a contrite heart, O God, thou wilt not despise. . . . Then shalt thou be pleased with the sacrifices of righteousness, with burnt offering and whole burnt offering: then shall they offer bullocks upon thine altar (Psalm 51:16–17, 19).

The truth-seeker must have a broken heart and a contrite spirit so that "order might [must] reign in the soul." Thus, the ladder of escape from the Oakeshottian prison of conditionality is first fashioned by developing a broken heart and a contrite spirit. The broken heart and contrite spirit are fundamental attributes, and when possessed by the truth-seeker, these attributes invite the Lord to respond with the gift of faith. We are often taught that faith comes by obedience; but, more specifically, faith is enhanced by obedience.[20]

Truly faith comes to us as a gift (see 1 Corinthians 12:9). Paul taught clearly that as we embrace Christ, our lives become inter-woven with Him and with His values and vision. In Galatians 2:20, Paul explains this relationship:

> I am crucified with Christ: nevertheless I live; yet not I, but Christ liveth in me: and the life which I now live in the flesh I live by the faith of the Son of God, who loved me, and gave himself for me.

It is out of this relationship, forged from a broken heart and a contrite spirit, that our souls accept His reordering of values, and thereby we are able to receive the gift of faith. Unless our souls are ordered by having Christ live in us, the gift of faith cannot be real-ized. However, once the truth-seeker has obtained the gift of faith, he or she has now moved into the position of transcendence from the Oakeshottian prison of conditionality. With this in mind, the ladder begun by a broken heart and a contrite spirit is fashioned next by faith, which faith provides the truth-seeker the ability to, in the words of Charles Taylor, "turn the soul's gaze from the darkness to the brightness of true being. . . . Just as the physical eye can only be turned by swiveling the whole body, so the whole soul must be turned to attain wisdom."[21] Thus, the soul has now turned from seeking objects to pursuing subjects. Paul shared the same prin-ciple when he taught that once we find Christ, "we walk by faith, not by sight" (2 Corinthians 5:7). Faith thus becomes the second attribute that allows the truth-seeker to escape the walls of conditionality.

With faith, certitude is within our grasp. Alma taught that faith was the final prerequisite to certitude produced by the process-of-thought method. Once the truth-seeker becomes confident in walking by faith, he or she is now ready to discover truth that is not fooled by the senses, neither is it an object of sense. It comes from the ultimate source of truth, the Savior Himself. Alma gives the truth-seeker this ultimate key to certitude:

> And now, behold, are ye sure that this is a good seed? I say unto you, Yea; for every seed bringeth forth unto its own likeness. Therefore, if a seed groweth it is good, but if it groweth not, behold it is not good, therefore, it is cast away. And now, behold, because ye have tried the experiment, and planted the seed, and it swelleth and sprouteth, and beginneth to grow, ye must needs know that the seed is good. And now, behold, is your knowledge perfect? Yea, your knowledge is perfect in that thing, and your faith is dormant; and this because you know, for ye know that the word hath swelled your souls, . . . that your understanding doth begin to be enlightened, and your mind doth begin to expand (Alma 32:31–34).

These verses inform the truth-seeker that laying a foundation of faith is an essential step on the path to certitude. Notice that it is faith that has produced "perfect" knowledge. Once that knowledge is obtained, faith becomes dormant. It is also important to note that faith does not go away, but instead forms the final foundation to transcendental truth and is the final building block to the super-structure of the bridge that transcends the Oakeshottian prison of conditionality. Should faith be removed, the superstructure of absolute knowledge will also collapse and leave the truth-seeker void of certitude, in an antecedent state of *a priori* conditionality.

Oliver Cowdery discovered this truth early in his experience with the Lord. Through the Prophet Joseph Smith, the Lord said to Oliver:

> Verily, verily, I say unto thee, blessed art thou for what thou hast done; for thou hast inquired of me, and behold,

as often as thou hast inquired thou hast received instruction of my Spirit. If it had not been so, thou wouldst not have come to the place where thou art at this time. Behold, thou knowest that thou hast inquired of me and I did enlighten thy mind; and now I tell thee these things that thou mayest know that thou hast been enlightened by the Spirit of truth (D&C 6:14–15).

Oliver was not able to recognize the fact that the Lord spoke truth to him *every* time he inquired because the nature of his faith was insufficiently strong to bear the weight of that truth. Oliver's soul wasn't yet ordered by an interwoven relationship with the Lord, and therefore he could not receive the type of faith necessary to bear the weight of absolute truth. Oliver never learned completely to confront the Lord in the manner discussed above and by not doing so, he was led into the abyss of doubt. It was not until the end of his life that he was able to transcend these walls. After Joseph Smith's martyrdom, Oliver "came to himself,"[22] and with the right kind of faith returned home to the outstretched arms of a forgiving Church. Even though Oliver had many experiences that caused him to pierce the veil, to see heavenly messengers, and to receive ordinances from on high, Oliver's faith was never sufficient to bear the weight of these experiences and, as his faith crumbled, so did the perfect knowledge promised by Alma also collapse. He could never finish the ladder necessary to transcend the Oakeshottian prison wall of conditionality. As time passed, the certitude Oliver obtained turned to doubt and questioning. It took Oliver Cowdery a lifetime to develop the right faith by which the transcendental ladder could be built, which would lead him beyond the prison walls of conditional truth.

The Book of Mormon points the truth-seeker, again in the words of Paul, to "a more excellent way" (1 Corinthians 12:31).

With respect to developing the kind of faith that will exceed the bounds of conditionality and lead to certitude, the experience of the brother of Jared provides an infallible illustration of how this is done. This example is particularly appropriate in a world that has ignored the value of *a priori* truth. The brother of Jared is a particularly tender example because he seems to be like us today in that he had little time for meditation and thought. He was abruptly brought from the object-of-sense method of discovering truth when the Lord rebuked him for not calling upon His name. In Ether 2:14–15 we read:

> And it came to pass at the end of four years that the Lord came again unto the brother of Jared, and stood in a cloud and talked with him. And for the space of three hours did the Lord talk with the brother of Jared, and chastened him because he remembered not to call upon the name of the Lord. And the brother of Jared repented of the evil which he had done, and did call upon the name of the Lord for his brethren who were with him. And the Lord said unto him: I will forgive thee and thy brethren of their sins; but thou shalt not sin any more, for ye shall remember that my Spirit will not always strive with man.

It seems that perhaps the brother of Jared was praying, but not "call[ing] upon the name of the Lord," which means he was not making the Lord the subject of his faith. The Lord was the object of his prayer, but the brother of Jared was not confronting the Lord as The Truth and, as such, the source of certitude. The brother of Jared was seeking solutions to the problems of the Jaredites much as we do today: seeking knowledge by measurement, by skill, and by wit. All of these are tools of the object-of-sense method. He had, like Oliver Cowdery, neglected to call upon the Lord in such a manner that the Lord could get through to him. The brother of Jared repented of his sin, and turned his soul's gaze, as Taylor suggested, from darkness to light by developing the kind of faith recommended by Alma. So successful was he that in the next chapter of Ether, we read of a consummate transcendental experience, produced by the right kind of faith—one of the greatest ever to be recorded in scripture. After repenting and reordering his soul, in the third chapter of Ether, the brother of Jared was able to put Alma's guide to the truth-seeker to the ultimate test. As Alma required, faith was to be the foundation to receive perfect knowledge; the right kind of faith would produce certitude; the right kind of faith is the attribute most required to transcend the Oakeshottian prison walls of conditionality. The brother of Jared was able, due to his newfound faith, to pierce the veil and obtain that perfect knowledge of which Alma spoke.

It is clear that the faith of the brother of Jared moved from object to subject. It is that faith, formed by experiences in the past, from both methods of inquiry, that becomes our preparatory faith. This faith, however, is insufficient to transcend the Oakeshottian prison walls. It is absolutely necessary, but incomplete. The required faith, which lays the final plank, the "leap of faith" required by both Kierkegaard and Taylor, is redemptive faith. This faith is produced by ordering the soul with preparatory faith; then, the moment the truth-seeker crosses the bridge, lifted up by the ladder of redemptive faith, that certitude is found. The concept of being "lifted up" over the prison walls of conditionality is very significant and meaningful to the humble followers of Christ. Great parallels exist in the Savior's own life. We see that at the very moment when the Christ was lifted up upon the cross, doubt among the disciples was at its apex. It was then, at that very moment, that most of them fell back on their preparatory faith. They reordered their souls by deep self-searching[23] and calling upon the Lord, and then they were able to wait for the moment of resurrection, in which their faith became redemptive and allowed them to transcend the prison walls of conditionality. It was then that they knew with absolute truth that our Lord was all He said He was. This certitude needed to be sustained by their redemptive faith, as Alma explained, for the Lord was with them for only forty more days. It was in the crucible of doubt that Descartes declared and acknowledged his need to know better the author of his being so that his senses would not be deceived. It was in the crucible of crucifixion that the Savior showed us that a contrite spirit relies totally upon the Father; and in that same crucible the truth-seeker confronts the reality of the resurrected Lord with the words of Thomas, upon receiving certitude, "My Lord and my God."[24]

This redemptive faith comes from deep within the soul itself. It is produced by ordering the soul with the vision and values of our Savior and then having the courage to accept these values as our own. Responding to the new "gaze of the soul," as Taylor suggests, Kierkegaard's "leap of [redemptive] faith" is taken when the truth-seeker allows Christ to live within him or her and, as Paul stated earlier, the life lived in the flesh is made alive "by the faith of the Son of God" (Galatians 2:20). Christ's faith becomes our faith. In receiving such certitude, Thomas was commanded to "be not faithless." It was then that he was admonished to receive the gift of redemptive faith (John 20:28). Thomas's flesh was made alive by the faith of the Son of God. It is His faith that becomes our faith, and it is His faith that is redemptive and causes the truth-seeker to know, with certitude, The Truth. We have made him the object and the subject of our faith. Moroni explains the process, which involves our being "remembered and nourished by the good word of God, . . . to keep [us] continually watchful unto prayer, relying alone upon the merits of Christ, who was the author and the finisher of [our] faith" (Moroni 6:4).

Moroni taught that as an expression of our preparatory faith, we make Christ the author of our faith; but, in the confronting act, where the truth-seeker is willing to rely alone, solely, on the merits of Christ, reordering his or her soul with the values and vision of the Christ, that redemptive faith becomes a reality. With this reality, Christ thus becomes the finisher of our faith and the producer of certitude.

It is the Lord who will choose the moment of confrontation. He will prepare us by becoming the author of our faith, and He will allow us to grow from study, "as all have not [redemptive] faith" (D&C 88:118); and it is He who will choose the moment to confront us, when our faith is sufficiently prepared. As was shown in the examples above, each truth-seeker has a personal, tailor-made path toward certitude. This unique path cannot be encapsulated in the four or ten "steps to certitude." Each truth-seeker is unique, but the methodology is the same. Look at the example of the fifty great men and women who appeared to Wilford Woodruff in the St. George Temple in 1877[25] to have their saving ordinance work done. These men and women are evidence enough to show the Lord is no respecter of persons when it comes to eventually obtaining certitude. Each of these men, for great purposes established by the Lord, were able to reach an assurance, a level of certitude particular to their endeavor while on earth. But in a final sense, the decisive certitude was provided by recognizing Christ as the finisher of their faith—and the subject of their faith. They came to the recognition that the Lord, as part of being the finisher of their faith, had allowed them the certitude to proceed and receive all the saving ordinances in the house of the Lord.

As Latter-day Saints, having had the precious gift of the Holy Ghost conferred upon us, we have a unique benefaction that allows Latter-day Saint truth-seekers to acquire certitude through a confronting moment with the Author and the Finisher of our faith. The search for this moment is intensely personal, as the Savior suggested in Luke 17:20–21, when He taught the Pharisees after they demanded that he tell them when the kingdom of God should come. "The kingdom of God cometh not with observation: Neither shall they say, Lo here! or, lo there! for, behold, *the kingdom of God is within you*" (emphasis added).

It is this personal search, the personal shift of the "gaze of the soul" that places the feet of the truth-seeker on an unalterable path, which if successful, will lead him or her to certitude. Then, as we wait upon the Lord, our wait will cause us to seek Him in meekness with a broken heart and a contrite spirit, with preparatory faith. We thereby make Him the author of our faith. The profound leap of redemptive faith was illustrated by President Hugh B. Brown in an address to the student body at Brigham Young University in May 1969:

> Our reactions to the ever-changing impacts of life will depend upon our goals and ideals. "The vision that you glorify in your mind, the ideal that you enthrone in your heart, this you will build your life by, this you will become." Every life coheres around certain fundamental core ideas whether we realize it or not, and herein lies the chief value of revealed religion. But while I believe all that God has revealed, I am not quite sure that I understand what he has revealed, and the fact that he has promised further revelation is to me a challenge to keep an open mind and be prepared to follow wherever my search for truth may lead. . . . Our reactions to the ever-changing impacts of life will depend upon our goals and our ideals. And I would like to leave that thought with you to ponder.
>
> Again I emphasize, there is *no final goal*. Life must continue to expand, to unfold, and to grow, if it is to continue to be a good life. These things are indispensable, and in this

connection age makes little difference (thank goodness for me!). There is opportunity for all to expand and to grow and to be and to become. . . .

We have been blessed with much knowledge by revelation from God, which, in some part, the world lacks. But there is an incomprehensibly greater part of truth, which we must yet discover. Our revealed truth should leave us stricken with the knowledge of how little we really know. It should never lead to an emotional arrogance based upon a false assumption that we somehow have all the answers—that we in fact have a corner on truth. For we do not. Whether you are in the field of economics or political science, history or the behavioral sciences—continue to search for the truth; and, maintain humility sufficient to be able to revise your hypotheses as new truth comes to you by means of the Spirit or the mind. Salvation, like education, is an on-going process.

One may not attain salvation by merely acknowledging allegiance, nor is it available in ready-to-wear stores or in supermarkets where it may be bought and paid for. That it is an eternal quest must be obvious to all. Education is involved in salvation and may be had only by evolution or unfolding or developing into our potential. It is in large measure a problem of awareness, of reaching out and looking up, of aspiring and becoming, pushing back our horizons, seeking for answers and searching for God.

In other words, it is not merely a matter of conformity to rituals, climbing sacred stairs, bathing in sacred pools, or making pilgrimages to ancient shrines. The depth and height and quality of life depends upon awareness, and awareness is a process of being saved from ignorance. Man cannot be saved in ignorance. Man is saved by inquiry, by revelation, by knowledge borne of faith and being reconciled to God through the atonement of our Lord and Savior, Jesus Christ.[26]

It can be seen in President Brown's explanation of seeking truth that he has suggested the quest for knowledge is eternal and that there will be no final goal in this life. He shares an important point that the pursuit of certitude leads us down a path in which an ongoing process is commenced. This reach for redemptive faith is done as we look up, aspire for answers, and become more developed in the eyes of the Lord. It is done by pushing back the horizons of ignorance produced as we near the limits of the Oakeshottian prison. We must continue to seek for answers by searching for God. Salvation from ignorance transforms itself into the pursuit of exaltation, which then becomes the ultimate goal of the truth-seeker's search.

The Lord has in fact made this promise to all Latter-day Saint truth-seekers. He declared to us all, in Doctrine and Covenants 93:

> Verily, thus saith the Lord: It shall come to pass that every soul who forsaketh his sins and cometh unto me, and calleth on my name, and obeyeth my voice, and keepeth my commandments, shall see my face and know that I AM (D&C 93:1; final word is not capitalized in original).

Elder Bruce R. McConkie, in his final address to the Latter-day Saints, clarified this point when he contemplated his impending death and said, "I testify that he is the Son of the Living God and was crucified for the sins of the world. . . . But I shall not know any better then than I know now that he is God's Almighty Son."[27] For Elder McConkie, certitude was attained long before that day by sacred moments of confrontation in which his preparatory faith was transformed into redemptive faith. This was done in intensely private moments as a "leap of faith," even redemptive faith over the walls of the Oakeshottian prison. He transcended the object of sense into confronting the subject of Christ, the pinnacle of *a priori* knowledge. Both prophets and philosophers have pointed out this path.

For the Latter-day Saint truth-seeker, the assurance found by this consensus of the secular and the sacred, by men and women of our faith and by those not of our faith, demonstrates that the move from preparatory faith to redemptive faith is one of certitude produced by making the Savior the subject of our faith. It leads to the source of absolute truth long sought by great men from Plato until the present time. It is a long process unique to each person, and it may not even be completed in our lifetime. However, the methodology of how the path is engaged and traversed is universal and can be accessed with remarkable success. For each of us, the path is private, personal, and redemptive.

The invitation to the path of certitude is provided by Isaiah. He counsels us, "The work of righteousness shall be peace; and the effect of righteousness quietness and assurance for ever" (Isaiah 32:17). It is this quietness and assurance forever that is produced by our redemptive faith. It is in that moment, when we successfully transcend the Oakeshottian prison of conditionality through redemptive faith, that we encounter thereby the Lord, and thus come to know "The Truth."

Notes

1. *Marx's Critique of Hegel's Philosophy of Right*, edited by Joseph O'Malley, translated by Annette Jolin and Joseph O'Malley (Cambridge, England: Cambridge University Press, 1970).

2. Gregory A. Prince and William Robert Wright, *David O. McKay and the Rise of Modern Mormonism* (Salt Lake City: University of Utah Press, 2005), 40; emphasis added.

3. Michael Oakeshott, *On Human Conduct* (New York: Oxford University Press, 1975), 27.

4. George Q. Cannon, in *Discourses of Wilford Woodruff and His Counselors* (Salt Lake City: B.H.S. Publishing, 1988), 2:293.

5. James E. Talmage, *Improvement Era* 4 (October 1901): 909.

6. Bruce R. McConkie, *Mormon Doctrine* (Salt Lake City: Bookcraft, 1966), 578.

7. Gordon B. Hinckley, "What Are People Asking about Us?" *Ensign,* November 1998, 71. In the interview with Larry King, President Hinckley stated: "The figures I have are from—between 2 percent and 5 percent of our people were involved in it. It was a very limited practice; carefully safeguarded. In 1890, that practice was discontinued. The president of the church, the man who occupied the position which I occupy today, went before the people, and said he had prayed about it, worked on it, and had received from the Lord a revelation that it was time to stop, to discontinue it then. That's 118 years ago. It is behind us. . . . I condemn it, yes, as a practice, because I think it is *not doctrinal.* It is not legal."

8. Thomas Kuhn, *The Structure of Scientific Revolutions* (Chicago: The University of Chicago Press, 1970), 83, 98; Albert Einstein, "Autobiographical Vote," in *Albert Einstein: Philosopher-Scientist,"* edited by P. A. Shilpp (Evanston, Illinois, 1949), 45.

9. David Hume, *An Enquiry Concerning Human Understanding,* edited by Anthony Flew (LaSalle, Illinois: Open Court Publishers, 1988), 87.

10. David Hume, "Abstract of a Treatise on Human Nature," in *An Enquiry Concerning Human Understanding,* edited by Anthony Flew (LaSalle, Illinois: Open Court Publishers, 1988), 34–35.

11. René Descartes, "Sixth Meditation," in *Meditations on First Philosophy* (Cambridge, England: Cambridge University Press, 1996), 53–54.

12. Soren Kierkegaard, "Concluding Unscientific Postscript," translated by David F. Swensen, in *Ethics and Values—Basic Readings in Theory and Practice* (Boston: Pearson Custom Publishing, 2002), 103.

13. Max Weber, *Selections in Translation,* edited by W. G. Runciman (Cambridge, England: Cambridge University Press, 1993), 18–21.

14. Jacobellis v. Ohio, 378 U.S. 184 (1964) http://en.wikiquote.org/wiki/ Potter_Stewart; accessed May 14, 2007.

15. Charles Taylor, *Sources of Self—The Making of the Modern Identity* (Cambridge, Massachusetts: Harvard University Press, 1989), 115.

16. Plato, "Apology," in *The Trial and Death of Socrates,* translated by G. M. A. Grube (Indianapolis: Hackett Publishing, 1975), 389.

17. Taylor, *Sources of Self,* 123.

18. Neal A. Maxwell, *Even As I Am* (Salt Lake City: Deseret Book, 1982), 4; emphasis in the original.

19. Ibid., 19.

20. In Luke 17, the apostles asked the Lord to increase their faith. The Lord explained in a parable that performance of duty would enhance their faith. In verses 7–10 He explained:

"But which of you, having a servant plowing or feeding cattle, will say unto him by and by, when he is come from the field, Go and sit down to meat? And will not rather say unto him, Make ready wherewith I may sup, and gird thyself, and serve me, till I have eaten and drunken; and afterward thou shalt eat and drink? Doth he thank that servant because he did the things that were commanded him? I trow not. So likewise ye, when ye shall have done all those things which are commanded you, say, We are unprofitable servants: we have done that which was our duty to do."

It is clear from the above that keeping the commandments increases faith and produces a broken heart and a contrite spirit. It is the broken heart that creates the condition to receive the gift of faith.

21. Taylor, *Sources of Self,* 123.

22. See Luke 15:17.

23. The soul-searching of the disciples is particularly poignant in Matthew's account of the denial of Christ by Peter:

"Now Peter sat without in the palace: and a damsel came unto him, saying, Thou also wast with Jesus of Galilee. But he denied before them all, saying, I know not what thou sayest. And when he was gone out into the porch, another maid saw him, and said unto them that were there, This fellow was also with Jesus of Nazareth. And again he denied with an oath, I do not know the man. And after a while came unto him they that stood by, and said to Peter, Surely thou also art one of them; for thy speech bewrayeth thee. Then began he to curse and to swear, saying, I know not the man. And immediately the cock crew. And Peter remembered the word of Jesus, which said unto him, Before the cock crow, thou shalt deny me thrice. And he went out, and wept bitterly" (Matthew 26:69–75).

24. In John 20:24–28, Thomas's experience is recorded: "But Thomas, one of the twelve, called Didymus, was not with them when Jesus came. The other disciples therefore said unto him, We have seen the Lord. But he said unto them, Except I shall see in his hands the print of the nails, and put my finger into the print of the nails, and thrust my hand into his side, I will not believe. And after eight days again his disciples were within, and Thomas with them: then came Jesus, the doors being shut, and stood in the midst, and said, Peace be unto you. Then saith he to Thomas, Reach hither thy finger, and behold my hands; and reach hither thy hand, and thrust it into my side: and be not *faithless*, but believing. And Thomas answered and said unto him, My Lord and my God" (emphasis added).

25. *Discourses of Wilford Woodruff*, 3:431–40.

26. Hugh B. Brown, *Speeches of the Year*, Brigham Young University, May 1969.

27. Bruce R. McConkie, "The Purifying Power of Gethsemane," *Ensign*, May 1985, 11.

Choosing Your Lifestyle

Sarah Jenelle Monson

Bachelor of Arts in Journalism, Brigham Young University

Question:

A few years ago I had a bleak couple of months. Two LDS friends in other states called to tell me they were leaving the Church for a homosexual lifestyle. Another friend confided that he had also stopped attending Church and doubted he would ever feel like going back. A boy I was dating confessed he had a serious problem that prevented his temple worthiness. All around me, friends bemoaned their single status and complained that living the gospel "just hadn't worked for them." It was the first time in my somewhat sheltered spiritual life that I confronted personal apostasy in people I knew well, and it seemed to happen all at once. It felt like everyone I knew was doubting the gospel or calling it quits.

Experiences with one friend at that time are still especially memorable to me. He had broken his neck in a skiing accident and was trapped in an orthopedic halo and back brace, resting on painkillers in a smelly bachelor apartment. My roommate and I volunteered to clean for him, and while we grimaced through this weekly task, we let him vent his frustrations. His list of grievances with the Almighty began with the broken neck, but extended to the hypocrisy of Church members, the stupidity of dating, the impossibility of chastity, and the general unfairness of the universe. Maybe it was just the painkillers talking, but he made a compelling case for despair. He seemed to embody the unhappiness of all my wayward friends, and I was frustrated by my inability to find satisfying answers to his questions. His hopelessness was contagious. Even though I didn't agree with him that living the commandments was impossible, it did begin to look like living them *with joy* was. The path ahead looked dreary and unrewarding.

Now, a few years later, I am happy to report that I survived those difficult months of doubt, and I have since seen many friends thrive in the gospel and move forward with faith in fulfilling lives. Even the friend with the broken neck made a full recovery, physically and spiritually. But my other friends who lost their faith at that time have not come back, and I still have a lot of friends struggling to stay the course.

In our late twenties, the challenges seem even trickier. There are still long stretches where we plod uphill against doubt, discouragement, and temptation, wondering why some anticipated blessings haven't materialized. From single friends I hear, "Do you really think this is worth it?" and bitter jokes about "If I'm not married by [insert age here], I'm just going to [enter tempting forbidden activity here]." Not that marriage solves everything; by now I know people who have faced divorce, betrayal, and all kinds of heartbreak. From some married friends, I hear disillusionment in statements like, "It's harder than you think it will be, you know," and "The fact is, I just really don't like having children right now," and "I feel like I'm doing nothing with my life." It sometimes seems there are a million ways to get lost. Some of us lose our way through apathy, or escape into entertainment (the video gamers, the compulsive TV-watchers), while others head the other direction toward obsession (the extreme sportists, the workaholics). I've seen friends lose their focus, their personal happiness, and their closeness to God in all of these ways. Some come back; some don't.

My friends who wander were all once strong. At one point they knew the restored gospel was true, that God loved them, that there was a plan for their life, and that their choices mattered. I believe their initial spiritual experiences and convictions were real . . . but I also believe in the reality of their current pain. This is confusing, challenging stuff. How do I help them? How do I avoid wandering myself?

Because by now I also know it could happen to me. Today, right now, I find joy and comfort in the restored gospel, and I have no intention of giving up the fight. But I have come through my dark times, too, and I know it would be foolhardy to assume I could never be blindsided by a serious crisis of faith. Everyone I know has passed through the valley of doubt and disillusionment. Some are still down there. How do we come through it? Has it always been this hard, or does my generation face unique challenges to stay the course? What are we to do when all the evidence of our senses says, "It's not worth it," when the promised blessings of gospel living seem not to come, or we don't feel the burning of the Spirit like we did before?

* * *

Susan Easton Black

Professor of Church History and Doctrine at Brigham Young University

Answer:

I doubt I would have driven through traffic in southern California to see just anyone baptized in 2002; but I was acquainted with Joanna and knew of the obstacles she had overcome to enter a baptismal font, and I didn't want to miss being a part of her new-found commitment. Upon entering the stake center, I found the chapel pews filled with well-wishers like me. I quietly took a seat on a folding chair in the cultural hall. After listening to an inspiring talk on baptism, I left the hall hoping to find a place near the font to watch her baptism. Due to the numbers present, few of us actually saw Joanna enter the font or heard the words spoken before she was immersed in the water. Yet all present sensed that her heartfelt feelings that day would always be cherished.

I am confident that no one imagined on that day that within six months Joanna would not be attending church. It wasn't that she asked to have her name removed from Church records; she just found one reason after another to not attend Sunday meetings. Could it be that she was offended at the baptism? Was she fully converted to the gospel of Jesus Christ? Are there underlying issues in her life that need to be understood and addressed? Are the requirements of faithful membership in The Church of Jesus Christ of Latter-day Saints too restrictive for her lifestyle? What can be done to rectify the situation? Will new home teachers help? Should the bishop become more involved? What about the ward mission leader?

Questions like these that are spawned by the Church inactivity of Joanna are not new. Yet solutions are slow in coming. A friend, a calling, and a plate of cookies have led more than one less active or prodigal to return to Church fellowship—but not all. Wanting a solution and hoping to find it through the process of research, writing, and prayer, I present the dilemma of inactivity within The Church of Jesus Christ of Latter-day Saints—the problem of the faltering steps.

The Issue

The issue of commitment (or lack thereof), often defined as a willingness to retain in remembrance and action baptismal covenants, is not a twenty-first century phenomena. Its roots reach back to the nineteenth century—an era when Joseph the Prophet walked the well-trod streets of New York, Ohio, Missouri, and Illinois. Of the thousands who followed his footsteps, only 130 are mentioned by name in the Doctrine and Covenants.[1] Of those named, biographical information reveals that seventy-two, or 55.38 percent, died as faithful members of the Church.[2] Forty-four of those named, or 33.92 percent, died outside of Church fellowship.[3] Church status of the named others is unknown.[4]

The faithfulness of one and the faltering steps of another are analogous to the Savior's parable of the ten virgins, which portrays only five virgins steady in their gospel commitment (Matthew 25:1–12). The parable, closely illustrating the religious commitment of Joseph Smith's era, declines in application when discussing the long-term effects of migration from Nauvoo to the Salt Lake Valley and the polygamy raids in Utah. Few who boast of being a descendant of Latter-day Saint pioneers can claim that 50 percent of their Mormon ancestors faithfully attended Church, partook of the sacrament, or kept sacred commandments. The harassment and persecution faced by yesterday's pioneers, which has often been given as an excuse for their lack of faithfulness, is nearly extinct among twenty-first century Mormons. Yet the gnawing issues of inactivity, retention, and lack of commitment are still present.

Figure 1

Individuals Mentioned in the Doctrine and Covenants Differed in Their Gospel Commitment

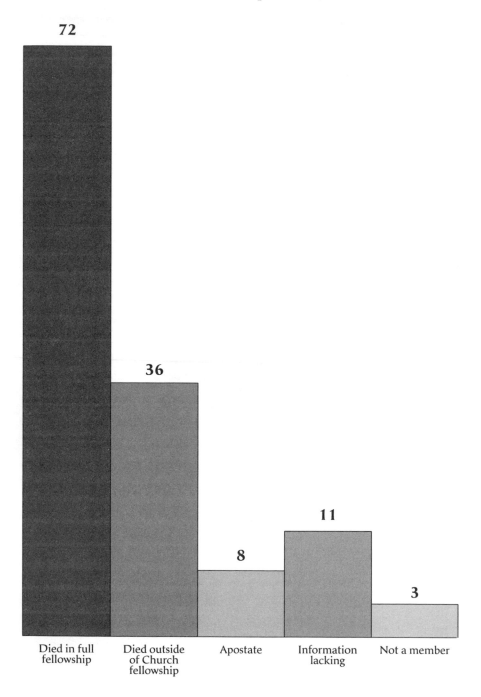

There is not a ward or branch in the Church that is exempt from its devastating effects. With the Church now stretching worldwide, this means that inactivity is present throughout the globe. President Gordon B. Hinckley has spoken of the global reach of the Church:

> There is not a city in the United States or Canada of any consequence which does not have a Latter-day Saint congregation. It is the same in Mexico. It is the same in Central and South America. Likewise in New Zealand and Australia, in the islands of the sea, and in Japan, Korea, Taiwan, the Philippines. In Europe our congregations are everywhere.[5]

The Church grows at the rate of a million members each three-and-a-half years. Of those numbers, how many are like Joanna? How many chapels built this year have empty pews? How many sessions in holy temples are canceled because the Joannas of the world fail to enter?

I believe a solution to inactivity within the Church is overdue. I am not alone in that belief. President Hinckley has stated:

> I worry greatly about those who drift away—what we can do to bring them back. . . . Every convert is precious. . . . There is no point in doing missionary work unless we hold on to the fruits of that effort. The two must be inseparable. . . . This loss must stop. It is unnecessary. I am satisfied the Lord is not pleased with us."[6]

I feel a great desire to help Joanna, but how? This question begs for an answer—an answer for Joanna and for all who have entered the sacred covenant of baptism and no longer enjoy the fellowship of the Saints.

Case in Point: A More Global View of Inactivity

On a six-nation, twenty-city tour of South America—in which ground was broken for temples in Cochabamba, Bolivia, and Recife, Brazil—President Hinckley spoke in Santiago, Chile, to a large gathering of Saints in November 1996. The importance of holding family home evenings, paying tithing, attending the temple, and the sacred role of parenting were the topics addressed. President Hinckley promised the membership in Chile that if they would hearken to his words, they would not want for shelter or food, and the destroying angel would pass over them as he had the ancient children of Israel. His promises in 1996 may have seemed unnecessary to the Chileans, who then were enjoying a period of unparalleled national prosperity.[7] However, within a few years the prosperity Chile had known dramatically faded. Severe drought, crisis in international markets, unemployment, and political intrigues had brought Chileans to an economic crossroad.

On April 25, 1999, nearly three years later, President Hinckley addressed an estimated 53,000 Latter-day Saints in Chile once again. For those who recalled his earlier address, his words seemed reminiscent:

> I wish to implore you that you live worthily in order that you may go to the house of the Lord and participate in the marvelous blessings that one can have only in that place. . . . We have thousands and tens of thousands [in Chile] that don't go [to the temple]. . . . I plead this morning that you put your lives in order. . . . You who have not been in the House of the Lord, I beg you that you begin today to repent of the past in order to put your lives in order and seal to yourselves those who you love most.

He continued, "Partake of the sacrament every week, gather

your families around you to have family home evening, read your scriptures and talk with them, be friendly with them, pray with them, gather them to you." He then admonished the members to "pay your tithing in order that you can be worthy of the blessings of the Lord."

Then President Hinckley wondered aloud,

> I don't know how [God] will bless you if you don't live worthy, I don't know if he can bless you if you are not worthy of his blessings. . . . If you live the gospel, if you live in faith, if you do what you should do, not only you will be blessed but all this people will be blessed because the Lord of the Heavens will smile with love for you and the land where you live. . . . And as his servant I make you this promise, Just do it."

President Hinckley ended his address with these words, "I leave my own testimony and blessings and love in the name of Jesus Christ, Amen."[8] After his solemn "amen," the prophet waved good-bye to the Chilean Saints. In response, handkerchiefs were waved aloft as an expression of heartfelt love for the Lord's anointed.

Local Chilean leaders were heartened by the outward expressions of love for the prophet. They felt confident that their members would now obey prophetic counsel and awaken to their sacred responsibilities. The hope remains today, but too often in individual cases it still awaits realization. More than one frustrated Church leader has asked, "Reactivate, but how?" What brings one member back to Church is the reason another gives for turning away.

Seeking a Solution to the Faltering Steps

A solution that binds, that fits Joanna and thousands like her—and perhaps even future converts—must be sought in humble prayer to God. Such a prayer will respect the agency of each convert yet express abiding love and confidence that each will be true to baptismal covenants. As I have prayed about the solution for my friend, I have been drawn again and again to Joseph Smith—History in the Pearl of Great Price. Within that sacred text, parallels between Joanna and Joseph Smith's youthful experiences have sparked new thoughts—thoughts that speak of a solution to the faltering steps.

The Quest for Religious Truth

The poignant story of young Joseph begins with a spirit of revivalism that "commenced with the Methodists, but soon became general among all the sects." So pervading was the quest for religious truth, it seemed to the young boy that "the whole district of country seemed affected by it, and great multitudes united themselves to the different religious parties, which created no small stir and division amongst the people" (Joseph Smith—History 1:5). Joseph "wanted to get religion too, wanted to feel and shout like the rest but could feel nothing."[9]

"Priest contending against priest, and convert against convert" over conflicting Christian doctrine left him confused as to which denomination was accepted by God. "It was impossible for a person young as I was, and so unacquainted with men and things, to come to any certain conclusion who was right and who was wrong," wrote Joseph (Joseph Smith—History 1:6, 8).[10] Searching the Holy Bible for answers led him to a passage in the epistle of James, "If any of you lack wisdom, let him ask of God, that giveth to all men liberally, and upbraideth not; and it shall be given him" (James 1:5).

In accordance with the directive to ask God, "on the morning of a beautiful, clear day, early in the spring of eighteen hundred and twenty" young Joseph stepped into the woods near his family farm to ask God to unravel the confusion. As he "kneeled down and began to offer up the desires of [his] heart" he was nearly overcome by "the power of some actual being from the unseen world." In this moment of great alarm, he exerted "all [his] powers to call upon God to deliver [him] out of the power of this enemy" (Joseph Smith—History 1:14–16).

> I saw a pillar of light exactly over my head, above the brightness of the sun, which descended gradually until it fell upon me. It no sooner appeared than I found myself delivered from the enemy. . . . When the light rested upon me I saw two Personages, whose brightness and glory defy all description, standing above me in the air. One of them spake unto me, calling me by name and said, pointing to the other—*This is My Beloved Son. Hear Him!*" (Joseph Smith—History 1:16–17).

As Joseph listened, Jesus Christ told him that the creeds of the contesting Christian sects were "an abomination in his sight," and the professors of those creeds "teach for doctrines the commandments of men, having a form of godliness, but they deny the power thereof" (Joseph Smith—History 1:19).

The divine answer received was definitive. There was no mistaking the Lord's directive to Joseph Smith that day in Palmyra. Likewise, converts like Joanna search for an answer in scripture and on bent knee. When that answer comes, it is so definitive to them that they are willing to change even lifelong habits to embrace the truthfulness of the gospel of Jesus Christ. Like youthful Joseph, they listen to the word of God and seek to obey His counsel.

Sharing Religious Truth with Significant Others

Soon after the First Vision, Joseph Smith shared glimpses of his manifestation from God with a minister in Palmyra. Instead of rejoicing over the boy's vision, the minister treated his "communication not only lightly, but with great contempt, saying it was all of the devil, that there were no such things as visions or revelations in these days; that all such things had ceased with the apostles." The clergyman then withdrew from the boy and cast aspersions upon him. Fools listened to the clergyman and then derided the sacred; they heaped contempt and mockery upon the boy until such derision became Joseph's common foe. "Though I was an obscure boy, only between fourteen and fifteen years of age, and my circumstances in life such as to make a boy of no consequence in the world," Joseph mused, "yet men of high standing would take notice sufficient to excite the public mind against me, and create a bitter persecution" (Joseph Smith—History 1:21–22).

The opposition caused great sorrow for Joseph (Joseph Smith—History 1:23). Townsfolk labeled him "lazy," "illiterate," "superstitious," "disorderly," "a drunkard," "an imposter," and "addicted to vice and the grossest immoralities."[11] They claimed he was "lounging, idle; . . . and possessed of less than ordinary intellect."[12] When resident Thomas Taylor was asked, "Why didn't they like Smith?" He answered, "To tell the truth, there was something about him they could not understand; some way he knew more than they did, and it made them mad."[13]

Could it be that Joanna shared news of her baptism with significant family members and friends? Instead of recognizing her joy, did these significant others mock her religious decision? Did they bring ministers of other persuasions to dissuade her baptismal commitment? Was their verbal persecution or ostracism too difficult for

Joanna to bear? Was she too willing to return to old friends or to old ways?

When Actions Don't Mirror a Godly Walk

Adding to Joseph's difficulties were his own actions. He "frequently fell into many foolish errors, and displayed the weakness of youth, and the foibles of human nature" (Joseph Smith—History 1:28). What he had observed as a contradicting message in the preacher's walk and talk was mirrored in his own youthful demeanor. However, he confessed, "I have not, neither can it be sustained, in truth, been guilty of wronging or injuring any man or society of men."[14] Yet for a boy who had seen God the Father and Jesus Christ and had suffered "severe persecution at the hands of all classes of men, both religious and irreligious, because I continued to affirm that I had seen a vision," his foolish actions caused him to feel "condemned for his weakness and imperfections" (Joseph Smith—History 1:27, 29).

Unfortunately, such comments also describe Joanna. Cares of the world, family pressures, and satanic enticements dimmed the bright change of heart she felt the day of her baptism. Her light is now hid as if under a bushel. But she, like young Joseph, has not become as salt that has "lost his savour [and is] . . . good for nothing, but to be cast out, and to be trodden under" (Matthew 5:13). She is of worth—of infinite worth to God.

Can the work of God's kingdom go forward without her? Of course. The Lord has promised that no unhallowed hand can stop the work from progressing; "as well might man stretch forth his puny arm to stop the Missouri river in its decreed course" (D&C 121:33). The work will go forward. Yet to quote President Hinckley, "Every convert is precious. . . . This loss must stop. It is unnecessary."[15] I agree.

Your Standing Before God

I suggest that the solution for the loss lies within Joseph Smith's history contained in the Pearl of Great Price. After three-and-a-half years of being buffeted by friend and foe, on the night of September 21, 1823, Joseph had reached a pivotal point in his life. He wanted to know his standing before God. Perhaps, like Joseph Smith, Joanna is now on her knees in supplication before the Lord. Could it be that she wants to know her standing before God? For Joseph, the very act of calling upon God in September of 1823 provided the answer. As he prayed, a light filled his room and caused it to be lighter than at noonday. An angelic personage appeared in that light and called Joseph by name, for he knew the young man praying for guidance (Joseph Smith—History 1:33). Joseph was not just a number or a statistic gone bad; he was an individual known by God and His messenger. Similarly, less active members like Joanna have been identified through the long and arduous process of record keeping. Records have been checked, updated, and revised. Every effort has been made to know the whereabouts of each Joanna who has entered the waters of baptism. Each is known by God and by his representatives.

God Has a Work for You to Do

The similarity of the Joseph Smith story continues. After the angel called Joseph by name, he announced that "God had a work for [Joseph] to do" (Joseph Smith—History 1:33). He then explained through repetitive visits the work Joseph must accomplish for the Lord and His children. The message, in part the solution to the faltering steps, is found in that announcement. "God has a work" for each convert. For the less active, this bold announcement may be daunting. For some, the assignment of speaking in sacrament meeting led to their inactivity. How can they accept that God has a work for them to do, especially when they may have wrongfully assumed that the Lord no longer knows their name or that their casual embrace of gospel principles renders them useless to the Lord?

The sincere answer is that the Lord is feeling after His children and wants them back. The Primary song "Dare to Do Right" bears a meaningful testimony:

> You have a work that no other can do;
> Do it so bravely, so kindly, so well,
> Angels will hasten the story to tell.[16]

Each convert needs to believe that the Lord knows his or her name and has an important work for each one of us to accomplish in building His kingdom and Church upon the earth. This belief will enable converts to feel a renewed sense of purpose and confidence. "Where do I begin?" will soon be the question that replaces "I'm not interested in being involved."

Conclusion

The return to activity will be more circular than a linear, step-forward approach. Truths will need to be grasped again. If the individual is not careful, the sharing of these truths with significant others will again leave him or her with faltering steps. To prevent a repeat of earlier days, as the convert returns to fellowship a more mature member must express sincere joy and unrestrained friendship. This member should be one who has felt and feels the prompting of the Holy Ghost and has shown and shows a commitment to live God's laws. Just as Moses needed Aaron and Hur to hold up his arms to guarantee victory for the Israelites, those who have lost their way need help in the conversion process to succeed (Exodus 17:12).

Joseph Smith needed help to succeed in the work he was called to do. After the first angelic visit on September 21, 1823, he "lay musing on the singularity of the scene, and marveling greatly at what had been told to me by this extraordinary messenger" (Joseph Smith—History 1:44). Instead of leaving Joseph alone with his musings, the heavenly messenger appeared again at Joseph's bedside and "related the very same things which he had done at his first visit" (Joseph Smith—History 1:45). This scene was repeated through the night and the next morning. The sum total of the repeated events made particularly deep impressions on the mind of young Joseph Smith (Joseph Smith—History 1:46). These impressions and the angelic visits continued for successive years.

Joanna stands at the crossroad like Sariah, Sam, and Nephi, who stood at the headwaters in Lehi's dream and "knew not whither they should go" (1 Nephi 8:14). Yet it is not just Joanna; it is the inactives in Chile and the inactives throughout the world. It was Lehi who issued the clarion call, "Come . . . and partake of the fruit, which was desirable above all other fruit" (1 Nephi 8:15). Like Father Lehi, President Hinckley has made that call in our day. Faithful members heed that call by being willing to "warn, expound, exhort, and teach, and invite all to come unto Christ" (D&C 20:59). They invite the less active to love God the Father and His Son Jesus Christ and to do as Moroni 7:48 directs: "Pray unto the Father with all the energy of heart, that ye may be filled with this love." For when the faithful love another into gospel righteousness, they are not just "in the service of [their] fellow beings"—they truly are "in the service of [their] God" (Mosiah 2:17). Although that service may be a "small part in moving the work of the Lord on to its magnificent destiny,"[17] it is time to be up and doing. Joanna needs to be "nourished by the good word of God, to keep [her] in the right way, to keep [her] continually watchful unto prayer" (Moroni 6:4). She needs friendship. She needs love. The question is, "Who will help?" I humbly pray, "Please let it be me."

Notes

1. For further information on this and the following lists, see Susan Easton Black, "The Importance of the Individual in the Lord's Revelations," *The Heavens Are Open: The 1992 Sperry Symposium on the Doctrine and Covenants and Church History* (Salt Lake City: Deseret Book, 1993).

2. Seventy-two died in full fellowship with the Saints: Jesse Baker, Ezra T. Benson, Samuel Bent, Titus Billings, Seymour Brunson, Reynolds Cahoon, Gideon Carter, John S. Carter, Simeon D. Carter, William Carter, Zebedee Coltrin, Oliver Cowdery, David Dort, James Foster, David Fullmer, Algernon S. Gilbert, John Gould, Oliver Granger, Thomas Grover, Levi Hancock, Solomon Hancock, Emer Harris, Martin Harris, Henry Herriman, Elias Higbee, Solomon Humphrey, William Huntington, Orson Hyde, Vienna Jacques, Aaron Johnson, Luke Johnson, Heber C. Kimball, Joseph Knight, Newel Knight, Vinson Knight, Thomas B. Marsh, Daniel Miles, Isaac Morley, John Murdock, Noah Packard, Edward Partridge, David Patten, William W. Phelps, Orson Pratt, Parley P. Pratt, Zera Pulsipher, Charles C. Rich, Willard Richards, Samuel J. Rolfe, Shadrach Roundy, Lyman Sherman, Henry Sherwood, Don Carlos Smith, Eden Smith, George A. Smith, Hyrum Smith, John Smith, Joseph Smith Jr., Joseph Smith Sr., Samuel H. Smith, John Snider, Erastus Snow, Daniel Stanton, John Taylor, Robert Thompson, Peter Whitmer Jr., Newel K. Whitney, Frederick G. Williams, Samuel Williams, Wilford Woodruff, Brigham Young, and Joseph Young.

3. Eight of the forty-four became apostates—John C. Bennett, Ezra Booth, John Corrill, John A. Hicks, William Law, William McLellin, Robert D. Foster, and Symonds Ryder.

4. To date, information about the enduring faithfulness of the following eleven individuals is unknown: Major Noble Ashley, Stephen Burnett, Philip Burroughs, Jared Carter, Asa Dodds, Ruggles Eames, Selah J. Griffin, Jacob Scott, Micah Welton, Calves Wilson, and Dunbar Wilson. Three were not members of the Church: Lilburn Boggs, James Covill, and Alvin Smith (who died before the Church was restored).

5. Gordon B. Hinckley, "Look to the Future," *Ensign,* November 1997, 68.

6. Interview with Gordon B. Hinckley, February 7, 1996, as cited in Sheri L. Dew, *The Biography of Gordon B. Hinckley: Go Forward with Faith* (Salt Lake City: Deseret Book, 1996), 531; Hinckley, "Converts and Young Men," *Ensign,* May 1997, 48; Hinckley, "Some Thoughts on Temples, Retention of Converts, and Missionary Service," *Ensign,* November 1997, 50–51.

7. Interview with Elder Eduardo LaMartine, an Area Seventy, August 2, 2000, Santiago, Chile.

8. Speech of Gordon B. Hinckley, April 25, 1999, Santiago, Chile; transcript typed in Spanish, then translated into English.

9. Alexander Neibaur's recording of Joseph Smith's testimony, May 24, 1844, as cited in Milton V. Backman Jr., *Joseph Smith's First Vision* (Salt Lake City: Bookcraft, 1971), 177.

10. Joseph Smith, *History of the Church of Jesus Christ of Latter-day Saints,* 7 vols. (Salt Lake City: Deseret Book, 1976), 1:3–4.

11. Eber D. Howe, *Mormonism Unvailed* (Painesville, Ohio: E. D. Howe, 1834), 249, 259.

12. Ibid., 248.

13. *Juvenile Instructor,* October 1, 1882, 17:302.

14. *Latter-day Saints' Messenger and Advocate,* December 1834.

15. Hinckley, "Converts and Young Men," 48; Hinckley, "Some Thoughts on Temples, Retention of Converts, and Missionary Service," 51.

16. "Dare to Do Right," *Children's Songbook* (Salt Lake City: The Church of Jesus Christ of Latter-day Saints, 1989), no. 158.

17. Hinckley, "Look to the Future," 67.

Index